CONSUMER ETHICS IN A GLOBAL ECONOMY

CONSUMER ETHICS IN A GLOBAL ECONOMY

How Buying Here Causes Injustice There

Daniel K. Finn

Georgetown University Press / Washington, DC

The publisher is not responsible for third-party websites or their content. URL links were active at time of publication.

Library of Congress Cataloging-in-Publication Data

Names: Finn, Daniel K., 1947– author.
Title: Consumer Ethics in a Global Economy : How Buying Here Causes Injustice There / Daniel K. Finn.
Description: Washington, DC : Georgetown University Press, 2019. | Series: Moral traditions series
Identifiers: LCCN 2018058554 (print) | LCCN 2019015491 (ebook) | ISBN 9781626166974 (ebook) | ISBN 9781626166950 (hardcover : qalk. paper) | ISBN 9781626166967 q(pbk.: qalk. paper) |
Subjects: LCSH: Consumption (Economics)—Moral and ethical aspects. | Consumer behavior—Moral and ethical aspects. | Commerce—Moral and ethical aspects. | Social ethics.
Classification: LCC HB835 (ebook) | LCC HB835 .F56 2019 (print) | DDC 178—dc23
LC record available at https://lccn.loc.gov/2018058554

♾ This book is printed on acid-free paper meeting the requirements of the American National Standard for Permanence in Paper for Printed Library Materials.

20 19   9 8 7 6 5 4 3 2 First printing

Printed in the United States of America.

Cover design by John Barnett, 4 Eyes Design.
Cover image Frame China/Shutterstock.com. Female laborers work in a cloth factory, Anhui province, East China.

To Mela

Contents

Acknowledgments

I am indebted to many people who have inspired, shaped, and/or improved this volume. First among these is undoubtedly British sociologist Margaret S. Archer, whose lifelong work in helpfully conceptualizing the social world lies beneath a fundamental premise of the book to understand global markets as social structures. Both a colleague and a friend, she has graciously encouraged me in a process that presents to readers outside of sociology a somewhat simplified version of her more precise (and necessarily more technical) conception of social structures. I am also deeply indebted to her US colleague in sociology Douglas Porpora, whose publications and conversations have greatly improved my "outsider's" grasp of the issues.

I have gained much from the observations and critiques of colleagues when I have presented portions of this analysis at the Society of Christian Ethics, the Catholic Theological Society of America, the Association for Social Economics, and the College Theology Society. A number of people have made important suggestions for improvement to the text itself, including David Cloutier, Christina McRorie, Mary Hirschfeld, Daniel Daly, Patrick Henry, Dennis Barrett, and Jacob Finn. I am also grateful for the assistance of Christopher Heitzig, Megan Myers, Mary Korman, Rebecca Franta, Natalie Landwehr, Maxwell Martin, and Jack Barsody.

Some of the arguments in this volume have appeared earlier in journals or books to which I have contributed. These debts are acknowledged in the chapters where they are incurred.

I am grateful to generous editors at Georgetown University Press: Al Bertrand, Hope LeGro, and Glenn Saltzman. My deep thanks go to Mrs. Judy Shank, who tirelessly prepared the many rounds of revision of the manuscript.

Introduction

Recent years have seen a long series of industrial disasters in factories in the developing world where products are made for sale in the US and other wealthy nations. A boiler explosion and subsequent fire led to the collapse of a five-story building in the Tongi industrial area outside Dhaka, Bangladesh. Luckily, it happened at night and killed "only" 35 workers, injuring more than 50.[1] At the Qinghe Special Steel Corporation's steel processing plant in Tieling, China, 32 workers faced a brutal death when thirty tons of molten steel fell from an overhead ladle, spilled onto the floor, burst through a door, and engulfed the room where the workers were meeting.[2]

In the garment industry, faulty electrical switches in the Ali Enterprises factory in Karachi, Pakistan, led to a fire that consumed a four-story building that had no emergency exits. In all, 262 people died.[3] At the Ha-Meem garment factory in Ashulia, Bangladesh, faulty wiring started a fire on the ninth floor that spread to the tenth and killed 29, injuring more than 100. The factory makes clothing for Gap and Wrangler.[4] Also in Bangladesh, the Rana Plaza factory collapse in 2013 killed 1,134 workers and injured 2,500, and a fire in the Tazreen Fashion factory, a nine-story building without fire escapes, caused the horrific death of 117 seamstresses, with another 200 injured.[5]

Upon investigation, some of these disasters might turn out to be unanticipatable accidents, while others may be the result of malfeasance by some individual, rendering them events of deep injustice to the victims involved. In all of them, as we will see, the market plays a role.

Are consumers who bought the products made by these workers in any way morally responsible for those injustices? And what about the far more frequent, less severe injustices, such as the withholding of wages, the denial of bathroom breaks, forced overtime, and harassment of various sorts? Could buying a shirt at the local department store create for you some responsibility for the horrendous death in a factory fire of the women who sewed it half a planet away?

Some people explicitly deny the possibility. Andrew J. Spencer, for example, asks whether "purchasing a shirt may bring direct moral accountability for human rights violations in a distant country." His answer is that "such an understanding of account-ability is not livable because no consumer can know the ethical merits of the entire supply chain of a given product."[6] The problem with such an answer is that although ignorance can mitigate one's responsibility, it is not a blanket excuse. If I enjoy roll-ing large stones down steep mountainsides, the fact that I cannot see that, much far-ther down, some hiker is hit and injured does not relieve me of responsibility for my actions. Surely we must first decide whether we as consumers are morally responsible for injustices that occur at the other end of the supply chain. Then, if we have such a responsibility, we must ask how we might become better informed about what is occurring there and what we might be able to do about it.

Most economists, of course, try to avoid moral judgments in their science. Eco-nomics sees itself as specializing in the identification of causes, not values. But within the vast majority of economists, conservative or liberal, who can be labeled as part of the "mainstream"—from Milton Friedman to John Maynard Keynes, from N. Greg-ory Mankiw to Paul Krugman—there is little capacity for identifying any causal link between consumer and seamstress. The market is thought of as largely abstract and disembodied: it offers consumer and seamstress alike a menu of choices (of shirts in one case, jobs in another), and each makes a choice that seems best to them. If asked, most economists would say that any one consumer has no perceptible impact on dis-tant producers, and so, in practical terms, no one consumer causes anything to occur half a planet away.

The aim of this volume is to articulate a view of markets that makes clear the causal relation between consumers and producers that provides the material foun-dation for the moral claim that consumers are complicit in—and so in some degree morally responsible for—the injustices suffered by the distant producers of the things they buy.

Outline of the Volume

Part I of this volume, comprising the first three chapters, introduces the issues. Because an individualistic mind-set is one of the contributing causes for our inability to see these connections, chapter 1 reviews why modern industrialized societies, particularly the United States, are as individualistic as they are. As sum-marized by philosopher Charles Taylor, the cultural movement over the past eight hundred years has not been a story of the development of science and individual-ism causing the shrinking of religious belief and its stress on community. Instead, a long series of reforms *within* Christianity, including the thirteenth-century rise of lay movements like the Franciscans, moved Christian piety toward greater responsibility of individual Christians for their own spiritual lives. While there are many advantages today of this historical trend, individualism has many destruc-tive effects. Most relevant for this volume is the way an individualistic bias blinds us to the impact of social structures on moral agency. Two examples illustrate:

the linguistic dominance of English in the world today and the influence of gerrymandering in US elections.

Chapter 2 surveys the history of contemporary mainstream economics to uncover why it has so strong an individualistic bias that the mainstream paradigm in economics fails to recognize the systemic, structural forces that shape the decisions of persons and businesses in daily economic life. It recounts the four crucial contributions of John Stuart Mill to later mainstream economics: deductivism, individualism, empiricism, and the is/ought distinction. It traces the shifts of focus in economics from wealth maximization to utility maximization, from economic decisions to all decisions under scarcity, and from endorsing maximization by consumers as a realistic claim to employing it only as a helpful though unrealistic assumption. The chapter concludes with a brief outline of the problems within economics today arising from Mill's intellectual bequests.

Chapter 3 briefly reviews three philosophical attempts to improve our moral analysis of structural injustice: by Iris Marion Young, Onora O'Neill, and Christopher Kutz. Each presses us to get beyond an individualistic ethic. But because all three accept the dominant understanding of causality today, none bases moral agency in a causal connection between consumer and distant producer. Young and O'Neill ground this moral responsibility in a "social connection" with the producers that is implicit in the action of purchasing the shirt, even if it is not in the consciousness of the consumer. By contrast, Kutz bases the responsibility for collective harms on "participatory intention." A fundamental problem is that all three refer to the impact of social structures without providing a description of what structures are or how they operate. An inquiry is needed into that discipline specializing in the analysis of social structures: sociology.

Part II, the next four chapters, provides the analytical resources needed to adequately describe the contemporary global economy. Chapter 4 introduces "critical realism," a view of the world and of science as an endeavor to describe the forces and mechanisms that make things happen in that world. Critical realism proposes a philosophy of the natural sciences that aims to replace 250 years of empiricism since David Hume. Taking cues from what scientists do in the lab, Roy Bhaskar, the principal founding voice of critical realism, rejects the decision to limit human knowledge to what is perceptible by our five senses. Instead, reality comprises three nested realms: the empirical (everything perceived), the actual (everything that occurs, which includes the empirical), and the whole of reality (the empirical, the actual, and the forces that cause things to occur). Critical realism objects to the assignment of causal power to scientific laws. The book does not hit the floor due to the law of gravity. It hits the floor due to the force created by the relation between the book and the earth, with neither the relation nor the force directly perceptible by our five senses. Scientific "laws" are only helpful human summaries, created to name natural forces. And due to the "emergence" of novelty in nature, we should see the world as "stratified," as having different "levels," so that a higher level—say, water or human consciousness—cannot be fully explained by the characteristics of their constituent parts.

Chapter 5 investigates the application of these principles of critical realism to social structures. With competing views of structures on offer in sociology, a few fundamental philosophical commitments essential to theology are helpful to outsiders in choosing among them. Eliminating from consideration those views that are either individualistic (and reject the reality of structures) or holistic (and reject the freedom of individuals), critical realist sociology is advocated as most adequate. A social structure is a system of relations among preexisting social positions into which persons enter. Like the relation between the book and the earth, such relations are not sense-perceptible but are ontologically real, and, as a result, structures are as well. When we take on, for example, the position of rider on a city bus, that preexisting position is in relation to the preexisting position of bus driver, which another person has taken on. Both driver and rider face restrictions and opportunities generated by the relation of the two positions. Critical realist sociology makes clear how structures are ontologically real: they emerge from the actions of individuals but then have an existence at a "higher" level. They have their causal power by nondeterministically altering the decisions that persons within them make. Most frequently, persons sustain structures by making decisions in accord with the restrictions and opportunities they face, but they can resist this causal impact and, if enough others join in, they transform the structures.

Chapter 6 focuses on power, a much-maligned characteristic of human relations. Although many people instinctively think that power is a bad thing—for it can surely be used for evil purposes—the fact is that most power occurring in most of life is good and constructive. Focusing on power as constrictive—by imposing restrictions on others—and "enticive"—by offering opportunities to others—we can see that parents exercise power over their children, teachers over their students, and city council members over their fellow citizens. This understanding of power allows us to better describe the power of social structures, which is actualized (only) when persons make decisions within those structures in the face of restrictions and opportunities those structures generate. And because over the long run we typically make and remake the same kind of decisions within the same social structures, those structures also have a kind of constitutive power. They not only shape our decisions at the moment; over time they shape our characters as well.

Chapter 7 applies this view of structures and power to the market as a social structure. The great advantage of the market is its capacity to relay information very quickly over long distances by means of price changes so that individuals and businesses can quickly adjust to changing conditions. Like all social structures, markets generate restrictions (e.g., rising prices or the threat of a loss) and opportunities (e.g., ways to buy more cheaply or to make a profit) that shape decisions made within them. Because social structures are ontologically real, we can understand the global market for shirts as a long chain of relations between social positions, starting with the relation between consumer and clerk at the store, all the way to the other end of the supply chain to the relation between the factory floor manager and the seamstress. This establishes a causal relation between consumer and seamstress that is quite real even though different in kind from the conception of causality implicit in empiricism.

Part III comprises the final three chapters. Chapter 8 addresses the character of sinful social structures. These have been identified in Catholic social thought as evil forces in the world, but without any analytical clarity about what a social structure is or how a structure would be sinful. Employing the critical realist understanding of social structures, taking a cue from Pope Benedict XVI, and employing Karl Rahner's description of the characteristics of original sin, the chapter comes to two conclusions. The first is that sinful social structures are sinful in the way original sin is sinful: they influence our choices without canceling our freedom. Second, any assessment that a structure is sinful requires two kinds of judgment. On the one hand is the more obvious judgment that outcomes of structural forces are morally destructive. On the other is the often-implicit choice of a "casual typology," a set of assumptions about "how things work" in the particular kind of structure we are examining.

Chapter 9 brings together the various insights from earlier in the volume to describe the character of economic ethics in a stratified global world. It reviews the choices among alternative causal frameworks, noting that the decision to employ critical realism is itself a (more basic) choice of a causal framework, which thereby eliminates explanations of social phenomena that are either collectivistic or individualistic. But it points out that each of us faces a choice of a more specific causal framework that explains "what causes what" in whatever social structure we are investigating: whether our place of work, the global market for shirts, or the Tuesday morning garden club. It then examines two important issues as examples of how the critical realist analysis can assist moral judgment. The first is whether it is more important to improve the rules of the economic system or increase personal virtue (typically a difference between the political left and right). The second is the importance of trust and reciprocity in economic life. The chapter concludes with the judgment that because we as consumers are causally related to the distant producers of the goods we buy, each of us has a moral responsibility (along with many others, of course) for the injustices that markets cause in the lives of those people.

Chapter 10 addresses what we can do in light of such moral obligations. At a most basic level, one option is to alter our consumption patterns by purchasing "fair trade" or "ethical trade" products and favoring brands known for their efforts to ensure responsible production. Another is to participate in efforts to alter the policies and practices of large firms. The case of Nike is a helpful example. And because consumers are citizens as well, it is important to make the issue of labor standards in manufacturing—both domestically and abroad—a part of one's agenda as a voter. Particularly in elections for national office, attitudes toward justice in less industrialized nations are critical.

The volume's conclusion gives a detailed summary of the argument and a one-paragraph précis:

A social structure is a system of relations among preexisting social positions into which persons enter. Structures affect moral agency because the incentives and disincentives they generate tend to alter the decisions of persons within them. Personal moral responsibility requires not only virtuous decisions within structures (resisting restrictions and opportunities that encourage morally evil decisions) but also effective efforts to alter social structures so that restrictions and opportunities make morally good decisions more likely and, in the long run, shape us to be morally better persons.

To understand and respond to the moral challenges of global markets, we need a new way of thinking about them. As Christina Traina has put it, the shift required is akin to the move in physics from Newtonian mechanics to the theory of relativity.[7] The more comprehensive view incorporates the earlier approach as a subset, while the earlier approach exhibits no awareness of the more comprehensive vision.

Conclusion

Put simply, this volume applies insights of critical realist sociology into the causal powers of social structures to understand better the causal impact of markets—and our participation in them—in the injustices that occur in the lives of the distant people who produce the goods we buy. The constraints of space do not allow the application of these same insights into social structures to the vast array of problems in social life. Racism remains a scourge for people of color. "The very conditions on which human civilization has depended for the last 12,000 years are threatened by human ideologies, actions, and systems that perpetuate climate change."[8] Health care, immigration, economic inequality, sexual harassment, war, homelessness, and religious freedom around the world require a sharpened analysis. Still, the analysis provided in this volume provides an example of how these other pressing moral problems might be similarly illuminated.

Central to each of these problems, and particularly the issues addressed in this volume, is the pervasive influence of individualism on how we understand ourselves and the world around us. To this we now turn.

Notes

1. Associated Press, "23 Killed in Bangladesh Factory as Boiler Explodes and Sparks Fire," *Los Angeles Times*, September 10, 2016, http://www.latimes.com/world/la-fg-bangladesh -factory-fire-20160910-snap-story.html; Shahnaj Begum, "Probes Find No Real Cause of Tampaco Fire," *Daily Observer*, September 28, 2016, http://www.observerbd.com /details.php?id=35571.

2. Associated Press, "32 Workers Killed in China Steel Plant Accident," *NBC News*, April 18, 2007, http://www.nbcnews.com/id/18170087/ns/world_news-asia_pacific/t/workers -killed-china-steel-plant-accident/.

3. Declan Walsh and Steven Greenhouse, "Inspectors Certified Pakistani Factory as Safe as Before Disaster," *New York Times*, September 19, 2012, http://www.nytimes.com/2012 /09/20/world/asia/pakistan-factory-passed-inspection-before-fire.html; Pauline Overeem, Martje Theuws, and Mariette van Hijstee, "Fatal Fashion," *SOMO*, March 1, 2013, https://www.somo.nl/fatal-fashion-2/.

4. Saad Hammadi and Matthew Taylor, "Bangladesh: Workers Jump to Their Deaths as Fire Engulfs Factory Making Clothes for Gap," *Guardian*, December 14, 2010, https:// www.theguardian.com/world/2010/dec/14/bangladesh-clothes-factory-workers-jump-to -death; "At Least 28 More Garment Workers Die in Bangladeshi Factory Fire," *Clean Clothes Campaign*, December 14, 2012, https://cleanclothes.org/news/2010/12/14/at -least-28-more-garment-workers-die-in-bangladeshi-factory-fire; Maher Sattar, "Bangladesh's Garment Workers Brave Deadly Fires to Make Luxury American Clothing," *Huffington Post*, May 2, 2012, https://www.huffingtonpost.com/2012/05/02/bangladesh -garment-workers-american-luxury-clothing_n_1470922.html.

5. Jason Burke, "Rana Plaza: One Year On from the Bangladesh Factory Disaster," *Guardian*, April 19, 2014, https://www.theguardian.com/world/2014/apr/19/rana-plaza-bangladesh -one-year-on; Vikas Bajajnov, "Fatal Fire in Bangladesh Highlights the Dangers Facing Garment Workers," *New York Times*, November 25, 2012, http://www.nytimes.com/2012 /11/26/world/asia/bangladesh-fire-kills-more-than-100-and-injures-many.html.

6. Spencer, review of *Distant Markets, Distant Harms*, 549–52.

7. Traina, "Facing Forward," 174.

8. Veerabhadran Ramanathan, "How Faith, Reason and Environmental Protection Go Hand in Hand," *The Hill*, May 25, 2018, http://thehill.com/opinion/energy-environment /389401-how-faith-reason-and-environmental-protection-go-hand-in-hand.

PART I
Our Situation

CHAPTER 1

Understanding Our
Individualistic Cultural Bias

The University of St. Thomas in St. Paul, Minnesota, has worked hard to strengthen its Catholic character. As a diocesan institution, it does not have the benefit of a sponsoring religious order and thus must articulate its specifically Catholic character, while many comparable institutions feel more at ease stressing the charisms of their founding religious congregations.

The University has two seminaries, one for college students and another for college graduates. It has a lively mission office and a center for Catholic studies, which encompasses a degree major for students, the Habiger Center for Catholic Leadership, and the John A. Ryan Institute for Catholic Social Thought. Its commitment is impressive.

The University also has a wonderful motto, used in nearly all its literature in print and online: "All for the Common Good." Ironically, however, every time the motto appears it is followed by two letters: "TM." This five-word endorsement of the common good as the pervasive purpose of the University is a legal trademark, registered with the US Patent and Trademark Office, whose website explains, "A trademark is a brand name." A trademark is "used or intended to be used to identify and distinguish the goods/services of one seller or provider from those of others."[1] No organization can use this phrase without the permission of the University of St. Thomas.

Having long taught at the primary football rival of St. Thomas, I want to be clear that I say this not to impugn the motives of its leaders but to make a point about the pervasive individualism of the culture and economy in which we all live. "Branding" has become a powerful goal for most Catholic colleges and universities today. In addition, without the trademark some other entity could copy the motto, seek a trademark, and, if successful, prevent St. Thomas from using it.

The irony that anyone would seek property rights over a phrase endorsing the common good takes place within broader structural and cultural realities. How is it that we find ourselves in a situation where the self-interest of institutions and individuals "has to" constrain even bona fide efforts to further the common good?

Introduction

Our goal in this volume is to answer a question: Are we as consumers causally (and therefore morally) responsible for the harms that markets cause to distant others who make the products we buy? Most of this volume—chapters 4 through 8—is dedicated to presenting a constructive argument that produces a view of how markets work. This first chapter, however, provides a brief overview of the individualism that makes answering the question so difficult. It will review early developments in the long history of individualism, starting some eight hundred years ago and ending with the individualistic biases of American culture today. It will explore two examples—English as a dominant language and gerrymandering—to illustrate how an individualistic perspective is empirically inaccurate.

The Long Road to Individualism

The evolution of individualism in Western culture occurred over many centuries, in tandem with several other developments, including the rise of science and the shrinking of religion in so many parts of life. One of the most insightful accounts of this long road to individualism is provided by the philosopher Charles Taylor in his monumental study *A Secular Age*.[2] In it, he disputes what he calls the standard "subtraction" story of science and secularization that most people take for granted.

According to this subtraction story, religion—from primitive tribes to the medieval Christian church—sees the natural world as "enchanted." In Christian theology, the story goes, God is deeply involved in nature, which is vividly embodied in the festivals, carnivals, Ember days, blessing of crops, and other Christian appropriations of pagan culture. With the development of modern science, people started to be interested in the natural world "for their own sakes" and not just as some form of service to God.[3] Over centuries, from the Middle Ages to the modern period, trust in science and the value of individual autonomy increased, and religion receded. Responsible intellectuals then confronted a "disenchanted" natural world with no religious concerns. From Taylor's point of view, this story about the subtraction of religion to create modern individualistic, secular society is deeply mistaken—and the true story is much more interesting.

As have many before him, Taylor credits the Protestant Reformation with an important role in this process. Martin Luther, John Calvin, and other reformers rejected Catholic sacramentals (crucifixes, oils, salt, holy water, palms, ashes, etc.) as distorting elements of "magic," and they pressed for "the abolition of the enchanted cosmos." Instead, "sanctification depends entirely now on our inner transformation, our throwing ourselves on God's mercy in faith."[4] In contrast to the subtraction story, this move toward a disenchanted world and the increasing importance of the individual arose out of a conscious affirmation of Christian faith and not a rejection of it.

But Taylor cautions that this recognition of the Protestant Reformation is far from the complete history, because the Reformation was simply the most dramatic in a long line of efforts at reform within the church. Consider even official church policy. The Fourth Lateran Council, held in 1215, required that individual Christians annually participate in the sacrament of auricular confession, out of a concern to deepen the faith of the people, representing an endorsement of "a new individuality" in Catholic piety.[5]

Even more important, Taylor argues, was the rise of new movements of lay people in the thirteenth century—the Franciscans being the best example—that pressed for a lay spirituality in the world. These events in effect aimed to move the center of gravity of the apostolic life out of the monastery and into the world three centuries before Martin Luther posted his ninety-five theses on the door of the Castle Church in Wittenberg. It put greater emphasis on the role of ordinary believers. And, in later intellectual developments by Franciscan thinkers such as Bonaventure, Duns Scotus, and William of Occam, "it ends up giving a new status to the particular as something more than a mere instantiation of the universal."[6] Such developments represented a conceptual foundation for a growing appreciation of the uniqueness of each individual person. Its importance should not be underestimated. As Taylor puts it, "Though it couldn't be clear at the time, we with hindsight can recognize this as a major turning point in the history of Western civilization, an important step toward that primacy of the individual which defines our culture."[7]

Simultaneously, within another strain in the Catholic intellectual tradition Thomas Aquinas imported the insights of Aristotle into Christian philosophy and theology and proposed that we understand the natural world as having its own rules, that is, natural law. God is certainly responsible for the creation of this system, but Taylor credits Aquinas with "the autonomization of nature," another step on the road to the disenchantment of the natural world.[8] As with the Franciscan tradition, this Dominican insight was deeply tied to faith and not a rejection of it.

The trajectory from the thirteenth century to our day is a long and complicated one, but Taylor points out that it eventuates in the existence of "the buffered self": the human person is an "agent who no longer fears demons, spirits, magic forces."[9] Persons are identified more and more as subjects with rational control over their lives and less and less with ties to religious or cultural communities. As a result, "it is not surprising that the agent trained in this discipline falls easily prey to ideologies of atomism."[10]

In sum, Taylor rejects the subtraction story of Western culture because it is wrong to think that a departure from religion drove these changes. Rather, "a more conscious and zealous dedication to God . . . largely fueled the process of disenchantment."[11] The Old Testament conviction that religious faith is fundamentally a covenant between God and his people slowly erodes; religion becomes an individual commitment and an individual choice. Similarly, the stress on individual responsibility for one's faith eventually leads to a reconceived view of society as simply constituted by individuals and not an organic community.

As this brief history of the development of individualism in the West reveals, the rise of economics as a separate discipline in the nineteenth century cannot be blamed for the individualistic bias of contemporary culture in advanced industrialized societies today. The individualistic economic mind-set is clearly an effect, and not the cause, of a longer historical process. Nonetheless, the discipline of economics has since become a powerful progenitor of individualism today, both for its undeniable influence on government policies in nearly every nation on earth and for its pedagogical influence on the millions of college students around the globe who each year take Econ 101 and, to one extent or another, come to adopt its view of the world. We will examine the individualizing characteristics of economics in chapter 2.

Habits of the American Heart

In her study "A Brief History of Individualism," Nadia Urbinati observes that the American individualism of the mid-nineteenth century was experienced as a positive force precisely because it was structured by an equality of condition (generating a strong sense of self-respect) and a politics of rights (accompanied by "a strong sense of responsibility toward the community").[12] Emerging from a European historical context, where family lineage was far too influential, Americans celebrated the opportunity to "start anew," both nationally and personally. Eventually, however, the sense of responsibility to the common good withered, whether under the influence of the British conservatism of Edmund Burke or the later economic individualism of Friedrich Hayek.

A similar account, fleshed out in more detail, is provided by Robert Bellah and colleagues in *Habits of the Heart*. The authors conducted a large number of one-on-one interviews with Americans to better understand the relation of individualism and social commitment in the United States.[13] The book opens with a description of Brian Palmer, a successful businessman living in San Jose, California. After years focusing on work and his own advancement within the corporation, Brian experienced a divorce, a reexamination of life values, and a new marriage, which led to a shift of his concern toward family. Yet when asked to describe the reasons behind this change, "his new goal—devotion to marriage and children— seems as arbitrary and unexamined as his earlier pursuit of material success. Both are justified as idiosyncratic preferences rather than as representing a larger sense of the purpose of life."[14]

When asked about other moral convictions, such as his opposition to lying, Brian says, "Why is integrity important and lying bad? I don't know. It just is. It's just so basic. I don't want to be bothered with challenging that. It's part of me. I don't know where it comes from, but it's very important."[15] As the authors put it, Brian "lacks a language to explain what seem to be the real commitments that define his life, and to that extent the commitments themselves are precarious."[16]

As interviews of others affirm, Brian's combination—having particular moral commitments along with an inability to explain a foundation for them beyond personal inclination—typifies much of American culture today. The authors attribute this situation to a shift in the character of American individualism over the last two centuries.

The United States, they argue, was founded on two versions of individualism: biblical and civic. Biblical individualism arrived on the shores with dedicated Christians who were escaping religious persecution in England. These were strong individuals standing up for their beliefs. But as John Winthrop, the first governor of the Massachusetts Bay Colony, said just before disembarking in 1630, "We must delight in each other, make others' conditions our own, rejoyce together, mourn together, labor and suffer together, always having before our eyes our community as members of the same body."[17] Biblical individualism was deeply rooted in communal commitment.

By the time of the founding of the republic a century and a half later, a second, more secular form of individualism had appeared. Civic individualism held up the ideal of "the active citizen contributing to the public good."[18] The Founding Fathers of the nation made few religious arguments, but, similar to biblical individualism, their civic principles also aimed for "a web of interconnection by creating trust, joining people to families, friends, communities, and churches, and making each individual aware of his reliance on the larger society."[19]

As the economic vitality of the United States grew during the nineteenth century, advocates of both biblical and civic individualism recognized the need for a public moral consensus that could lend meaning to the rapidly emerging economic order. Out of the economic and cultural shifts over the years came two other forms of individualism that continue to undermine community today.

Utilitarian individualism "takes as given certain basic human appetites and fears . . . and sees human life as an effort by individuals to maximize their self-interest relative to these given ends."[20] Expressive individualism is founded on the assumption that "each person has a unique core of feeling and intuition that should unfold or be expressed if individuality is to be realized."[21] For both, Bellah and colleagues argue, "the touchstones of truth and goodness lie in individual experience and intimate relationships."[22] Largely gone is any articulated sense that daily meaning is wrapped up in commitments that the individual hasn't personally chosen.

In short, one of the fundamental messages of this study is that, remarkably, Americans are more involved communally than their language allows them to acknowledge. International comparisons find that they are more frequently and deeply engaged in civic organizations and voluntary associations than their peers in most other industrialized nations. The Brian Palmers of the nation are indeed involved in coaching youth sports and encouraging truthfulness among the young, even though the language they use to articulate the reasons behind such activities has veered dramatically toward the individualistic and idiosyncratic. Unfortunately, this generates an individualistic bias in how we think and talk about daily life—and makes it much more difficult to recognize how we are related to the distant producers of the things we buy.

The Individualistic Bias in Everyday Experience

Because so much of the culture around us describes us individualistically and encourages us to live individualistically, it is often difficult for us to recognize the larger structural forces that shape our choices; we think "we're the cause of our own actions." Of course, to a large extent that is true. As we saw in the previous section, the culture itself is a major force in this process. However, it will be helpful to look at two examples of how social structures shape our decisions in ways that seem so "natural" that they can be almost invisible within our awareness of the world.

Language

First, consider the interplay of language and social structure.[23] English has become the world's global language. Approximately 360 million people speak English as their first language. According to a Harvard Business School report, 1.75 billion people on the planet speak English at a useful level, most having learned English as a second or third language.[24] English has become so important as the language of international commerce that Hiroshi Mikitani, the CEO of Rakuten—Japan's largest online marketplace—mandated that English would be the company's official language of business, even among the firm's Japanese executives during business meetings in Japan.[25] What does this have to do with the rest of us?

We will see in more detail in chapter 5 how sociologists describe social structures that generate opportunities and restrictions to which individuals within those structures must react. Consider the options open to me as an English-speaking tourist. I can travel to scores of nations around the world without knowing the local language and still be assured that many people there will understand English and will facilitate my journey. This ease of travel is enabled by the structure of languages in the world. But consider citizens of Brazil, or Sri Lanka, or Italy. Should they wish to travel to China or Germany or Malaysia, they will face a significant restriction. They will have to hire a translator, learn the local language, or learn English, each of which imposes a significant cost, in order to cope from day to day on such a trip.

An individualistic interpretation of these linguistic facts will think of them as nearly "natural," something like the presence of gravity that keeps us from floating away into space. A less individualistic understanding recognizes that the ease of travel I enjoy as an English speaker is generated by socially constructed facts that originated in human history due to, for example, the reach of the British Empire in the eighteenth and nineteenth centuries and the influence of American business and military prowess in the twentieth.

Gerrymandering

Consider a second example, from electoral politics.[26] In the United States, every seat in the House of Representatives is open for election every two years. When the election is over, we often say that "the people have spoken." While there is much truth to this, it is also seriously misleading. There are a number of difficulties to overcome in ensuring that the views of the citizens eventuate in a Congress that reflects those views. The distorting effect of "dark money" in political campaigns is well known, but here the focus is on gerrymandering: the design of election districts to favor the candidates of one political party over another.[27]

Consider a hypothetical example, where all voters in the United States are unwavering members of either the Democratic or Republican Party and each always votes along party lines. Presume further that 60 percent of all voters are committed Republicans and that the vast majority of Republicans live in heavily Republican congressional districts (for example, districts where 80 percent of voters are Republican). Assume that most Democrats live in less heavily Democratic districts (say, with 60 percent of voters being Democrats).

Because a winner needs only 50 percent plus one vote, any additional votes for a candidate above the 50 percent mark are "wasted." In Democratic districts, the extra "10 percent" of Democratic votes above the needed 50 percent are wasted. Put more precisely, one in six Democrats (17 percent) cast wasted votes. In Republican districts, the extra "30 percent" of Republican votes above the 50 percent are wasted votes. That is, three in eight Republicans (37 percent) cast wasted votes. Because so many more Republican votes are wasted, Democrats could win a majority of the seats in the House of Representatives even though more citizens vote Republican.

This fundamental fact of electoral politics often leads the majority party in state government (where election districts are defined) to draw the boundaries of election districts to favor their own party's candidates for both state and national elections. Some states have found more equitable solutions, such as assigning a three-judge panel to redraw election districts, but many states still allow the partisan political process to do so.

Gerrymandering by the Republican Party in North Carolina brought a 2016 court order to redraw two districts that are heavily African American, one of which zig-zagged its way some ninety miles through the state. By putting so many minority voters in one district, many of their votes are sure to be wasted. As Democratic State Senator Josh Stein objected, "North Carolina is a 50-50 state, and yet this map all but guarantees that 10 out of 13 in our congressional delegation will be Republican."[28] Gerrymandering by the Democratic Party in Maryland in 2012 created a narrow pinwheel-shaped district for Congressman John Sarbanes, apparently to put him up for reelection in all of the state's key media markets and facilitate his later run for the US Senate.[29] The overall relevance of gerrymandering in the United States is amply illustrated in the elections of 2010. All Democratic candidates for the House of Representatives together received approximately one million more votes than did all Republican candidates, but the election resulted in a thirty-four-seat advantage for the Republican Party.

The purpose of this example is not to criticize one party or another, nor even to examine the injustice of the gerrymandering process, unjust though it is. The point is that interpreting election outcomes as simply the result of voting by individuals ("the people have spoken") conceals the causal impact of structural forces at play and far overstates the causal efficacy of individual voters. Employing a distinction from the philosophy of science, we might call Election Day voting the "precipitating" cause of the election of candidates. As such, it is but one cause among others (like the shape of election districts) that together cause the outcome of the election. A similar oversimplification is evident in individualistic interpretations of global travel, economic markets, and a host of other aspects of social life. A more careful examination of the character of social structures and their causal impact in the lives of individuals will come in chapter 5.

Conclusion

This chapter has briefly sketched out the history and character of the individualism that typifies so much of daily life in advanced industrialized nations today. In principle, individualism is no more dangerous to an authentic humanity than is collectivism. But because of the historical eclipse of collectivist political options following the collapse of the Soviet Union and the steady transformation of China, individualism is today by far the greater threat to personal human flourishing and the common good.

Yet even though individualism today makes it difficult for most people to understand the complex relationships in global social structures, might not the discipline of economics offer a solution? One might reasonably suppose that economics would be able to explain the causal impact of consumers on the distant factories that produce the things they buy. Unfortunately, economics suffers from a similar, though more "rational," individualism.

Notes

1. US Patent and Trademark Office, "Trademark Basics."
2. Taylor, *A Secular Age*.
3. Taylor, *A Secular Age*, 90.
4. Taylor, *A Secular Age*, 79.
5. Taylor, *A Secular Age*, 69.
6. Taylor, *A Secular Age*, 94.

7. Taylor, *A Secular Age*, 94.
8. Taylor, *A Secular Age*, 91.
9. Taylor, *A Secular Age*, 135.
10. Taylor, *A Secular Age*, 142.
11. Taylor, *A Secular Age*, 143.
12. Urbinati, "A Brief History of Individualism."
13. Bellah et al., *Habits of the Heart*.
14. Bellah et al., *Habits of the Heart*, 6.
15. Bellah et al., *Habits of the Heart*, 7.
16. Bellah et al., *Habits of the Heart*, 8.
17. Bellah et al., *Habits of the Heart*, 28.
18. Bellah et al., *Habits of the Heart*, 142.
19. Bellah et al., *Habits of the Heart*, 251.
20. Bellah et al., *Habits of the Heart*, 336.
21. Bellah et al., *Habits of the Heart*, 334.
22. Bellah et al., *Habits of the Heart*, 250.
23. I am indebted to Margaret Archer for this example.
24. Neeley, "Global Business Speaks English."
25. Neeley, "Global Business Speaks English."
26. I am indebted to Margaret Archer for my Americanized version of her example. Archer, *Realist Social Theory*, 54–55.
27. This feature of US elections, or, more concretely, the predictable fate of a third party that gets 20 percent of a nationwide vote but wins no seats in Congress, is the reason most other nations employ some form of proportional voting.
28. Hrafnkell Haraldsson, "Scalia-less SCOTUS Lets Stand Lower Court Ruling Against NC Gerrymandering," *Politicus USA*, February 20, 2016, http://www.politicususa.com /2016/02/20/scalia-less-scotus-lets-stand-court-ruling-nc-gerrymandering.html.
29. Deb Belt, "Maryland's 'Praying Mantis' District Among Worst in Gerrymandering," *Annapolis Patch*, January 13, 2016, http://patch.com/maryland/annapolis/marylands -praying-mantis-district-among-worst-gerrymandering-0.

CHAPTER 2

Why Economics Sees
Markets Individualistically

If the Bangladeshi seamstress who put the stitches in the collar of the shirt I am wearing died in a factory fire six months after the shirt was made, do I have any moral responsibility for her death simply because I bought the shirt? Most people would agree that if I helped to cause her death, I would have some degree of moral responsibility. But did I really play a causal role in her death simply by buying the shirt?

Most economists would answer "no." Surely, most would say, the fault lies with the government inspectors who failed to enforce safety standards or the factory owners who did not install fire escapes. The market for shirts offers me alternative retailers at which to shop and a choice of shirts once I enter a store. Similarly, the woman in Bangladesh faced various alternatives for employment and made a choice, given her options. Her wages as a seamstress were far below the average in industrialized nations, but most probably were above the average in her nation. In economics the market is understood as an opaque "black box" that coordinates the decisions of producers and consumers, but there is no need to look inside the box to understand the connections between the people involved, because each participant has a vanishingly insignificant impact on the market as a whole.

Introduction

This chapter will examine the history of the discipline of economics to get a better view of the self-imposed limitations on scientific method that economists have chosen to live by. Contemporary economics as a discipline is absolutely essential to any understanding of global markets and the everyday economic life of ordinary people. Yet, in spite of the many insights it offers, over the last two centuries the discipline has in several important ways become less helpful, both from the point of view of formal ethical reflection and from the perspective of the general public. Critically

important are the discipline's radically individualistic understanding of social interaction and its peculiar commitment to empiricism and to an empirically untenable
view of how humans make choices. Chapter 4 will step back to review the parallel
problems existing in the philosophy of science and will propose a better alternative
for understanding how science operates: critical realism. Chapter 5 will investigate
the view of critical realist sociology on how social structures have causal impact.
Chapter 7 will apply this analysis to markets as social structures to make clear how
we as consumers do indeed stand in causal relationship to the distant others who
make the products we buy.

Two Centuries of Economics

During the 2,100 years between Aristotle and Adam Smith, everyone assumed that
considerations of economic life were a part of the discipline of philosophy. Smith,
widely considered to be the father of modern economics, was a moral philosopher
who never used the word "economics." The first university chair in "political economy" was established at the University of Naples in 1754; its first occupant was
Antonio Genovesi, a philosopher and Catholic priest. In 1805 Thomas Malthus
was named England's first "professor of political economy," while the first formal
chair in the discipline in Britain was not founded until 1825, at All Souls College, Oxford University. Political economy as a separate academic discipline in the
English-speaking world is only about 200 years old.

When the discipline that we today call "economics" moved out of the philosophy
department and established its own methods and principles, it did so in an intellectual environment dominated by a growing respect for the methods of the highly
successful natural sciences and by the utilitarian analysis of both ethics and science
provided by Jeremy Bentham. Much has changed over two centuries, but mainstream economics today remains deeply shaped by these forces, particularly as articulated by the most influential nineteenth-century British scholar in both economics
and philosophy, John Stuart Mill. This chapter reviews the most important developments that have left today's economists with a paradigm that is unable to analyze, and
in most cases unable even to recognize, the causal links between consumers in the
developed world and the producers half a planet away who make the things they buy.

The Four Bequests of John Stuart Mill

The four most basic methodological commitments in the history of British and
American economics were espoused, though not necessarily invented, by John Stuart Mill. First, in his articulation of the philosophy of social science, Mill argued
that the social world is so thoroughly characterized by a complex "plurality of
causes" and an intricate "intermixture of effects" that examining particular cases to
discern general patterns (i.e., relying on induction) is doomed to failure. Instead,

he proposed that political economy must be a "deductive science" on the model of "mature" sciences like physics, which begins, for example, with a general principle such as gravity and then proceeds to explain events to the extent that the law of gravity can account for them.[1] As we will see, most economists today would officially reject Mill's claim that economics is a deductive science, but in their actual work they do indeed proceed with a strong dose of deductivism. Nearly every empirical investigation (typically employing economic regression analysis) is accompanied by the deductivist claim that rational, utility-maximizing decisions by economic actors lead to the outcomes under study.

Contributing to the British inclination toward deductivism in economics was the widely held conviction, often attributed to David Hume, that "mankind is much the same in all times and places." This belief underlay Adam Smith's depiction of the economic exchange of beavers for deer by primitive societies, something anthropologists today assure us did not occur. As he lived more than a century before the appearance of anthropology as a discipline, Smith might be forgiven for the error. But the German historical school of economics in the mid-nineteenth century[2] — and heterodox economists ever since[3] — have been deeply critical of the mainstream assumption that people of all cultures, continents, and centuries can be adequately understood by means of a single (deductivist) model of human decision-making.

Second, the individualism that characterizes economics today became canonized through Mill's choice of the general deductive principle with which political economy began. "Political economy borrows from the pure science of mind" the laws of "the phenomena of mind which are concerned with production and distribution."[4] "Political economy considers mankind as occupied solely in *acquiring and consuming wealth*, and aims at showing what is the course of action . . . if that motive . . . were *absolute ruler* of all their actions."[5] That is, individuals attempt to maximize their wealth. Two secondary principles are included: attempts to maximize wealth are mitigated by an "aversion to labour" and the "desire of the present enjoyment of costly indulgences."[6]

Writing half a century earlier than Mill, Smith attended to the motivation of individuals in economic life. After all, it was he who argued that "it is not from the benevolence of the butcher, the brewer, or the baker that we expect our dinner, but from their regard to their own interest."[7] But Smith did not restrict the explanation of economic behavior to self-interested activity.[8] Things were different for Mill. The combination of the dominant individualistic utilitarianism of the day and his own philosophy of science (needing a fundamental principle in a deductive science) led to his basing the discipline on the maximization of wealth.

Here Mill was borrowing generously from the utilitarianism of Jeremy Bentham, who argued that the desire to increase pleasure and reduce pain was not only the empirically best explanation for why people do what they do but was also the morally best rule for how people ought to act.[9] Mill insisted that political economy should not engage in moral judgments, but he found Bentham's empirical analysis adequate for certifying the maximization of wealth as the starting principle of economic analysis.

We should be clear, however, that Mill understood that people are motivated to do many things in life for reasons other than wealth maximization. As he said, no political economist "was ever so absurd as to suppose that mankind are really thus constituted," but "this is the mode in which science must necessarily proceed."[10] Unlike later economists, Mill was not proposing a general description of how people make all decisions. His point was that an economic event could be considered explained if it could be shown to be the result of the desire to maximize wealth.

The third principle Mill left to later economics is empiricism: the belief that the ultimate source and test of reliable knowledge is what our five senses can detect. Thus, any hypothesis about why some economic event has occurred must be "tested against the facts." The twentieth century's turn to econometrics has led to a reliance on statistical techniques that didn't exist in Mill's day, but the same assumption reigns: any hypothesis explaining why something happens must be tested to see if it can explain similar things that happened in the past.

The fourth principle Mill bequeathed to economics is the conviction that the discipline aims only to describe what *is* going on in the world and leaves judgments about what *should* go on to policy makers, philosophers, theologians, and ordinary citizens. Mill's version of this principle carried with it a strict sense of epistemological humility (which the discipline would later largely abandon). Policy makers must rely on the insights of many sciences as well as their own value judgments. The job of economists and other scientists is to receive from policy makers a goal, investigate its "causes and conditions," and send back "the proposition . . . that the performance of certain actions will attain the end."[11] Thus economists, as scientists, must humbly admit that they do not have a broad enough perspective to endorse or oppose particular policy positions.

Connecting Market Prices to the Values of Consumers

The era of "classical" political economy began with Adam Smith and came to an end with the disciples of John Stuart Mill. "Neoclassical" economics began in 1871 with a change in the discipline's conception of how individual persons make decisions. British economist William Stanley Jevons expanded on Mill's claim about the maximization of wealth to arrive at maximization of "utility"—the happiness, fulfillment, satisfaction, or whatever an individual might consider worthwhile.[12] Jevons is also responsible for the introduction of calculus to elegantly depict in mathematical terms the notion of "maximization." With these two innovations, Jevons employed what is today called "marginal utility theory" to solve the age-old "diamonds/water paradox," a primary roadblock to explaining how a product comes to have a particular price in the market. His solution brought about a dramatic increase in the self-confidence of the discipline.

Why is it that water is far more critical for human life than diamonds but its price is far lower? The answer is that the total value of a product does not determine its price; instead, the price is determined by the value to the buyer of the last unit purchased (the "marginal" unit). Put simply, if I could obtain only one cup of water per week, I would be willing to pay far more for that one cup than for a diamond. But, of course, I drink a lot of water each week, so I do not put a very high value on the last cup. The principle of "diminishing marginal utility" names this reality. For example, as we consume more and more potatoes per week—moving, for example, from two to four to five per week—we value the additional "final" potato per week less and less. In psychological terms, consuming only one or two potatoes per week makes them special; as we eat more and more per week, we tire of them. Because we pay the same price for each of those potatoes, the final ("marginal") dollar we spend on potatoes produces less utility the more potatoes we buy each week.

This is true for each of the products we buy. As we purchase more and more meat or bread or books or movie tickets or gasoline each week, the satisfaction (utility) generated by the last dollar spent on each item decreases. The economist thus asks us to think of our consumption decisions not in terms of the total satisfaction (total utility) that any particular product provides but in terms of its marginal utility—the satisfaction provided by adding one more dollar's worth of consumption per week. Put more plainly, if you have already decided how to spend all but the last dollar of your budget for the week, you would choose to spend that last dollar where the extra dollar's worth of one product produces more utility than that dollar would produce if spent on any other product. You would buy more of whichever product has the highest marginal utility for you at the time.[13]

This allows the economist to speak of the individual "demand curve" for each product. For example, at any particular price for gasoline—whether one, two, three, or four dollars per gallon—we will decide how much to buy based on the marginal utility of the last dollar's worth of gasoline we buy per week (compared to the satisfaction we would get from spending that extra dollar on some other things we buy), all based on our own values. A demand curve is exactly this: If the price of gasoline is X, how much will you buy? If the price is Y, how much will you buy? And in turn, the demand curve for the whole market for gasoline is simply the sum of all the demand curves of all the individuals in the market who buy it: it tells how many gallons of gasoline all consumers together will be willing to buy at any particular price. From this perspective, market demand can be traced directly to the values of consumers.

By 1891 the American economist John Bates Clark had applied this same sort of analysis to the decisions of producers of goods, through "marginal productivity" analysis. Analogous to diminishing marginal utility for consumers is increasing marginal cost for producers, and analogous to the particular tastes of each consumer are the producer's particular conditions of production (costs and efficiency of labor, costs and size of the production facility, etc.). Where consumers try to maximize their utility, producers try to maximize their profits. Thus, just as each individual consumer has a demand curve for each particular product, each individual producer has a supply curve that indicates how much he is willing to produce at any particular price of that product in the market. The supply curve for each product in the overall market is simply the sum of all the supply curves of individual producers.

Thus, the market price for a product is the price at which the number of units of the product that utility-maximizing people are willing to buy is equal to the number of units that profit-maximizing producers are willing to sell. If we consider all products and services together, the interaction of all this is called "general equilibrium analysis," which was first articulated in 1871 by the French mathematician and economist Léon Walras.[14] Following Mill's example, this theory explains the prices and quantities of products in the marketplace by tracing them back to the maximizing decisions of individual consumers and producers.

There are two great advantages provided to economics by this marginal analysis of human decision-making of both consumers and producers. The first, and more apparent, is the systematic conception of how individuals make rational consumption and production choices, where rationality is defined in a precise mathematical way. For those who held up the natural sciences as the ideal model for social science, this analysis stood economics head and shoulders above sociology, political science, and psychology.[15]

The second advantage is that general equilibrium analysis provides an often-unacknowledged moral legitimation for the economist's reliance on markets. Most important, the demand curve for gasoline or potatoes or automobiles or haircuts is understood to be rooted in the valuations that individual consumers place on the various products among which they choose in accord with their own values. Similarly, the supply curve for each of these products is founded on the decisions of the suppliers of goods and services. Because suppliers are assumed to be simply maximizing profits, they are also assumed to be simply responding to the value-based choices of consumers. This analysis is the foundation of the notion of "consumer sovereignty": a conviction that the value-based decisions of consumers determine what gets produced and sold in the market.[16]

There have been many refinements in economics since the late nineteenth century, but this basic model for understanding the economy—the neoclassical economic paradigm—remains at the core of the discipline today. Recent developments in "behavioral" economics, however, now raise serious questions about the assumptions behind this "orthodox" economic view of the world. Time and again behavioral economists find that people don't decide things as the paradigm assumes. Nonetheless, the neoclassical economic paradigm is articulated in the microeconomic theory courses taught in nearly every university, and its view of human decision-making and interaction is largely shared by the vast majority of both conservative and liberal economists today.

Broadening the Definition of Economics

Three further changes in the discipline that are relevant to our task occurred in the twentieth century. All three happened while maintaining the four founding bequests of John Stuart Mill.

The first occurred when economists came to think of their discipline as examining all human choices and not merely those in the realm of economic life. In 1935

Lionel Robbins proposed the definition of economics that is now accepted by most economists and appears in nearly every introductory economics textbook: "Economics is the science which studies human behavior as a relationship between ends and scarce means which have alternative uses."[17] That is, economics is the study of not just decisions related to economic life but any sort of decision where limited resources play a part (which includes just about every human decision, since financial means are a part of so many decisions, and the use of time—also a scarce resource—is a part of all of them).

This shift in the definition of the discipline was made possible by the move from maximizing wealth to maximizing utility, even though Jevons, who had made the move from wealth to utility, had argued that political economy should be restricted to "the lowest rank of feelings": "A higher calculus of moral right and wrong would be needed to show how a man may best employ his wealth for the good of others as well as himself. But when that higher calculus gives no prohibition, we need the lower calculus to gain us the utmost good in matters of moral indifference."[18]

With Robbins' expanded definition, economists jettisoned the recognition by Mill and Jevons that economics does not apply to all human decisions. Mill had cautioned against overconfidence in economics when noneconomic ("disturbing") causes intervene. In these cases, "it never can fall within the province of Political Economy; it belongs to some other science; and here the mere political economist, he who has studied no science but Political Economy, if he attempt to apply this science to practice, will fail."[19]

But once the discipline expanded its purview to include all forms of choice in conditions of scarcity, Mill's limits—and his disciplinary humility—evaporated. This new definition of the discipline—that whether investing in the stock market or serving dinner to the homeless, the persons involved will always be attempting to maximize their utility—allows economists to apply their models to both selfish and altruistic behaviors. The best-known example of this idea comes from the work of Gary Becker. Economists in Becker's line have applied economic analysis to such noneconomic topics as crime and punishment, dating and marriage, addiction, and even suicide.[20]

Making Economics More Empirical

The second shift occurred in 1938 when Paul Samuelson published his work on "revealed preference theory."[21] Economists had for decades been criticized for basing their discipline on a view of human decision-making (marginal utility theory) that both psychologists and the man on the street found woefully inadequate. Philosophers of science in the first quarter of the twentieth century were confidently moving to more and more empiricist standards, indirectly challenging economists to start not with assumptions about how people decide things but with the facts of experience.[22]

Samuelson's insight was that the supply and demand analysis (and the mathematics behind it) did not have to depend on a theory about what happens inside the human mind. The standards of empiricism in science are strict, and economists, after all, know nothing about what goes on inside the human brain. Marginal utility theory has no justification in economics, and economists cannot "borrow" it from psychology as Mill had done, since twentieth-century psychology rejected it completely.

Samuelson argued that economics can remain as robust as before if it merely traces the demand analysis back to (hypothetical) consumers' choices, not to their thinking about choices. At least in theory, if each consumer can state a preference between any two possible bundles of goods, the mathematics of microeconomic theory will remain largely unchanged. All this occurs "in theory" since the choices among bundles here has one of the same problems as the analysis of people thinking about choices: those choices have to be assumed to behave nicely from a mathematical perspective. They had to be characterized by consistency, completeness, and transitivity, each of which frequently fails when dealing with actual choices of individuals. So this economics was still reliant on an empirically faulty view of choice, but at least it no longer needed to make claims about what happens inside people's heads.

Preserving Utility Maximization

The third change in the discipline occurred in spite of the persuasiveness of arguments about the inadequacies of utility theory because most economists were unwilling to give it up. Admittedly, a significant proportion of our everyday decisions are such that utility theory describes them reasonably well: they primarily involve trade-offs among things we value, under conditions of scarcity. Whether choosing which melon to buy in the grocery, which route to take when driving to a friend's house, which stores to patronize, or which source of daily world news to rely on, most of us most of the time aim for, and likely come close to attaining, more of our goals at a lower cost (of money, time, energy, or other resources) than other choices would do. Perhaps the best evidence behind this conviction implicit in the economic model is that when thinking about the choices of others whom we do not know, most of us most often assume they are seeking to further their own goals as well as they can.

In 1953 Milton Friedman proposed a pragmatic view of economic method, arguing that good scientific principles are almost never literally true and thus economics could use the assumption of rational maximization to generate hypotheses about why things occur in the world.[23] As long as those hypotheses were subjected to empirical testing, he claimed, it doesn't matter whether the assumption is true or not. Physicists, Friedman pointed out, assume that the law of gravity is simply true, even though the inverse-square relation is almost never perfectly accurate under real-world conditions. Similarly, economists can legitimately assume that people are maximizing utility in making decisions even if this isn't true.

In proposing this view of economic method, Friedman aimed to accomplish two things. The first is an endorsement of one of the fundamentals of empiricism: the claims (hypotheses) that economists make about why things happen in the world must be tested against the facts of economic life. The second, however, is a defense of the neoclassical view of human choice—utility theory—which economists were now officially allowed to employ, although without being allowed to really believe it because psychologists dismiss it as crude and inaccurate. The problem is whether they "really believe it." We saw John Stuart Mill's statement concerning his assumption that people are simply wealth maximizers; no political economist, he said, "was ever so absurd as to suppose that mankind are really thus constituted."[24] What would today's mainstream economists say about the assertion that people "really are" utility maximizers? Very few would call it absurd. In violation of the methods of their own discipline, a sizable majority would likely endorse it with conviction. They thereby illustrate what Charles Taylor has called "the recurring ambition of our rationalist civilization to turn practical reflections much as possible into calculation."[25] Andrew M. Yuengert has investigated this issue in depth in his book *Approximating Prudence*.[26]

Friedman and contemporary economics thus maintain (in somewhat revised form) all four of the principles on which Mill founded economics: Friedman's defense of utility theory retains the deductive and individualistic basis, and his insistence that concrete hypotheses must be tested against the facts sustains the essence of Mill's empiricism. And, like Mill, Friedman insists that all this is done merely in description of what's occurring in the world without adding any of the economist's value judgments.

Problems with the Neoclassical Paradigm

Neoclassical economics today provides many valuable insights for gaining an understanding of contemporary economic life. This final portion of the chapter will review several fundamental problems with the neoclassical paradigm, but it should remain clear, especially to justice-oriented critics of economics, that the discipline provides valuable analysis. To take but one example, Nobel prize–winning econometrician and Chicago-school economist James Heckman has conducted a number of studies of the results of the Perry Preschool Program in Ypsilanti, Michigan, where low-income, low-IQ three- and four-year-olds were given an excellent preschool education. By following those individuals (and a control group that did not get that education) for forty years, Heckman is able to demonstrate that a dollar spent well in educating such children leads to greater economic returns to government (less time in prison, lower welfare costs, etc.) than people can get from investing in the stock market. His impeccable credentials have bolstered many efforts to increase spending on preschool education.[27]

It will be most helpful to review the problems created by the contemporary versions of the four fundamental commitments that John Stuart Mill bequeathed to economics: reliance on a deductive mind-set, an individualistic view of social interaction, a commitment to empiricism, and the goal of a value-free social science.

Deductivism and Individualism

The first and second of these commitments are intimately related. Mill argued that the plurality of causes and intermixture of effects in social life requires political economy to begin with a deductive principle that people try to maximize their wealth. As we have seen, this principle was later expanded to the view that everyone seeks to maximize their utility, and this broader approach then allowed for the general equilibrium analysis, which today understands prices in the market as explained by the choices of producers and consumers.

The problem here is a fundamentally individualistic assumption: that social interactions are explained when they can be traced back to their "origins" in the decisions of individuals. Neither Mill nor later mainstream economists provide an adequate warrant for the assumption that wholes are explained by tracing them back to their constituent parts. In fact, much market behavior questions this assumption.

To take but one example, the fundamental "orthodox" economic model assumes that the tastes of consumers are "exogenous": consumers have whatever tastes they have and economics does not ask where those preferences come from. "Heterodox" economists (and a growing number of behavioral economists in the neoclassical camp) criticize this assumption. They might ask, for example, why it is that many consumers are willing to pay more for a pair of jeans that looks like it's several years older than a new-looking pair. Consumers are deeply influenced by the culture around them, and many of the institutions of culture—television, movies, social media, and so on—are owned by profit-seeking businesses that aim to influence those preferences. And what about Madison Avenue advertising? There has probably never been a male who admitted that his choice of a beer was influenced by TV beer commercials, but the big brewing companies know otherwise and spend billions each year on advertising around the world.[28]

If, the critics ask, people's tastes and preferences are not simply exogenous but are shaped by their culture and, in particular, by producers aiming to increase their profits, why should the discipline of economics assume it has *explained* the price of jeans or the quantity of beer sold each year simply by tracing it back to the desires of consumers? Would not a more complete and less individualistic analysis also need to explain why people want what they want?[29] Behavioral economics has in recent years creatively investigated such questions, but this work has not altered the fundamental model taught in most microeconomic theory courses.

Empiricism

The third principle economists today inherited from Mill—a commitment to empiricism—presents further problems. Nearly all neoclassical economists endorse the fundamental empiricist assumption that any hypothesis designed to explain events must be tested against "the facts." There is a valuable epistemological humility in this principle, as it would prevent an economist from allowing her own political commitments to sway her scientific findings. Mainstream economists today rely almost universally on econometric analysis that uses advanced statistical techniques to examine data about what has happened in the world to test possible explanations. Nonetheless, there are three fundamental problems here.

The first problem we have just seen: the individualistic assumption that wholes are explained by their parts. Empiricism assumes that everything in, say, biology, could be explained—if we only knew enough—by the laws of chemistry. And everything in chemistry could be explained—in principle—by the laws of physics. Economics tends to assume that everything in the social world can be explained by the decisions made by individuals and groups. We will review in detail the problems with this argument in chapter 4.

The second concerns problems inherent in the statistical processes that careful econometricians recognize but which have been widely ignored in the use of statistics in economics. Critics of the mainstream, such as Philip Mirowski, have long argued that the discipline's focus on the statistical significance of proposed statistical explanations eclipses the far more important question of the "real" significance of the results for actual problems in the world.[30] This "cult of statistical significance" distracts not only the economists doing the work but the editors who act as gatekeepers for publication in the leading economic journals.

Third, the "facts" against which hypotheses are tested are limited to those that can be represented quantitatively. But many of the things that are contributing causes to economic events are not easily quantifiable. For example, whether people are educated is influential in the analysis of poverty around the world, but the statistic used to measure education is typically the number of years of schooling completed, even though everyone recognizes huge differences in the quality of this "one year of schooling," both within and between nations. Causally important realities that are more difficult to quantify—such as the level of trust among workers in a firm or the traditions of civic virtue among citizens in a nation—are even more likely to be dealt with coarsely or ignored altogether in econometric analysis.

Value-Free Science

The fourth principle inherited from Mill is the view of science as "value-free." Once again, the intention behind this goal is a good one: to prevent the economist's own political convictions from skewing scientific results. Yet this commitment causes two crucial problems.

The first is based on the economist's notion that economics does not distinguish between morally good and morally bad motives or goals (because it aims to be value-free), even though it nonetheless considers itself capable of endorsing or rejecting particular policies. In the assumption that people maximize their satisfaction or happiness, no distinction is made between Mother Teresa (whose life was dedicated to helping the poor) and the thief in Kolkata (who preys on them). Both are assumed to be maximizing their self-interest (Mother Teresa's interests happen to include helping others). One might think that any discipline that declines to distinguish good from bad would not then attempt to choose between better and worse policies.

Yet the vast majority of economists endorse free international trade and oppose price controls. Contrary to Mill's epistemological humility, many economists today are overconfident. Since any policy has both morally bad effects and morally good effects, how can an economist committed to a value-free science conceivably defend taking a position as a scientist for or against either policy?

The second problem with making a claim to being value-free is that economists believe they can have a value-free impact on policy makers, who in turn employ the economic information they receive when making value judgments in policy. But this belief requires an understanding of just *how* policy makers make decisions, and although most economists presume politicians maximize their utility, since Samuelson the official standards of the discipline state that economists cannot know what goes on inside the human mind. If you claim no understanding of what goes on inside people's heads, how could you possibly be sure of the character of your influence on others? And, since the same disciplinary ignorance applies to the working of one's own brain, how could you even be sure your own analysis is *not* tainted by your values?

In sum, the official mainstream economic paradigm asserts that it knows nothing about human psychology and yet it claims to understand human behavior as a relation between our goals and the scarce means we have to achieve them.[31] Many economists think they are doing value-free economics while at the same telling their students that some public policies are good and some are bad. Most economists believe that policy makers should do as economists say, due to the truth of economic insights, and most economists prize freedom as a moral good. Officially, however, economics can say nothing about what goes on inside the heads of people, and it cannot distinguish between vice and virtue, good and bad. This should lead economists to greater humility in making public policy recommendations.

Conclusion

This chapter has reviewed the development of the discipline of economics to understand better the individualistic bias that renders it unable to articulate the structurally causal links between consumers and the distant others who produce the products those consumers buy. It has outlined how deductive, individualistic, descriptive, and empiricist assumptions have both led to greater disciplinary confidence and generated an incoherent disciplinary self-understanding. Economics today has rich contributions to make but is simultaneously profoundly flawed.

In the face of the failure of economics to provide a scientific account of the connection between consumers and the distant producers of the products they buy, and in light of the individualistic biases of contemporary culture, a number of philoso-phers have attempted to devise alternative ways for understanding science, as the next chapter investigates.

Notes

1. Mill, *A System of Logic*, 619–30.
2. See, for example, Roscher, *Principles of Political Economy*.
3. See, for example, Veblen, "Why Is Economics Not an Evolutionary Science?"
4. Mill, "On the Definition of Political Economy," 132–33.
5. Mill, "On the Definition of Political Economy," 138.
6. Mill, "On the Definition of Political Economy," 138.
7. A. Smith, *The Wealth of Nations*, 14.
8. Smith criticized "those who are fond of deducing all our sentiments from certain refine-ments of self-love," rejecting the view that all actions arise from self-interest. A. Smith, *The Theory of Moral Sentiments*, 54.
9. Bentham, *Introduction to Principles of Morals and Legislation*.
10. Mill, "On the Definition of Political Economy," 139.
11. Mill, *A System of Logic*, 653–54.
12. Jevons, *The Theory of Political Economy*, 136–44. Jevons's invention of utility theory was replicated by two others on the continent: Léon Walras and Carl Menger. The three came to the same solution to the diamonds/water paradox entirely independently of the others and nearly simultaneously. See Walras, *Elements of Pure Economics*; and Menger, *Principles of Economics*.
13. Mathematically this means that the marginal utility of the last dollar spent on every product will be equal. If product A has a higher marginal utility than product B, you could (and would) increase your overall satisfaction by buying less of B (which will cause its marginal utility to rise) and more of A (whose marginal utility will fall).
14. Walras, *Elements of Pure Economics*.
15. Mirowski, *More Heat than Light*.
16. The phrase "consumer sovereignty" seems to have been coined by William Hutt, in "The Concept of Consumers' Sovereignty."
17. Robbins, *An Essay on the Nature and Significance*, 16.
18. Jevons, *The Theory of Political Economy*, 93.
19. Mill, "On the Definition of Political Economy," 151.
20. See, for example, Becker, "Crime and Punishment," 169–217.
21. Samuelson, "A Note on the Pure Theory," 61–71.
22. The most extreme example here is the Vienna Circle, a group of philosophers whose logical positivism was the high-water mark for empiricism in Western philosophy. Self-critique from its own members (e.g., Gödel's Theorem) was already reducing enthusi-asm among philosophers for such extreme forms of empiricism, but news does not travel fast across disciplinary boundaries, and economists have been slow to respond.
23. Friedman, "The Methodology of Positive Economics," 3–34.
24. Mill, "On the Definition of Political Economy," 139.
25. Taylor, *Human Agency and Language*, 17.

26. Yuengert, *Approximating Prudence*.
27. See, for example, Heckman et al., "Understanding the Mechanisms."
28. Anheuser-Busch InBev, the world's largest brewing company, spent more than $5 billion on global advertising in 2014. See Tripp Mickle, "AB InBev's Carlos Brito Explains Shuttering of Busch Media, Hiring of WPP," *Wall Street Journal*, October 31, 2014, http://blogs.wsj.com/cmo/2014/10/31/ab-inbevs-carlos-brito-explains-shuttering-of-busch-media-hiring-of-wpp/.
29. For a fuller list of the problems associated with the neoclassical account of decision-making, see Finn, "What We Should and Should Not Learn from Economics," 217–34.
30. Ziliak and McCloskey, *The Cult of Statistical Significance*; Miroski, "Three Ways to Think about Testing in Econometrics," 25–46.
31. In a rejection of empiricism, the Austrian school of economics makes similar claims about human choice but bases those claims not on empirical generalizations but on a philosophical assumption about the necessary structures of human choice. See Von Mises, *Human Action*.

CHAPTER 3

Are Consumers Responsible for Injustices a World Away?

In her memoir, *A Border Passage*, Leila Ahmed provides this account of her family's visits to the beach near the city of Cairo as a young teenager.

> One could not go to the beach without seeing people, dressed in rags, who were crippled or blind and destitute. Arriving at the entrance trying not to see, trying to drop our coins without seeing too precisely what was wrong, turning our heads away, forced at the start of every carefree day at the beach to be aware, even as we tried to shut out such thoughts, of what we did not want to be aware of: the injustice of life and the terribleness of some people's lives, the awful things that can befall people and that could at any moment befall any of us. The injustice of life—not, as we saw it, our injustice. It was not we who had made the world the way it was, not we who made the poor poor, any more than it was we who were responsible for people having accidents or falling sick or being born blind or anything else. That was the way life was. The idea that we were responsible for society or that there was anything, besides giving generously, that we could do about the inequality was unfamiliar to me then.[1]

Leila Ahmed's point here, of course, is that later in life she was able to look back at her earlier understanding as letting herself off the hook of moral responsibility for the suffering of others. This volume asks whether we—consumers who are prosperous—have done the same.

Introduction

We saw in chapters 1 and 2 how an individualistic culture leaves people less able to sense the structural forces that shape their lives and why the discipline of economics has a similar astigmatism. Still, many citizens do feel morally responsible for the injustices suffered by the distant producers of the things they buy. This chapter will examine three philosophical approaches that set out to explain *why* consumers have that responsibility, even though each fails to recognize the causal link between consumer and producer.

Some philosophers who assert we have that responsibility also attribute insincerity to those who defend the innocence of consumers and the markets that deliver the products they buy. British philosopher Onora O'Neill, for example, asserts that the powerful exploit the vulnerable while claiming to treat everyone justly:

> Well organized exploitation of others' vulnerabilities is often coupled with bare-faced assertion of their invulnerability: the powerful assume, accurately enough, that the weak must go along with their proposals, yet then interpret their compliance, outrageously enough, as evidence of informed, legitimating consent. Once exaggerated assertions about others' capacities and capabilities are smuggled in, vulnerable people to whom they are misascribed may come to be thought of as entitled to just dealing in the market but not to the help they may need. Here too activity speaks louder than words, and displays the assumptions actually made about others accurately and more honestly.[2]

The problem, of course, is that the two actions referred to here—exploitation and legitimation—are typically performed by different persons or groups. Factory managers rarely write treatises on the justice of markets, and the scholars endorsing the justice of markets don't hire seamstresses in Bangladesh. Typically those scholars hold managers—and not consumers—accountable for the abuse of workers.

The task is formidable for scholars who assert that consumers—because of their purchases—do indeed have some degree of moral responsibility for the injustices suffered by distant workers who make the products consumers buy. They must answer the question: Why?

Arguments for Consumer Responsibility

Throughout history humans have debated what is right and wrong. No one asks whether the fish acts morally when it eats a minnow, nor whether the eagle is morally justified when it swoops down and grasps the fish in its talons. Yet human persons are rightfully brought up short and led to moral reflection when they witness one human victimizing another. From the most ancient of world cultures to the present, people have deliberated about right and wrong.

Traditional Ethics

Most of this history of ethical reflection—whether by philosophers in ancient Greece, prophets in ancient Israel, or the Buddha in ancient India—focused on the decisions of ordinary people in everyday life. Some attention was undoubtedly paid to the proper role of government and even to what we would today call the institutions of civil society. However, even there ethical reflection in a predemocratic age was generally understood to produce moral advice given to kings and princes, to the leaders of government, and to those of other organizations. That is, ethics was typically seen as a matter of individual persons making right decisions, given their station in life. The premodern world had few systematic critiques of, say, the economic or political structure of a nation, as these structures were typically presumed to be beyond human shaping, something like gravity or other "facts" of the natural world. We do not hope to change—and we surely sense no obligation to change— what we assume to be immutable.

Nevertheless, traditional ethical reflection, whether philosophical or theological, remains profoundly helpful today. Creative extensions of these resources to address issues of economic complicity—like Albino Barrera's book *Market Complicity and Christian Ethics*—benefit contemporary discussion.[3] Barrera's treatment of "economic compulsion" will be particularly helpful for the discussion in chapter 7.

Still, our Western ethical tradition arose prior to the development of scientific analysis of social structures and culture over the past century. As a result, the tradition is not fully adequate for sorting out the moral issues entailed. A central part of this inadequacy is the fact that the discipline of ethics, whether in philosophy or theology, has traditionally derived moral responsibility for harms caused to others from a form of individual causal efficacy. Several contemporary philosophers have addressed this problem.

The Social Connection Model of Responsibility

One of the best-known philosophical arguments in favor of the responsibility of consumers for the injustices done to the lives of distant workers has been developed by Iris Marion Young.[4] Young argues persuasively that the usual "liability model" employed in legal analysis falls short in accounting for the consumer's role in such injustices. In the liability approach, "we must be able to say that he or she caused it." But in the case of what Young calls "structural injustice," the problem is that "we cannot trace this kind of connection." "It is not possible to identify how the actions of one particular individual, or even one particular collective agent, such as a firm, has directly produced harm to other specific individuals."[5]

Young argues that there surely are individuals such as factory owners and managers who can and should be held liable under the narrower liability approach to ethical assessment. When factory managers violate local labor laws, they are morally wrong and should be prosecuted. Local government officials who accept bribes and agree not to enforce health and safety laws are similarly guilty.[6] Yet she acknowledges the defense frequently offered by managers and owners of factories, that they are under tremendous pressures in a highly competitive economic environment, something that would mitigate their responsibility. Not all choices (e.g., paying wages comparable to those in the developed world) are within their list of options. And only a doctrinaire idealist would recommend closing all culpable factories since, as the owners would assert, "surely it cannot be better for these workers to have no job at all."[7]

Concerning these local factory owners and managers, Young observes that "there is some basis for their excuses."[8] The more difficult problem is a larger, global one. Clearly, unjust sweatshop conditions "further the interests of so many diverse actors differently related to the apparel industry, and are produced by a large number of individuals and organizations acting on those interests." This is, for Young, the essence of structural injustice.

Instead of the liability model, Young proposes "a social connection model of responsibility." Within this model, "all those agents who contribute to the structural processes that produce injustice share responsibility for remedying that injustice."[9] She is careful to distinguish this "forward-looking" responsibility to rectify injustice from any attribution of guilt or blame, which she argues should not be assigned to the distant participants in structural injustice.[10]

A second philosophical approach to the question of responsibility in distant harms is provided by Onora O'Neill, on whom Young herself relies. O'Neill begins with the question of the "ethical standing" of others when one makes a decision, an approach compatible with Young's. If another person deserves ethical standing when I make a choice, I ought to take that person's situation into consideration, at least to some extent. Thus, the question is: "To whom must we (or I) accord ethical standing in taking this action?"[11]

O'Neill explores the answer based not on which other persons we are *conscious* of having a connection to, since agents may "deny, ignore, dispute or repress" the fact that "their activity evidently takes for granted that those others are agents and subjects."[12] Such denials are frequently "strategies of selfishness" and "mask what activity acknowledges, and substitute a distorted account of its presuppositions."[13] Myriad times in human history husbands denied ethical standing to their wives and masters denied the same to their servants or slaves.

O'Neill's answer to this question is that our actions assume that other persons are taking actions related to ours, whether or not we reflect on that fact. As a result, we must accord ethical standing to those persons. In the case of distant producers of the clothing we purchase, although we may typically be unaware of it, our actions do commit us to the assumption that those others are producing things for our use. This action entails an obligation on our part. It confirms their standing as persons to whom our moral principles apply.

Building on O'Neill's analysis, Young goes on to argue that

> when I look for less expensive shirts, I presuppose all those practices of pres-
> sure and competition that minimize labor costs, as well as those that purport-
> edly increase productivity of production and distribution. To the extent that
> these practices result in harming workers, my intention to buy cheap shirts is

implicated in that harm, even though I do not intend the workers harm. . . .
Because my actions assume all these others are acting to the result that there
are clothes in nearby stores, those others come within the scope of my obligation, whether I like that or not.[14]

In this analysis of the moral standing of others in our decisions, O'Neill provides a more substantive reason for the "social connection" that Young posits in her
analysis. Young's summary is that "O'Neill's account shows that to the extent that we
depend on them as demonstrated by how we assume that they are acting in specific
ways as the basis of our own actions, we are obliged to attend to their well-being."[15]

How helpful is this sort of ethical reflection on the moral responsibilities of consumers? Young notes that "it is typical for people to deny a connection" to others
whose lives are affected by large social systems in which those people are involved.[16]
But we must ask whether either Young's social connection model or O'Neill's appeal
to ethical standing is sufficient as an ethical argument.

First, is it sufficient to simply *assert* that responsibility follows on distant participation? The question at stake here is whether participation in a social process generates
a moral responsibility for the harms to others produced by that process. It would seem
that Young's social connection does little more than identify the question and respond
yes. Second, Young talks of structural injustice but does not inquire into the character
of social structures, something that would, it seems, require attention to the analysis
of structures in that discipline that specializes in that analysis: sociology. Third, she
concludes, along with the liability model there is no causal connection between the
consumer and the seamstresses who sew the clothes. But what if there is a connection
that could be found by employing a more adequate understanding of causality?

O'Neill's argument about ethical standing may persuade more people, but just
how much is accomplished by conceding this standing? Some who might otherwise
refuse even to acknowledge the seamstresses in Bangladesh would have to admit they
are subjects and agents and worthy of our consideration. But, of itself, this would
not seem to create any moral responsibility for harms the seamstresses may suffer. I
might grant that those who make the products I buy deserve moral respect yet still
judge that my purchases create no moral responsibility for me concerning any harms
suffered by those workers. Libertarians, for example, say that the seamstresses in a
distant factory are treated justly as long as they know the conditions of the work and
they voluntarily agreed to do it. Moral respect is not sufficient to warrant responsibility for distant injustice. This presents us with the same problem left to us by Young.

The Participatory Intention Model of Responsibility

In his book *Complicity: Ethics and Law for a Collective Age*, legal philosopher Christopher Kutz addresses the problem of an excessively individualistic ethics. Like
Young, Kutz argues that we cannot correctly understand complicity—our role in collective wrongdoing—if we limit ourselves to the traditional methods and principles of

ethics. More specifically, he identifies the "individual difference principle" as power-fully—but erroneously—constitutive of moral attitudes. In addressing what someone might be morally responsible for, the principle says that "I am accountable only for the difference my action alone makes to the resulting state of affairs."[17]

The commonsense insight implicit in the individual difference principle is quite helpful in assessing most questions of interpersonal moral responsibility. If I drive my car too fast in a dense fog and am unable to stop before hitting a car stopped on the highway in front of me, I am accountable for the harm done. But if a third car behind me then crashes into mine and does even worse injury to the driver in front of me, it is that third driver who is responsible for the additional damage.

This approach is quite adequate for a host of individual encounters, and even does tolerably well, Kutz argues, for gauging collective harms caused by the "concerted acts" of, for example, "governments, companies, and cartels."[18] As Kutz summarizes it, the individual decision-makers in these organizations are morally responsible for the collective harms caused.

But the excessive individualism implicit in the individual difference principle "is responsible for the difficulties that common sense and moral theory alike have,"[19] when it comes to "unstructured collective harms," such as environmental damage, that are caused by "a confluence of individual behavior."[20] To illustrate, Kutz examines the World War II firebombing of Dresden, Germany.

During a three-day period in 1945, over a thousand US and British planes and eight thousand pilots, bombers, navigators, and gunners dropped thousands of tons of bombs and incendiary devices on Dresden, destroying some fifteen square miles surrounding the city center and killing tens of thousands of innocent civilians. The point of the example here is not to investigate whether the destruction of Dresden was morally right or wrong. Kutz is correct to report, "I accept the general consensus, among both historians and philosophers, that the Dresden raids in particular, which came after an Allied victory was already assured, were both strategically valueless and inhumane."[21] The relevant issue for our purposes here is to consider the ethical method for assessing the accountability of a single crewmember.

Of course, those approving and planning the attack were primarily responsible for the destruction and killing. Yet here we consider the pilots, whom Kutz would also hold morally responsible, whether or not we approve of the raids morally. (And, for the purposes of this example, we assume—unrealistically, due to military conscription and discipline—that every pilot willingly flew his assigned missions.) There were so many planes dropping so many bombs that any one pilot could be argued to have had only a tiny influence on the ultimate conflagration. In fact, had any one plane not participated in the raid, it is quite likely that there would have been no perceptible difference in the result. So, by the individual difference principle, no single crewmember of any plane could be held morally accountable, a conclusion that amply demonstrates the inadequacy of traditional individualistic moral analysis of collective harms. Whether or not you think the firebombing was morally justified, the pilots are surely morally accountable for their actions.

Kutz goes on to ask about the accountability of the pilots in planes that ran into engine trouble and had to turn back without participating causally in the destruction. He argues that even those who turned back without dropping a single bomb also bear responsibility for the firebombing because of their intention to participate in the plan carried out by others. As with traditional ethical analysis, causal efficacy as well as the *intention* to exert causal efficacy can generate moral responsibility.

Ultimately, Kutz concludes that because "each crewman's causal contribution to the conflagration, indeed each plane's, was marginal to the point of insignificance,"[22] ethical analysis of collective harms cannot, in the end, rest on the *causal* effects of individual actions. "The notion of participation rather than causation is at the heart of both complicity and collective action."[23] As he puts it, "The salient connection between agent, act, and victim is essentially one of meaning rather than causality."[24] Kutz's own project goes on to attribute moral accountability for collective harms to "participatory intention."

While Kutz's line of argument—relying on participatory intention—may prove fruitful for his purposes, it is inadequate to resolve the problems of economic ethics addressed in this volume, primarily because of his willingness to give up on the role of causality in the moral assessment of collective harms. There are two reasons for this.

First, Kutz's argument overstates his case. Although the causal efficacy of each pilot is vanishingly small as part of one thousand flights, one can still ask what the causal effect of a single plane's bombs would have been had it been the only plane to rain down destruction on Dresden. While the damage would not have been as extensive, there would indeed have been a localized firestorm with both death and ruin. Surely the damage from one plane would amount to far more than one one-thousandth of the total destruction actually inflicted on the city by a thousand planes. Each pilot had a fearsome causal capacity.

Second, and more important, the focus of this volume is an analysis of the complicity of those who participate in markets that generate harms for distant others. Here there are a pair of critical differences between the example of the bombing raids and economic markets.

On the one hand, although one pilot acting alone would create a significant portion of the damaged caused by the raid, no single consumer in the absence of other consumers in the market would have any effect across the globe. On the other hand, unlike the pilots—both those who dropped their bombs and those who turned back with engine trouble—participants in the market have no intention to cause harm to those who produce the products they buy.

The Challenge for Ethics

Thus, the problem for ethics is how to articulate the moral responsibility that arises from our participation in markets even though none of us makes a perceptible difference in the harms markets help to cause, and none of us intends those harms in the first place. Young, O'Neill, and Kutz all acknowledge the challenge, but because they all accept the dominant view of causality, they decide they must look elsewhere for moral traction on the problem. Another way to say this is to recognize that the individual difference principle starts with a helpful understanding of the relation of causality and moral responsibility but employs an inadequate view of causality. On the one hand, the principle is correct in its assumption that if I play a causal role in the injustices suffered by others, I have a moral responsibility to rectify the situation. On the other hand, the individual difference principle is unhelpful in the case of harms caused to the distant producers of the things we buy because it takes for granted an individualistic view of causality itself.

As a result, the challenge will require a shift in conceptual framework, beginning at the level of our understanding of causality in science (see chapter 4). The traditional assessment of moral responsibility entails a sort of arithmetic estimate of causal responsibility, rooted as it is at the level of individual action. However, an accurate evaluation of moral responsibility within social structures focuses on a field of structured relationships. Thus, we need to better understand what social science has to say about structures and the character of the causal forces within them, for two reasons.

First, few ethicists—in either philosophy or theology—would attempt an analysis of medical ethics without an understanding of the human physiology involved, of managerial ethics without a view of the firm, or of environmental ethics without some knowledge of environmental science. Responsible ethical reflection on structural injustice requires attention to the discipline that specializes in the study of social structures: sociology. In fact, moral assessments of structural injustice typically entail an implicit view of structures in any case. Alasdair MacIntyre comes close to this assertion concerning any moral system: "A moral philosophy . . . characteristically presupposes a sociology. . . . Even Kant, who sometimes seems to restrict moral agency to the inner realm of the noumenal, implies otherwise in his writings on law, history and politics. . . . We have not yet fully understood the claims of any moral philosophy until we have spelled out what its social embodiment would be."[25]

MacIntyre has spent far more time and effort in developing a historical, not sociological, description of such social embodiment, but the point is well taken regarding an understanding of the social structures within which so much of daily life occurs.

Second, whether within the social structure of the organization we work for, of the banking system that processes our credit card purchases, or of the local school system when we meet with the teacher of a fourth-grade son or daughter, nearly all of the actions we take daily occur within the restrictions and opportunities that structures present to us. If we want to know whether the simple act of purchasing a shirt establishes a relationship of moral responsibility between a purchaser and the women eight thousand miles away who sewed that shirt, we will need to understand the character of the social structure that connects them. That structure is called "the market." And the market generates causal forces that affect them both.

How Does the Market Cause Harm to People?

A fundamental premise of this volume is that if we, through the market, are part of the cause of injustices suffered by the distant producers of the goods we buy, then we have a moral responsibility to do something about that. Thus, the first step is to conduct an inquiry into causality, only later moving to a judgment about moral accountability. Our focus here is whether the market causes harms to others, regardless of whether those harms would be judged to be injustices. More concretely, for example, did the market cause the deaths of the 117 seamstresses who died in the Tazreen factory fire?

One might think that the owners of the unsafe building were "the cause" of the deaths because they did not install fire escapes, did not replace an unsafe electrical system (a short circuit seems to have started the fire), and decided to use this particular building in the first place. But factory managers make their decisions within social structures, just as we do. We saw in chapter 1 how it is descriptively inaccurate to say simply that legislators are elected "because of the votes citizens cast on election day," as this statement ignores the role of gerrymandering in the process. Both the decisions of voters and the social structure of elections—which includes determining the shape of the election districts—cause the outcome. We cannot accurately say that voters are the cause of the result without keeping these conditions in mind.

Similarly, to focus on the individual decisions of factory owners without attending to the structural circumstances shaping those decisions gets the causality wrong. The *Wall Street Journal* interviewed one of the managing partners of the Tazreen factory after the fatal fire. His response made clear the role of market forces in the disaster: "It's hard to continue to improve factory compliance and safety when there is ever increasing downward pressure on the prices that global retailers are willing to pay."[26] Under the threat of losing the contract to provide clothing, he may have felt he had little choice. He is saying that market pressures brought about his decisions, which eventuated in the deaths. As we will see in chapter 5, we can say that the market caused those deaths but did so by altering his decisions—as this is the only way that social structures cause anything to occur. Structures present restrictions and opportunities to persons within them that frequently change the decisions made.

Emdadul Islam, the Dhaka factory owner and director of Babylon Group, which employs more than ten thousand workers making clothes for companies such as Tesco and River Island, complains about the response of global buyers when he argues that workers deserve better wages and that he should be allowed to raise his prices to fund the change. "They seem to be void of any sense of that. They don't give a damn if it is a rational price or not. They say, 'I can get it cheaper next door so you should be even cheaper.'"[27]

Thus, the many multinational clothing brands in the world undoubtedly play a role in low wages. They are typically only indirectly involved, as they do not own the factories that make the clothes they market. They put pressure on their supplying factories to produce ever more efficiently, meaning at ever-lower cost, and in ways that are ever more responsive to the market's latest need for particular colors, fabrics, and styles. Some management strategies, such as "just-in-time" or "demand-flow" production, require more frequent changes and quicker completion of orders and put pressure on local manufacturers to impose mandatory overtime on workers already working six days a week.

We could, of course, turn the blame onto Macy's, Target, and other clothing retailers of the world, since it is their drive to make a profit that causes that ever-increasing downward pressure on price. But should we stop there? Why do these retailers push for lower prices? If you or I as consumers have a choice between two equivalent shirts, do we not buy the cheaper one? Are we not part of that downward pressure? Some consumers are poor enough that they have little choice but to buy the cheapest clothing available. But many of us can afford to pay a dollar more for each shirt we buy in order to finance higher wages and safer working conditions. Since the seamstresses making a shirt receive far less than a dollar in wages for the time it takes them to make it, a dollar would be plenty to double their wages. But markets on their own don't offer such options.

When we say that the market is a cause of harms—some of which are injustices—there is no claim that the market is the only cause; individual agents like the factory owner and other structural forces like local labor laws are also causes. But social structures exert their causal impact by altering the decisions that persons within them make. For example, were it not for the pressures of competition that threaten the factory owners, charging a higher price could have paid for the installation of fire escapes or higher wages.

Consider a less controversial example that the market has helped to cause: a change in golf clubs. Fifty years ago, golfers carried 1- and 2-irons in their bags and there was no such thing as a "gap wedge." But, year after year, golf club manufacturers slowly made each of the clubs "steeper," decreasing the angle of loft. Why? The lower the angle (i.e., the steeper the face), the farther the ball will travel. How did the market cause this? As expert club maker Tom Wishon put it, "Each year, in order to say their clubs hit further [*sic*], the club companies have been tinkering with the loft angles—lowering them a bit at a time each year."[28] A golfer is more likely to buy a new set of clubs once he knows that the new 6-iron carries farther than his old 6-iron.

There are, of course, other improvements in the technology of golf clubs, but distance is a prime selling point. The effect of all this is that no one carries a 1-iron anymore; a 3-iron today has almost the same loft as a 1-iron of fifty years ago. And many 9-irons today have the same loft as a 7-iron of the past. A gap has been created between the pitching wedge and the sand wedge (which was never intended for distance, so its loft wasn't changed). That gap is now filled, appropriately, by the gap wedge.

The market has been a cause of the change in golf clubs. It is, of course, not the only cause, because it causes things to happen only by changing the decisions of persons acting within the market. And those persons are also causes. The market offered golf club manufacturers the opportunity to sell more golf clubs if they merely reduced the angle of loft. The market also offered golfers the opportunity to hit the ball farther if they bought new clubs. These opportunities changed people's decisions.

Moral Decision in a Stratified World: An Example

This volume aims to demonstrate how the market as a social structure is a contributing cause of the injustices occurring in factories around the world, and how we consumers play a causal role in those injustices, which in turn creates moral responsibility. Critical to this understanding will be how moral decisions—whether by consumers, factory managers, or seamstresses—are influenced by the structures within which those decisions must occur. To get a preliminary insight into the difference that this sort of structural analysis can make, it will be helpful to consider a simple example closer to home.

Assume you are a midlevel manager at a local firm and you've been thinking about how much transparency (the sharing of information) should exist between superiors and subordinates within organizations. You think you could make better decisions if your superiors shared more information with you, and you're beginning to believe that your assistants would do better work if you shared more information with them.

If you were discussing this with friends over a drink after dinner at your home, you would face certain restrictions and opportunities as a host: you don't serve yourself before your friends, but you do get to decide when the group leaves the table for the easy chairs in the living room. (Even informal events entail structural and cultural forces.) But you might feel completely free to say everything that's on your mind about transparency, perhaps arguing vigorously that every person with authority in an organization has a moral obligation of great transparency, giving subordinates all the information that those in authority have. With your friends you'd likely have a lively give-and-take and would not worry about pressing your own position with vigor.

If you held the position of manager in a social structure called a business firm, consider how differently such a conversation would go were you to be talking with either your supervisor or a subordinate. Proposing such transparency to your supervisor could be perceived as an explicit complaint about current levels of secrecy, and in most cases you would be cautious about pushing too hard, respecting the structural constraints (including potential reprisals) you face when your supervisor articulates resistance to your ideas. Yet, even in discussing with your subordinates the possibility of your becoming more transparent, you as their manager may well have concerns that also arise from restrictions generated by the social structure. You may worry that your superiors might not approve of greater transparency and thus you ought not to hold out a promise of change to your subordinates. Alternatively, you may be concerned that, if you ultimately decide against greater transparency, the more clamorous members of your team might later use such a conversation as evidence of your insincerity in dealing with subordinates. Your workers do not have legal authority over your actions, but such dissatisfactions can be a potent force in your daily work. The point of the example is that social structures impose both constraints and opportunities that influence our decisions (addressed in detail in chapter 5).

Moral analyses that ignore the structural character of social life can, of course, still take into consideration your concerns about the reactions of your supervisor and subordinates. Judgments within any analysis must, as always, balance competing goals in the light of existing circumstances that limit what is possible. But an understanding of social structure can provide a more precise grasp of the character of those circumstances. Methodological individualists, for example, limit those circumstances to the actions and moral characters of the persons around you. Using a sociological insight into the way structural forces work, moral judgment can more adequately understand the context of decisions and assess both what is possible and how best to achieve a desired outcome.

Conclusion

This chapter continued our inquiry into the question: Are consumers responsible for injustices in the lives of people who make the products they buy? It reviewed the arguments of Iris Marion Young, Onora O'Neill, and Christopher Kutz, each of whom rejects an individualistic moral analysis to account for structural injustice. Because each accepts the dominant but inadequate view of causality, each concedes that the individual persons involved in systems of structural injustice do not play a causal role in the problem. This volume aims to outline a view of social causality that is more adequate for understanding social structures and, thereby, global structural injustice.

This understanding will allow us to see that in addition to the various market participants that play a role in economic injustice, markets themselves have a causal impact. Understanding how that impact occurs will require us to grasp how social structures generate restrictions and opportunities that shape the decisions made by persons acting within them. And comprehending how structures work requires us to ask more fundamental questions about science itself, such as, What *is* a scientific law? At first glance this effort might seem to be an unnecessary distraction. But to answer our question about the causal impact of consumers in global markets, we will first need to understand the critical realist view of science and how many people misunderstand the meaning of scientific law.

Notes

1. Ahmed, *A Border Passage*, 160.
2. O'Neill, *Towards Justice*, 109.
3. Barrera, *Market Complicity*.

4. Young, *Responsibility for Justice.*
5. Young, *Responsibility for Justice*, 95–96.
6. Young, *Responsibility for Justice*, 131.
7. Young, *Responsibility for Justice*, 131.
8. Young, *Responsibility for Justice*, 133.
9. Young, *Responsibility for Justice*, 142.
10. Young, *Responsibility for Justice*, 143.
11. O'Neill, *Towards Justice*, 97.
12. O'Neill, *Towards Justice*, 101.
13. O'Neill, *Towards Justice*, 107.
14. Young, *Responsibility for Justice*, 160.
15. Young, *Responsibility for Justice*, 160–61.
16. Young, *Responsibility for Justice*, 158.
17. Kutz, *Complicity*, 116–24.
18. Kutz, *Complicity*, 166.
19. Kutz, *Complicity*, 116.
20. Kutz, *Complicity*, 166.
21. Kutz, *Complicity*, 118.
22. Kutz, *Complicity*, 118.
23. Kutz, *Complicity*, 138.
24. Kutz, *Complicity*, 140.
25. MacIntyre, *After Virtue.*
26. Syed Zain Al-Mahmood, "Bangladesh Probe Calls Fatal Fire Sabotage," *Wall Street Journal*, December 17, 2012, https://www.wsj.com/articles/SB10001424127887323723 10457818526086034671 2.
27. Simon Parry, "The True Cost of Your Cheap Clothes: Slave Wages for Bangladesh Factory Workers," *Post Magazine*, June 11, 2016, http://www.scmp.com/magazines/post -magazine/article/1970431/true-cost-your-cheap-clothes-slave-wages-bangladesh-factory.
28. Rob McGarr, "Why Do the Lofts on Irons Keep Getting Stronger?," *Today's Golfer*, November 11, 2015, https://www.todaysgolfer.co.uk/news-and-events/general-news/2015 /november/if-you-ask-someone-what-club-they-hit-youre-either-vain-an-idiot-or-both/.

PART II
Critical Realism

CHAPTER 4

Critical Realism
and Natural Science

An article on the Big Bang in the popular science magazine *Discover* centered on the views of cosmologist Alexander Vilenkin, who hypothesizes that the universe could indeed have arisen out of nothing, in the sense that there was literally nothing—no space, no time, no matter—during the instant before the Big Bang. But Vilenkin goes on to observe that there would have had to exist something else beforehand—namely "the laws of physics." Why? Because "those laws govern the something-from-nothing moment of creation that gives rise to our universe."[1]

This account is a stark articulation of the belief that the laws of nature are mysterious independent forces—they would exist even if nothing else did. The underlying presumptions—that the laws of nature "set the rules" for how things relate to each other or "are the forces behind why things happen" in the natural world—are widely held today. As we will see, the school of thought called "empiricism" provides the prevailing account behind this mistaken view of laws.

What exactly *is* a scientific law? Could one exist even if nothing else did? Although asking such questions may seem distant from the economic and ethical issues this volume focuses on, the connection is the role of empiricism in our thinking about science and how empiricism leaves the discipline of economics inadequate to its task. Instead, a critical realist approach provides a better understanding of science and of human knowledge itself, and consequently is a more adequate description of how things operate in the natural and social worlds. This approach will, in later chapters, generate a better picture of markets and of our role as consumers within them.

Introduction

The aim of this volume is to develop an adequate description of the causal connection between first world consumers and third world producers in order to specify the character and extent of economic complicity in markets. As chapter 1 put the question, do I play any causal role in (and, as a result, do I bear some individual moral responsibility for) the harms that confront the seamstresses who made the shirt I am wearing? More broadly, are we as consumers responsible, to some degree, for the injuries that markets cause in the lives of the distant others who make the products we buy?

Chapter 2 reviewed many of the difficulties that an individualistic mind-set causes; it often prevents any awareness of the causal impact of the social structures within which we live, rendering it harder to recognize our moral responsibility for those impacts. Chapter 3 briefly recounted the history of mainstream economics, identifying the restrictions on economic science—limitations economists have chosen to impose on themselves—that exacerbate this problem. This chapter will briefly summarize the principles of empiricism within the philosophy of science and then explore the more helpful conception of knowledge, science, and the world provided by critical realism. Begun by the British philosopher Roy Bhaskar as a school of thought within the philosophy of science, critical realism is now employed within the social sciences. Chapter 5 will explore how a critical realist way of thinking about science provides a better description of social structures. Chapter 7 will employ this sociological view of social structures to develop a more accurate view of the market as a social structure.

Empiricism

Empiricism has ancient and medieval antecedents[2] but its full statement appeared with the British philosophers of the seventeenth and eighteenth centuries. In response to claims by Continental philosophers — that we are born with innate ideas about the world around us—John Locke instead claimed that all of our notions about the world come from our sense experience of it.[3] David Hume, born seven years after Locke died, extended this conviction and is widely credited as the father of empiricism. For Hume as well, experience is "our only guide in reasoning concerning matters of fact."[4] Our five senses provide the only reliable knowledge.

The most important scientific implication of this conviction concerns the view of causality it necessitates. Aristotle had identified four forms of causality: material, formal, efficient, and final. But if the only knowledge we can trust comes through our five senses, all we can say about cause and effect is that one follows the other. As Hume put it, "We have no other notion of cause and effect, but that of certain objects, which have always conjoin'd together, and which in all past instances have been found inseparable. We cannot penetrate into the reason of the conjunction."[5]

The conviction that we can have no access to how or why causality works has perhaps been most precisely articulated by John Stuart Mill in his description of the views of Auguste Comte: "We have no knowledge of anything but phenomena. . . . We know not the essence, nor the real mode of production, of any fact, but only its relations to other facts in the way of succession or similitude. . . . Their essential nature, and their ultimate causes, either efficient or final, are unknown and inscrutable to us."[6]

Mill's definition of causality is typical of the tradition. The cause of a phenomenon is "the antecedent, or the concurrence of antecedents, on which it is invariably and unconditionally consequent."[7] If phenomenon B always and unconditionally follows phenomenon A, then A is the cause of B. This is what causality means in empiricism. Thus, the physicist in the lab, by isolating experiments from outside influences, strives to discover these sorts of invariant sequences of phenomena to discover scientific "laws" that govern those phenomena. Laws, of course, are statements of those invariant sequences. The classic example here is Newton's "law of gravity."

This thinking leads to a conception of scientific laws as the causal "forces" in operation, even though it is a very thin version of causal force: it is no more than a statement about a sequence of phenomena. Nonetheless, when I let go of a book I am holding, it hits the floor "because of the law of gravity" since there is no more fundamental "how" or "why" to which empiricists think we can have access. And yet, as we see in Vilenkin's assumption, this thin view of laws as causal forces nonetheless leads some to believe that these forces are so fundamental that they would exist even if nothing else did.

Critical Realism

As a view of how science operates, critical realism arose out of a frustration with the inadequacies of empiricist interpretations of what scientists do.[8] Convinced of its errors, Roy Bhaskar set out to overturn 250 years of empiricism since Hume. Bhaskar makes clear that there are, and science can learn about, "ontologically real things" that cannot be perceived by our five senses.

The Critique of Empiricism: Closure in the Lab

Bhaskar's fundamental argument against empiricism is that it is not based on how science operates and therefore misunderstands what science is. In spite of its commitment to rely on experience, empiricism's view of the generation of scientific knowledge is far too passive. The mistake implicit here, Bhaskar argues, is that scientists don't just perceive events. Rather, they are active agents in constructing experiments and, through painstaking efforts, precisely excluding from the laboratory a multitude of intervening forces in order to focus on a small set of events. Bhaskar says that to arrive at a well-designed "closed" situation in the lab—so that the scientist might observe invariant sequences of events—three conditions are typically required: isolation, atomicity, and additivity.[9]

The first, isolation, is the most straightforward and easily understood requirement for a good experiment. The scientist sets up a carefully regulated context to eliminate external forces. To see if a feather will fall toward the earth like a pebble of equal weight, the scientist creates a vacuum in a long glass tube and watches the feather and pebble fall. But there are always external forces that are impossible (or too costly) to eliminate, so the scientist must assume those forces have no impact on the experiment at hand. A physicist conducting this sort of research about gravity, feathers, and pebbles may simply assume that the various kinds of the sun's radiant energy are inconsequential in this context and can be ignored. The basic neoclassical model of economics assumes that business firms aim to maximize their profits even though many firms say they also have other goals. The physicist's assumption may be appropriate, while the economist's may unfortunately support an individualistic view of economic life.

The second, atomicity, is the requirement that the most fundamental items under study must not have internal structures, or, if they do, their internal structures remain constant. That is, nothing that happens in the experiment is caused by changes *inside* those basic items. The aim of the experiment is to investigate the changes that occur as a result of changes in the external environment. Thus, a biologist may conduct experiments about the effects of the interaction between water, salt, and the cells of a cactus without taking note of the internal atomic structure of any of the molecules involved. But just *assuming* atomicity can be a serious mistake. Bhaskar uses the example of trying to predict the behavior of an elephant when it is prodded with a stick in one way or another. If biologists ignore the elephant's internal state (for example, whether it is asleep or not), they might be attributing too much (or too little) influence to the external causes they study.[10] Neoclassical economists typically assume that the tastes of individuals are a given, showing little interest in how tastes are acquired or changed. But if producers can alter consumers' tastes through advertising, atomicity fails and arguments about the beneficent efficiency of markets are cast into doubt.

The third condition, additivity, entails the assumption that "the behavior of aggregates and wholes can always be described in terms of the behavior of their component parts."[11] The idea that the organization of an experiment's elements is additive is closely related to the notion of atomicity. Later in this chapter we will examine the critical realist notion of "emergence," whereby the combination of elements can in some circumstances create a more complex thing that cannot be explained merely by the characteristics of its constituent parts. For now, a simple example may be helpful. Water arises from a particular combination of hydrogen and oxygen but has attributes that neither of those elements possesses. Water will put out a fire, while hydrogen and oxygen will feed it. Similarly, in economics, chapter 7 will argue that the market itself is a social structure whose influence cannot be explained merely as the aggregated effects of the individuals acting within it.

In sum, empiricism would have a strong case were these three elements—isolation, atomicity, and additivity—consistently used to characterize its scientific work. Bhaskar argues that they don't.

The Critique of Empiricism: Scientific Knowledge

Bhaskar agrees with empiricists that scientific experimentation does indeed allow us to observe invariant sequences of events in the lab. The process involved is a complex one, and the scientist is "a causal agent of the sequence of events, but not of the causal laws which the sequence of events . . . enables us to identify."[12] What empiricism misses, Bhaskar argues, is that in science there are two types of knowledge, based on the two objects of knowledge. To help distinguish them he employs a grammatical analogy, distinguishing between "transitive" objects of knowledge (which, like transitive verbs, point to something beyond themselves) and "intransitive" objects of knowledge (which, like intransitive verbs, do not point beyond themselves).

The first sort of thing that scientific work focuses on—the "transitive" objects of knowledge—are what scientists create. These are "the antecedently established facts and theories, paradigms and models, methods and techniques of inquiry available to a particular scientific school or worker."[13] Karl Popper made a similar claim in distinguishing three "worlds," the third of which consists of the products of human thought.[14] Crediting Thomas Kuhn's *The Structure of Scientific Revolutions* for raising the awareness that science is a human project, Bhaskar notes that "men in their social activity produce knowledge which is a social product much like any other, which is no more independent of its production and the men who produce it than motorcars, armchairs, or books, which has its own craftsmen, technicians, publicists, standards and skills and which is no less subject to change than any other commodity."[15] When Isaac Newton proposed the inverse-square law of gravity, he contributed significantly to the social stock of scientific knowledge. And when Albert Einstein found Newton's paradigm to be inadequate to explain cosmic events, he too contributed transitive knowledge in developing the theory of relativity.

The second sort of thing scientific work focuses on—the "intransitive" objects of knowledge—is what scientists try to explain. These are "the real things and structures, mechanisms and processes, events and possibilities of the world; and for the most part they are quite independent of us."[16] Empiricists claim that we have no access to such things because they lie beyond sense experience. But Bhaskar argues instead that the scientific enterprise makes little sense without the assumption that we do in fact have access to these intransitive objects of knowledge. In this he is part of a wider movement within philosophy and science sometimes referred to as "the ontological turn."[17]

In the lab the scientist creates a "closed" system, one carefully and often ingeniously designed to eliminate from the laboratory the multitude of forces that affect events in the "open" world outside. As the empiricist asserts, the scientist discovers invariant sequences of events in the lab. Each is a "constant conjunction of events" of which Hume spoke. But Bhaskar points out that we almost never see such invariant sequences of events in the open world, so why should one assume that the invariant sequences discovered in the lab do in fact also occur outside the lab? Bhaskar's answer is that science requires, and working scientists presume, that there are indeed real mechanisms operating in the world about which we come to learn in the laboratory. These mechanisms *generate* the events that our five senses can perceive. "It is only if we make the assumption of the real independence of such mechanisms from the events they generate that we are justified in assuming that they endure and go on acting in their normal way outside the experimentally closed conditions that enable us to empirically identify them."[18]

This exposes a deep irony in the empiricist view of scientific law. On the one hand, laws are understood to be nothing more than statements describing invariable sequences of events, with no insight into how or why such invariable sequences exist. On the other hand, empiricists claim that these flimsy statements called "laws" are indeed the reasons that events happen in the world. The book hits the floor "because of" the law of gravity. As Bhaskar puts it, "A causal law is analyzed in empiricist ontology as a constant conjunction of events perceived."[19] Why? Because a faulty empiricist epistemology requires it.

The Reality of the Transfactual

What empiricists call laws are, in the critical realist view of things, merely human descriptions of what is going on between real objects in the world. The book does *not* hit the floor because of the law of gravity. Rather, it hits the floor because of the relation of the book and the earth, and the force (not a "law") of gravity generated by that relation. If that relation were different—say, if the book were a billion miles away from the earth—the relation would have no impact on the book's movement. The law of gravity is a transitive object of knowledge: it is simply the scientist's summary of the effects of the ontologically real causal relationship between the earth and the book, which is an intransitive object of knowledge. This "law" could not exist without humans to formulate it, and, contrary to cosmologist Alexander Vilenkin's assumption noted earlier, the force of gravity could not exist if there were no objects in existence whose relation to each other generates it.

Bhaskar accuses empiricists of committing "the epistemic fallacy": reducing ontologically real relations in the world to no more than matters of human knowledge.[20] Empiricists interpret the ontologically real relation between earth and book as no more than a matter of our knowledge of its sense-perceptible consequences (that one event follows on another).

More accurately, although our senses cannot perceive the relation between book and earth, that relation is nonetheless quite real. Employing the empiricist definition of fact—that is, something that is sense-perceptible—Bhaskar calls these real but not sense-perceptible things "transfactual." Science does indeed study the relation between the book and the earth by its various experiments in the lab, and it does come to conclusions about this transfactual thing. The same is true of a magnetic field, which is also beyond what our five senses can directly detect.[21]

Even though we are speaking of what cannot be observed, there is no mysticism here. For critical realists, the central task of all science is to begin with our empirical grasp of the actual events we perceive in the world (especially the events scientists carefully orchestrate in the laboratory) in order to hypothesize about the invisible powers that cause those events to occur. As Christian Smith argues, "Scientific inquiry as a project should be concerned more with the structured properties of causal relations and mechanisms than with the regularity of observable sequences of events—theorizing unobserved causal dynamics is what the best of science actually does and is more important than measuring the strength of association between variables."[22]

One last question about causality is helpful here. Is the notion of the cause of an event limited to the one final change in a situation prior to that event? For example, consider a claim that the weight of snow on a roof causes a house to collapse. Can we say simply that the snow is *the* cause?

Among the causes of an event we should include the conditions present all along, not simply the final element added to the situation (the snow). If no other house collapses due to the snowfall, undoubtedly the shoddy construction of this particular house is also a cause of the collapse. In general, the philosophy of science has concluded that every event has multiple causes (including the preexisting "conditions"), even if one stands out recognizably as the precipitating cause.[23]

The Three Domains of Reality

To clarify the limitations of empiricism, Bhaskar distinguishes the empirical, the actual, and the real, each a "domain of reality" that includes the previous.[24] The empirical is the sum total of events that are perceived: all experiences. According to empiricism, we can know only the empirical. The actual is the sum total of everything that occurs: all events, including but not limited to experiences. The fall of a dead tree so deep in the Amazon that no one will ever perceive it is nonetheless an event. So, too, is an earthquake on a barren planet circling some star a billion

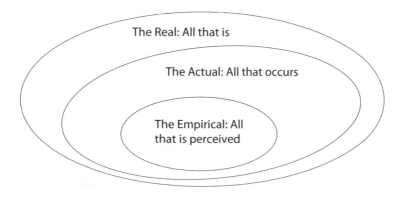

The Real: All that is

The Actual: All that occurs

The Empirical: All that is perceived

light-years from earth. Clearly the empirical is but a tiny proportion of the actual. The real includes everything that happens (all events, whether perceived or not) plus the causal forces—the powers or "mechanisms"—that bring about those events, including the relation between that Amazonian tree and the earth, a relation that generates the force of gravity that brings the tree down. As Bhaskar summarizes it, "Laws are then neither empirical statements (statements about experiences) nor statements about events. Rather they are statements about the way of acting of independently existing and transfactually active things."[25]

In critical realism it is foolish to limit science to only the empirical; the primary evidence is that it cannot account for how science actually operates. Empiricism describes neither what practicing scientists are doing nor what they understand themselves to be doing.

Emergence and Stratified Reality

The two types of scientific knowledge and the reality of the transfactual are two major contributions of critical realism; a third is the importance of "emergence" and the consequent "stratification" of the world. Emergence occurs when two or more "lower-level" elements combine to form a "higher-level" element that has different characteristics.[26] As we have seen, the simplest example is water. Although it is composed of hydrogen and oxygen and "emerges" from them, water's characteristics are quite different from either. Water puts out a fire, while hydrogen and oxygen feed it. This capacity of water to quench a fire is, then, "an emergent property," which in more general terms can be defined as a characteristic "that is not possessed by any of the parts individually and would not be possessed by the full set of parts in the absence of the structuring set of relations between them."[27]

Similarly, protons and neutrons have characteristics not present in the up quarks and down quarks that combine to produce them. The human mind emerges from and cannot exist without the electrochemical synapses in the brain, but the mind has properties different from those synapses and can act back on them, for example by drugs or brain surgery. Most important for the issue at hand in this volume is the origin of social structures: they emerge from the actions of individuals (many of them now dead), but, as we saw in chapter 2, those structures have characteristics and causal impact not reducible to the actions of individuals.

As Bhaskar has put it, "the operations of the higher level cannot be accounted for solely by the laws governing the lower-order level in which we might say the higher order level is 'rooted' and from which we can say it was 'emergent.'"[28] The phenomenon of emergence occurs in all areas of existence, and, as we have seen, some emergents are sense-perceptible (e.g., water) and some are transfactual (e.g., the human mind and social structures). In general, the world is "stratified" into different levels.

This understanding of emergent realities, which exist at a new, "higher" level than the elements that combine to create them, leads critical realists to reject "reductionism," the assumption pervasive in empiricist thought that all realities can be explained, at least if we know enough, by the functioning of their constituent parts. One classic statement of reductionism comes from Edward O. Wilson: "All tangible phenomena, from the birth of stars to the workings of social institutions, are based on material processes that are ultimately reducible, however long and tortuous the sequences, to the laws of physics."[29] Reductionism claims that "the causal power of the higher-level entity itself becomes redundant to the explanation."[30] This sort of elimination, of course, is the intention of methodological individualists in the social sciences, who see only persons and groups of persons, not social structures, as causes in the social world. Reductionism in the natural sciences is equally mistaken.

Consider a star as an emergent thing, and its capacity to emit light as an emergent property. A star emits light because of the relation of various nuclear particles under extreme pressure and temperature in its core. Those same nuclear particles would not emit light in many other situations (for example, being strewn at random evenly across space). "Thus the emission of light from a set of particles that would not otherwise emit it must be accounted for by the level and form of organization that constitute them into a star."[31] The star can be said to exert a "downward" causal effect on the particles, causing them to emit light. Any explanation of a star and its emergent properties as simply the result of the character of the elements that make up a star—reductively eliminating any causal role for the higher-level structure—is inadequate.[32]

This claim of reductionism—that all higher-level explanations can, in principle, be reduced to lower-level explanations—is often taken as a simple scientific fact by those who endorse it. Yet we must recognize that although reductionism makes sense within an empiricist philosophy of science, it does not make sense within some other schools of thought within the philosophy of science. It is not a scientific fact, for example, that the actions of the human mind can be ultimately explained by the physics that lie behind the chemistry that lie behind the biology of the brain. Reductionism is a philosophical choice, not a scientific fact, and it is tied to the rise of empiricism in Western history.

Emergence is equally important in the social world. Social structures emerge from the actions of individuals—typically actions taken long before we were born—and require the ongoing participation of individuals today for their continued existence. But structures have an independent existence and independent causal effects in the lives of today's individuals. As Christian Smith puts it, because reality is stratified, "social structures exist at a level other than and above personal human lives. That is the level of the distinctly social, constituted by interactive relationships, usually existent temporally for historical periods that transcend individual human lifetimes, and situated so as to be able to shape human mental and behavioral life."[33] Social structures are ontologically real, transfactual things; they exist at a "higher" level than individual persons or groups of persons (though without thereby entailing any greater explanatory importance or moral significance).

More generally, the world is stratified, with, for example, the biological existing "above" the chemical, the conscious above the biological, and the social above the individual person.

An Aside Concerning Religious Faith

We will soon use this analysis in the philosophy of science to improve our understanding of social structures, but it is worth first briefly noting an implication for fundamental theology and Christian faith. Hume's empiricism played a central part in his rejection of religious faith. As he put it sarcastically, since the only knowledge we can trust comes from our five senses, "the Christian Religion not only was at first attended with miracles, but even at this day cannot be believed by any reasonable person without one."[34] Applying a version of what later was called the distinction between synthetic and analytic propositions, Hume dismissed religious thinking: "If we take in our hand any Volume of Divinity or School Metaphysics, for Instance; let us ask, Does it contain any abstract Reasoning concerning Quantity or Number? No. Does it contain any experimental Reasoning concerning Matter of Fact and Existence? No. Commit it then to the Flames: For it can contain nothing but Sophistry and Illusion."[35] The eventual predominance of empiricism among Western intellectuals—including its rejection of any knowledge other than the sense-perceptible—was a significant cause (along with others) in the erosion of the persuasiveness of religion in the modern world.

Yet if intellectuals in our world today were to move from an empiricist to a critical realist philosophy of science, thereby acknowledging the ontological reality of things in the natural world that are not sense-perceptible, religious faith would regain a kind of intellectual respectability, even among nonbelievers, that it has not had for two centuries. Both natural science and religious faith learn and talk about things we cannot see or touch but that are susceptible to study.

Other philosophies of science have made similar claims—for example, those of Alfred North Whitehead[36] and Bernard Lonergan, SJ[37]—but typically these have come from theists who start with "strong" assumptions and have often entailed a complex system of concepts and neologisms that are a challenge to grasp even for a committed student. Bhaskar's work starts with "weak" assumptions and fewer conceptual complexities and provides a purely secular analysis of science. (Bhaskar observes that "it is entirely accidental that we exist"[38] and that "civilization is, like man himself, perhaps nothing more than a temporary rupture in the normal order of things."[39]) As a result, Bhaskar's work has a greater potential for having an impact on the empiricist mainstream.

In short, critical realism provides the philosophical foundation for a more adequate social science, one that enables us to identify causal relations that generate moral obligations. It also provides a scientific warrant for our knowledge of ontologically real things in the natural world that are not sense-perceptible—opening ontological and epistemological space both for the reality of spiritual "things" and for our (always limited) knowledge of them.

Conclusion

In this chapter we have reviewed how empiricism provides an inadequate understanding of science and knowledge. This may at first seem all too distant from the ethical concern of this volume. But as we saw in earlier chapters, a faulty view of causality, engendered by more than two centuries of empiricism, has prevented ethical reflection from recognizing the causal connection between consumers and distant producers.

We have outlined the critical realist alternative to empiricism as proposed by Roy Bhaskar. Essential here are the difference between transitive and intransitive objects of knowledge, the existence of transfactual (i.e., not sense-perceptible) things, and, most important, the significance of emergence and the stratified character of reality.

All of these issues arise in our understanding of the natural world and of natural science. In the next chapter we will investigate what critical realism means for our understanding of the social world, and in particular for sociology's insight into the origins, character, and causal impact of social structures. Later we will apply these same insights to the discipline of economics. We will see, for instance, that just as the book does not hit the floor "because of the law of gravity," so prices do not change "because of the law of supply and demand." We can then speak about how the decisions made both by us and by the seamstresses are shaped by the social structure we call the market for shirts, and how our decision to buy a shirt is causally related to the harms suffered by those distant women.

Notes

1. Steve Nadis, "What Came Before the Big Bang?," *Discover Magazine*, September 2013, http://discovermagazine.com/2013/september/13-starting-point.
2. For example, the Greek Stoic philosophers taught that the mind starts blank but acquires knowledge as the outside world is impressed on it. See Rist, *Stoic Philosophy*, 134–35.
3. Locke, *An Essay Concerning Human Understanding*.
4. Hume, *Enquiry*, 56.
5. Hume, *A Treatise of Human Nature*.
6. Mill, *Auguste Comte and Positivism*, 6.
7. Mill, *A System of Logic*, 245.
8. Bhaskar, *A Realist Theory of Science*. For a brief summary of his critique of Hume, see pp. 11–20.
9. Bhaskar, *A Realist Theory of Science*, 74–79.
10. Bhaskar, *A Realist Theory of Science*, 75.
11. Bhaskar, *A Realist Theory of Science*, 76.

12. Bhaskar, *A Realist Theory of Science*, 33.
13. Bhaskar, *A Realist Theory of Science*, 21.
14. Popper, "Three Worlds."
15. Bhaskar, *A Realist Theory of Science*, 21.
16. Bhaskar, *A Realist Theory of Science*, 22.
17. See, for example, Holbraad and Pedersen, *The Ontological Turn*.
18. Bhaskar, *A Realist Theory of Science*, 13.
19. Bhaskar, *A Realist Theory of Science*, 33.
20. Bhaskar, *A Realist Theory of Science*, 36–40.
21. Bhaskar, *A Realist Theory of Science*, 12.
22. C. Smith, *What Is a Person?*, 96.
23. See, for example, Mill, *A System of Logic*, 237.
24. Bhaskar, *A Realist Theory of Science*, 56–57.
25. Bhaskar, *A Realist Theory of Science*, 52.
26. For a helpful discussion of emergence, see C. Smith, *What Is a Person?*, 25–42.
27. Elder-Vass, *Causal Power*, 17.
28. Bhaskar, *A Realist Theory of Science*, 13.
29. Wilson, *Sociobiology*, 226.
30. Elder-Vass, *Causal Power*, 24.
31. Elder-Vass, *Causal Power*, 60.
32. This distinction is helpful in answering the question of whether an emergent thing could have been "predicted" from a knowledge of its constituent parts. On the one hand, just about everyone admits that often it could not have been anticipated from even a thorough description of those parts as separate entities. On the other hand, empiricists argue, once the emergent reality is understood, one element of a detailed description of any one of its parts *could* include that part's capacity to generate the emergent thing when combined with other elements under the right set of relations and conditions. Reductionists (including methodological individualists in social science) might then claim that a good explanation can be had by recourse only to the constituent parts. But as Elder-Vass explains, such a structuring set of conditions and relations among constituent parts is exactly what an emergent thing *is*, so it is a mistake to think that an emergent property can be explained simply by the characteristics of its parts. See Elder-Vass, *Causal Power*, 23–26. Moving the emergent thing's information back into the description of its constituent parts would require adding to the description of hydrogen the fact that if it is joined with oxygen, water will form. This is like including in a definition the word that is being defined.
33. C. Smith, *What Is a Person?*, 328.
34. Hume, *Enquiry*.
35. Hume, *Enquiry*, 256.
36. Whitehead, *Principles of Natural Knowledge*; Whitehead, *The Concept of Nature*.
37. Lonergan, *Insight*.
38. Bhaskar, *A Realist Theory of Science*, 250.
39. Bhaskar, *A Realist Theory of Science*, 10.

CHAPTER 5

Social Structures

Libertarian philosopher and economist Friedrich Hayek endorsed an extreme form of methodological individualism, going so far as to assert that "wholes" such as society "are never given to our observation but are without exception constructions of our mind."[1] For Hayek, "the economy," "war," and "a university" are no more than shorthand linguistic summaries of the actions and interactions of the individuals involved. On this account, "society" is nothing more than an aggregate term—an idea—created to conveniently sum up the actions of a large group of persons. It's no wonder, then, that Hayek goes on to argue that there is no such thing as social justice.[2] As he puts it, "the concept of 'social justice' is necessarily empty and meaningless."[3] If the social world has no reality beyond the actions of individuals, there's no way to judge a nonexistent world as either just or unjust. Justice pertains only to the morality of individual action.

Roy Bhaskar criticizes such individualistic assumptions about the world. "Whereas few people nowadays . . . would hold that a magnetic field is a construction of thought, the idea that society is [a construction of thought] remains quite widely held."[4] We saw in the last chapter how an empiricist view of knowledge entails a rejection of Bhaskar's conviction that the relation between the earth and the book—an invisible relation that generates the emergent force of gravity—is an ontologically real "thing" that scientists can and do study. Hayek was not an empiricist. He was, however, an individualist. And, as Bhaskar has put it, "Most individualists regard 'the social' as a synonym for 'the group.'"[5]

The reason that methodological individualists like Hayek can understand magnetic fields as quite real but misunderstand society as nonexistent is rooted in the difference between the natural and the social worlds. Emergent realities like water in the natural world have a relatively simple relation to the elements from which they emerge. Society, and all social structures, are emergent realities that have a more complex relation with the elements—the actions of individuals—from which they emerge. As Bhaskar puts it, "Society stands to individuals then as something that they never make, but that exists only in virtue of their activity."[6] Unlike structures in the natural world, social structures do not exist independently of the moral agency of the individuals subject to the structures' causal impact. If the people disappeared, there would be no social structure. As we will see, structures are maintained by ongoing human decisions to "go along" with the causal impacts of those structures, which at times are changed, but only through human decisions, typically made to resist that causal impact.

Introduction

The fundamental premise of this volume is that we can fully understand our *moral* responsibility as consumers in the market only if we recognize our *causal* role as consumers in the lives of distant others. Economics is the discipline that sets out to understand markets, but, as we saw in chapter 2, particular methodological commitments in mainstream economics prevent the discipline from making this kind of causal connection. Given the strong individualistic bias of our culture today, as examined in chapter 1, one of the fundamental challenges in developing an adequate understanding of social structures is the need to overcome our inclination to see those structures as no more than groups of individuals. Some economists, such as Ulrich Witt, have argued for an "evolutionary" economics that pushes beyond the individualism of the neoclassical paradigm and attends to the influence of social structures on individual economic actors.[7] Yet Witt makes little use of the discipline of sociology, which specializes in the study of those structures.

To that end, this chapter will first briefly review the four main options within sociology for understanding social structures, choosing among them by employing criteria fundamental to Christian theological commitments. It will examine the causal impact of structures on human decisions through the restrictions, opportunities, and incentives that structures generate, and will show how social structures emerge, are sustained, and at times are transformed through the actions of individuals. These insights will then be applied to economic life in chapter 7, which will examine the market as a social structure.

Philosophical Criteria for Employing Social Science in Catholic Theology

To understand social structures, theology needs to rely on sociology. Peter Henriot and Kenneth Himes, among others, have made helpful theological use of the classic work on "the social construction of reality" by Peter Berger and Thomas Luckmann.[8] An even more robust engagement with sociology is needed for an adequate conception of what social structures are and how they operate, as Daniel Daly and Matthew Shadle have shown.[9]

Yet a problem immediately arises: there are multiple explanations for social structures offered within sociology. Thus Christians face a crucial question: How might an outsider to sociology decide among the options it provides? The answer, in very brief form, is that some fundamental commitments in Christian, and particularly Catholic, theology render certain sociological options better than others.

This is a claim far different from that of John Milbank's "radical orthodoxy." In his book *Theology and Social Theory*, Milbank says that Christian faith requires narrative and historiography "but finds no room whatsoever for 'social science.'"[10] For him, "the social knowledge advocated is but the continuation of ecclesial practice."[11] He denies to the social scientist nearly all autonomous insight. Milbank is right that Christian theology must not naively accept whatever social scientists assert to be true. When science begins to tell us who we are—as social science theories of human decision have to do—a philosophical and theological judgment has to be made. But Milbank errs when he gives theology too much authority over science. At stake here is the appreciation of science attributed to Paul Tillich: that a strength of science from which theology should learn is its "humility before the fact." Theology has much to learn from sociology and the other social sciences, even though some options within any particular social science are intellectually unacceptable and none of the options can fully plumb the depths of a life of Christian faith.

Fundamental in deciding among competing social theories are the Christian understanding of moral agency and the character of the human person: created in the image of God, endowed with free will, and flourishing within community. Given the constraints of space, little attempt will be made here to justify the claims about philosophical commitments underpinning theology, but they are sufficiently general not to need defense here (even though the details of each are perennially debated among Christians).

To be useful to Christians, any social scientific perspective needs to be nondeterministic. That is, it must appreciate the radical character of human freedom. At the same time, however, it must recognize the constraints on that freedom, which individuals face in their daily lives within social structures. Persons in community act freely, even though under constraint. Social relationships in community, when functioning well, make personal flourishing possible.

Concerning a social scientific understanding of human community, Catholic social thought has always attempted, as Pope Pius XI put it, to "avoid the reefs of individualism and collectivism," each of which generates errors, both in its description of social life and in its prescriptions for improving that life.[12]

Collectivism has fallen out of favor in Western culture compared to its status a century ago, but its errors remain fundamental. Descriptively, it views the individual person as subsidiary to the community or state, whose life and decisions are causally far more significant than those of its members. Prescriptively, collectivism calls for the subordination of the life projects of individual persons to those of the collective.

Individualism has come to predominance in Western culture, particularly in the United States. While its errors are no more fundamental than those of collectivism, they are far more destructive today due to the prevalence of an individualistic mindset in intellectual discourse, popular culture, and the self-understanding of so many people. As described in chapter 1, one of the fundamental insights of the sociological study *Habits of the Heart*, by Robert Bellah and colleagues, is that Americans use a far more individualistic language to describe themselves than their communally involved lives would merit.[13] Descriptively, individualism understands social life as no more than the interaction of individual persons trying to achieve their goals, whether selfish or altruistic. Invisible in this view of life are the myriad of ways in which social structures influence—for good or ill—the persons within them.

The profoundly communal sense of human existence in Catholic thought has often been referred to as an "organic" view of social life, in which society is more like an organism than a network with only discrete individual-to-individual relations. A similarly Catholic view of institutional life led Pope John Paul II to speak of the "subjectivity" of society: "Authentic democracy . . . requires that the necessary conditions be present for the advancement both of the individual through education and formation in true ideals, and of the 'subjectivity' of society through the creation of structures of participation and shared responsibility."[14] According to this analogy, society "thinks out" its problems through the interactions of the many civil society organizations in vibrant democratic life.

Prescriptively, individualism stresses the primacy of individual rights and is deeply suspicious of law and government and any other institutions that might restrict personal freedom. In the Catholic view, however, law and structure, when properly constituted, are not threats to human freedom but actually enable and enhance it. More taxation is not always right, but taxation is not theft; it is the way a people pools its resources to accomplish common goals. Democracy does not pit the "us" of ordinary citizens against the "them" of government but is instead self-government, even when a political party we fundamentally disagree with has been elected to lead that government.

Beyond these commitments, Christian theology requires an additional philosophical conviction that entails a view of human knowledge. It can be stated quite briefly.

As seen in chapter 4, one of the primary philosophical developments that has led to a loss of intellectual respectability for religious faith over the last two and a half centuries is the conviction that our five senses are the only trustworthy source of knowledge. According to this empiricist view, those who espouse any religious faith violate this fundamental epistemological principle. On the contrary, however, Catholics, and nearly all other persons of religious faith, understand that we can know (with varying degrees of certainty, of course) far more than what we directly perceive through our five senses. As a result, any adequate social science should embody this broader view of knowledge as well.

Thus we can sum up this cluster of philosophical commitments that are helpful in sorting through the options within sociology by observing that Catholic thought is noncollectivist, nonindividualist, nondeterministic, and nonempiricist. (In fact, many other perspectives—both theological and philosophical—would also endorse these four criteria, but providing adequate warrants for this broader observation lies beyond the scope of this volume.) Theology can still learn from some of the insights of social scientific perspectives that are collectivistic, individualistic, deterministic, or empiricist. But when persons of faith import into their analysis a social scientific way of thinking about the world, they should choose one that shares rather than rejects theology's philosophical underpinnings.

What Is a Social Structure?

Because there are competing accounts of the character and influence of social structures, the next step in the argument of this chapter entails a review of those accounts and an evaluation of them employing the criteria just identified.

Four Options in Sociology

Sociologist Douglas Porpora has described the four most prevalent options within sociology for understanding the character of social structures.[15] In the first, social structures are "patterns of aggregate behavior." In the second they are "collective rules and resources that structure behavior." The third sees structures as "law-like regularities that govern the behavior of social facts." The fourth understands social structures as "systems of human relations among social positions." It will be argued here that this fourth, the critical realist position, is a more adequate description of social structures and will allow us to address questions of ethics within them.

The first two options are individualistic. There is considerable diversity within these perspectives, but, as Margaret Archer points out, the fundamental claim was well summarized long ago by Max Weber. For him, collectivities—whether business firms, families, or governments—"must be treated solely as the resultants and modes of organization of the particular acts of individual persons."[16] From this perspective, only persons have causal power and society is reducible to the interactions of those persons. More recently, sociologists such as George Homans[17] and Randall Collins[18] see structures as simply "patterns of aggregate behavior." Others, most notably Anthony Giddens,[19] view social structures as "collective rules and resources that structure behavior." The approach of Homans and Collins embodies the methodological individualism we saw earlier, but even Giddens describes the social world in an individualistic way. As Porpora puts it, "like Collins, Giddens denies that social relationships themselves have any independent causal properties."[20]

Individualism leaves ample room for an understanding of the freedom of the person, but it dramatically overstates that freedom. It acknowledges that human freedom is conditioned, influenced, and limited by the actions of other persons, but it eclipses the many ways in which such influences on freedom also arise from the causal impact of social structures within which individuals live out their daily lives. The example of the influence of gerrymandering on the outcomes of elections from chapter 1 is a case in point. Methodological individualists certainly know what gerrymandering is, but they view it as no more than a set of rules; the causal impact comes from persons in authority who enforce those rules.

The third perspective on the nature of social structures tends to collectivism, the roots of which stretch deep into the history of sociology. Auguste Comte explained that "society is no more decomposable into individuals than a geometric surface is into lines, or a line into points."[21] Social forces are seen as so influential in shaping human behavior that it is naive to attempt to explain this behavior by means of the choices of individuals. Émile Durkheim argued that "social life should be explained, not by the notions of those who participate in it, but by more profound causes which are unperceived by consciousness."[22] Social theories, from this perspective, must be holistic to be adequate. As Archer puts it, "Individuals are held to be 'indeterminate material' which is unilaterally molded by society, whose holistic properties have complete monopoly over causation."[23] Expressed in simpler terms, human persons are denied moral agency; they are little more than pawns pushed around on the chessboard of life by social forces.

More recently, collectivism within sociology is represented in the work of Peter Blau[24] and Bruce Mayhew.[25] They understand social structures as "law-like regularities that govern the behavior of social facts."[26] This approach tends to be quantitative and empiricist in relying on statistical analysis to uncover such regularities. The psychological level of experience is largely ignored, and social structures are assumed, as Porpora puts it, to operate "mechanically and naturalistically over the heads of individual actors."[27] This approach does not take seriously enough the reality of individual agency and freedom.

In sum, the problem with these first three ways of defining a social structure within sociology is that, according to Archer, individualism makes structure "inert and dependent," while collectivism leads to the "subordination or neglect" of agency.[28] The criteria outlined above—that any social science framework to be imported into our ethical analysis should be noncollectivist, nonindividualist, nondeterministic, and nonempiricist—leads to a rejection of these first three understandings of social structures.

The fourth conception of social structure within sociology is the critical realist approach taken by Porpora, Archer, and others. This view understands social structures as "systems of human relations among social positions."[29] Much more can be said about this simple definition, but it will serve our purposes well.[30] Its helpfulness to a descriptive understanding of the market as a social structure—and to a moral assessment of the responsibility of consumers within markets—will become clear in the exposition below.

The Causal Impact of Restrictions, Opportunities, and Incentives

We saw in the prior chapter how emergence characterizes much of the natural world. In her *Realist Social Theory: The Morphogenetic Approach*, Margaret Archer argues that over time human interaction generates "emergent properties" that have a facticity that endures in time beyond the actions (and often beyond the lifetimes) of the human agents within them, and that these properties influence (and often alter) the decisions agents make.[31] This causal influence of social structures comes in the form of socially generated (i.e., emergent) opportunities, restrictions, and incentives.

Consider how the structure of languages on the planet (discussed in chapter 1) influences a promising young scholar born in the United States. He speaks English, which happens to be a language understood by many other scholars in the world, not only those born in English-speaking countries. Thus he can write in his native tongue and have it understood by scholars around the world, an "enablement" or opportunity that is not similarly available to the many scholars who live in places like Poland, Argentina, or Japan. Such opportunities for the young American are not the conscious creation of any person or group but are emergent opportunities that have arisen in the relations among scholars due to the history of human interaction.

Restrictions are the negative side of the same reality. A scholar who grew up in Poland faces a linguistic restriction. In her relation to other scholars, either she will publish in Polish and be limited to a much smaller potential audience than her North American counterpart or she will have to publish in a second language.

These opportunities and restrictions are objective realities generated by the relations among scholars (and among larger language groups, of course). They are experienced (perceived psychologically) by any one scholar as either incentives or disincentives. The scholar from Poland has a strong incentive to learn a second language, most likely English, to overcome the restrictions she faces. The US scholar has little incentive to learn Polish, or any other language, due to the linguistic opportunities he faces—a fact that helps explain why European scholars typically speak more languages than do their American counterparts.

Of course, there are significant differences within nations, not just between them. The well-to-do in any nation face far more structured opportunities—regarding language and a multitude of other things—than the poor. Bright and promising children from poor families in Poland have far less chance than their wealthier Polish friends to live for a summer or attend school in an English-speaking nation. Within the United States, we know that the culture of achievement in strong suburban school districts is a significant advantage for children whose families can afford to live in suburban school districts. Recent economic studies have found significant benefits for children under age thirteen in families who moved from high-poverty neighborhoods to low-poverty neighborhoods. These children were more likely to attend college and have significantly higher eventual incomes than their peers in a control group who did not move.[32] The reputational advantages of elite colleges are another example of an opportunity available to the children of the wealthy and the most talented of the children of poverty. And the poor face far more restrictions in daily life, such as the random violence of many low-income neighborhoods or the majority's suspicion and stereotyping of minority groups.

How Do Social Structures Cause Things to Happen?

Critical realist sociology provides a more accurate account of the relation of moral agency and structure than does either collectivism or individualism. From the critical realist perspective, only persons are conscious agents. Social structures emerge from and are sustained by the actions of individual agents and have independent causal impact in the lives of those agents. But precisely how does that impact occur? In short, structures generate restrictions, opportunities, and incentives in the face of which persons in those structures make different decisions than they otherwise would make. That is, structures cause decisions to change (along with other causes, of course).

Consider the example of the social structure known as a university. Like all social structures, it is a system of relations among social positions. A university comprises many sorts of these relations among positions, including between president and employee, department chair and department member, coach and player, and so on, but the most basic is the relation between the social positions of professor and student. The standard route to becoming a member of a university faculty is to earn a doctoral degree. But a degree cannot make one a teacher; only having students can do that. And being a teacher is not merely a characteristic of an individual; it means taking on the social position of professor that already is in relation with the social position of student. Similarly, being a university student is the result of entering into the social position of student, which is in already existing relation to the position of professor.

In critical realism, the relation between the positions of professor and student is ontologically real. It has emerged over time from the active decisions of many persons. Like the relation between the earth and the book, it is transfactual (i.e., not sense-perceptible) but can be studied. Some scholars, such as economic sociologist Mark Granovetter, think that to attribute such reality to social structures amounts to the error of reification, conceiving of structures independent of the activity of persons.[33] But critical realist sociologists counter this interpretation. As Bhaskar puts it, a social structure "does not exist independently of human activity" and thus there is no reification involved.

University faculty members have considerable influence over the social dynamics within their classrooms, and a particular faculty member can have a unique personal relationship with any particular student. But all of what goes on in the classroom occurs within the restrictions, opportunities, and incentives generated by the preexisting relation between the positions of professor and student.

This relation provides students an *opportunity* to learn from well-informed persons; it provides professors an *opportunity* to channel student effort in ways conducive to learning and allows time and support for scholarly writing. Simultaneously, however, students are *restricted* by their professors' course requirements and faculty members are *restricted* by the expectations of their students and their departments (for example, to hold office hours, to give students grades, and to publish research in professional journals). Each person experiences these objective restrictions and opportunities psychologically as *incentives* embodied in the social structure (i.e., in the relation of positions). Students want to perform well to receive good grades that will enable them to get a job or earn a place in a graduate program. Faculty members want to do well to keep their jobs, gain tenure, and enjoy reputations as good teachers and scholars.

Whatever the personal goals of any particular individual, social structures have causal impact only through the ways that the opportunities, restrictions, and incentives affect the choices made by the individual actors who confront them when they enter into some social position within those structures. Structures cause outcomes only in and through the decisions of people trying to accomplish their goals within them.[34] In effect, restrictions are conditional penalties: if you do (or don't do) X, Y will happen to you. If you as a student don't complete the course requirements, you will fail. If you as a professor refuse to assign grades, you will be fired. If you as a Polish scholar don't find a way to publish in English, few others will read your work. Similarly, opportunities are conditional rewards. If you as a student come to class, you will learn more. If you as a salesperson exceed your monthly quota, you'll get a bonus.

The decisions of students, professors, scholars, and salespeople are influenced (and frequently changed altogether) by these causal forces. But this influence is not deterministic. As Archer puts it, it does not operate by "hydraulic pressure."[35] Instead, this influence has an effect only insofar as it affects the choices that individual agents make in trying to accomplish their goals (whatever these may be) while facing those opportunities, restrictions, and incentives.

Most people within most social structures "go along" with the opportunities they face, and their ongoing acquiescence to restrictions maintains the social structure as it is. This is "structural reproduction," in the jargon of sociology.

As with restrictions, the assistant professor is free to ignore the opportunities she faces. She need not use the university funds offered to her to travel to academic conferences, but the availability of such funds provides an incentive to participate. If she doesn't go to conferences, her scholarship will likely suffer and she may pay a high price at tenure review. The student is free to ignore the insights into a particular discipline that the professor provides, but gaining such insight is the basic reason for attending college, and sitting in a classroom with a well-informed expert is one of the easiest ways to do that. The salesperson may ignore bonuses but will have a smaller income because of it. Typically, people highly value the opportunities that are generated by the relations of the positions they take on. Anyone who wants to reduce those opportunities (thus changing the structure) faces considerable opposition from those currently benefiting from them. This, too, tends to maintain the structures as they are.

In sum, then, social structures do indeed cause things to happen. They generate restrictions and opportunities (experienced psychologically as disincentives and incentives) that frequently alter people's decisions. People are, of course, the cause of their own decisions, but this claim is incomplete without acknowledging that the decisions may have been made differently had no restriction or opportunity been present. Thus, when we say a social structure causes this or that to happen, we mean that it does so by influencing persons to take actions causing those effects. This insight will prove critical when we investigate how markets cause outcomes, both good and bad (chapter 7).

Emergence, Reproduction, and Transformation of Structures

We need to look more directly at how social structures come to be and how they are sustained or transformed.

How Do Social Structures Emerge?

The origins of social structures entails what Archer has called their "historicity of emergence."[36] As individual persons we almost always encounter social structures—whether the organization we work for, the government of the city we live in, the religious congregation where we worship, the music concert we attend, or the family we were born into—that existed prior to our own participation in them.[37] At the same time, we recognize that every social structure has indeed emerged from the interaction of agents in the past. Archer makes this point by citing Auguste Comte's aphorism that "the majority of actors are the dead."[38] Where an individualist view sees all things social as the result of "these people here present," critical realism recognizes the enduring effects on our decisions of the actions of people long gone.

Many structures emerge without the guidance of an overall plan by anyone involved and without any persons or groups who might be understood as their founders. Examples include the market for wheat, the government of the United Kingdom, courtship among young adults, the traffic system of Paris, the institutions of peer review in the natural sciences, and society itself. As Bhaskar describes it, "society stands to individuals then as something that they never make, but that exists only in virtue of their activity."[39]

But some particular structures—a business organization, for example—have a more concrete sense of a beginning, and some hold a deep respect for their founders. Examples here include the founding CEO of the firm where we work, the charter members of our religious congregation, the music group that has planned its own tour, or our parents. Yet whether or not a social structure has founders, it is critically important to recognize two things in this process of emergence.

The first, as Archer makes clear, is that the structures that emerge are not exactly what anyone involved had intended.[40] Agents have differing goals, so the actual structural outcome of their various actions will not satisfy anyone completely. And the process of emergence always entails a degree of unpredictability, with no one able to anticipate everything that eventually occurs. Sometimes things turn out so differently that even the founder of an organization is rejected by his own board of directors.[41] Or consider National Public Radio (NPR), the best-known national radio news service in the United States. It is an organization governed by its members, the local public radio stations around the nation. The initial purpose of NPR was to provide a network for reporting the national and international news that is broadcast by those local stations. Yet a controversy broke out when the board of NPR proposed that it should supplement its revenues by also selling its news broadcasts to satellite radio stations. Many member stations were aghast that NPR would do business with one of the leading competitors of the local stations.[42] While the divergence between original intent and eventual developments is not as stark as this, just about everyone who has started an organization, or even a committee to accomplish something within an organization, has found that things don't turn out as expected.

The second characteristic of the emergence of a social structure is that even when there are identifiable founders of a new organization, their initial actions occurred within the restrictions, opportunities, and incentives generated by preexisting social structures. Anyone starting a business, a university, a parish, a sports team, or a family has learned how such institutions "are supposed to" work. And each takes those initial actions as someone already holding a variety of social positions (e.g., as a citizen or member of a voluntary association) that exist in relation to other social positions, and these prior relations among positions generate restrictions, opportunities, and incentives that have a causal impact on the choices made. It is literally impossible to go back in history to a time when a social structure emerged from a situation in which no social structures had existed before.

Thus, individual activity (mostly of persons long dead) always precedes social structure, and social structure always precedes individual activity (of living persons). This is the historicity of emergence of social structures. As a result, when we consider what individual persons do within a social structure we must recognize that people don't *create* social structures. "Agential power is always restricted to remaking, whether this be reproducing or transforming our social inheritance."[43]

Structural Reproduction: Good and Bad

The fact that agents will be worse off if they resist restrictions, forgo opportunities, or ignore incentives means that most decisions within a social structure tend to "go along," sustaining the structure as it is. As Roy Bhaskar puts it, "People do not marry to reproduce the nuclear family or work to sustain the capitalist economy. Yet it is nevertheless the unintended consequence . . . of their activity."[44] Once a social structure is in place, it tends to endure. This is an inclination toward reproduction that can be good or bad, depending, of course, on the good or bad character of the structure's effects.

Consider the impact of social structures on the sense of agency experienced by the persons within them. A highly innovative technology company faces the risk of bureaucratization as it grows. Firms like Google expend great effort and considerable resources to see that the restrictions, opportunities, and incentives its employees face encourage, not thwart, creativity and initiative, in an attempt to maintain the advantages of a small startup to the greatest extent possible. The rationale behind the giving of grades in schools is similar: to encourage students to take responsibility for their learning by providing specific feedback on their performance.

Of course, structures can also be designed to subvert that agency. The most extreme example is a police state, where citizens trying to change the system are imprisoned and political parties are banned. From Stalin to Pinochet, Pol Pot to Batista, from Hitler to Kim Jong-un, tyrants have relied on structural restrictions to subvert the agency of their citizens. But many social structures impose lesser restrictions that discourage the agency of individual persons within them. Consider the business firm that is run on a strictly top-down philosophy. The CEO and management presume they know how things should operate and offer benefits (opportunities) to encourage a docile attitude and present restrictions that discourage employee initiatives.

The reproduction of structures can be good or bad, and a moral judgment is required to tell the difference. The same is true for the transformation of structures.

How Do Social Structures Change?

We know that social structures do change. The people of India rejected British control and created a democracy in 1947. African Americans fought against the racist structures of the United States in the civil rights movement of the 1960s and 1970s. Every day there are people trying to alter the restrictions generated by the social structures within which they live, whether at work, in the public square, or at the Tuesday night bowling league. What might lead to change of a social structure?

One possibility is that newly appointed leaders—whether CEO of a firm, chair of a government board, pastor of a parish, or president of a student club—want to alter certain characteristics of their organizations. Such changes are often difficult to bring about (because leaders also face restrictions generated by the structures they operate within), but rarely would such changes fundamentally alter their structures. After all, leaders are usually chosen to keep the organization running smoothly.

If we look at leadership from the perspective of critical realist sociology, we might understand the leader as someone who employs agency (of the leader as well as of subordinates) to establish good structures and transform bad ones—good and bad, of course, being a matter of judgment. The leader of an organization of any kind wants to set up a system of interaction where the members of the organization face both opportunities that, if taken up, will promote the organization's values, and restrictions that, if respected, will prevent actions that would thwart those goals. In this process the leader has the power of personal persuasion, attempting to convince members of the organization that it would be a good thing for them to do what the leader wants. Each leader also has "power over" members in the organization, exercised through some degree of control of some of the restrictions, opportunities, and incentives that members face. An essential element in leadership—and in the life of social structures more generally—is the use of this power, a theme we will address in the next chapter.

Yet significant structural change almost always arises not from the actions of formal leaders but from the conflict between persons enjoying many opportunities within a structure and others facing many restrictions. The hazardous factories of the nineteenth century became safer only after workers pressed national governments for the right to form unions, which then pressed both government and employers for stricter safety standards. African Americans fought for decades in the civil rights movement to reverse racist laws and social structures, a struggle that continues today. As Claudia Goldin and Cecilia Rouse have documented, concert orchestras began hiring women on a par with men only after women insisted that the hiring process, overseen by male musicians, was biased toward men and that auditions should occur with a screen that prevents the search committee from seeing the candidate.[45] Adjunct faculty members at US universities (those with part-time contracts and no prospect of tenure) are paid far less per course than tenured or tenure-track faculty even though their qualifications are often similar, and many adjuncts are trying to unionize to have the economic clout (the capacity to create restrictions and opportunities) to press their universities for better compensation.

Sometimes efforts to change social structures entail an unmediated confrontation, as when student protestors take over a university president's office to demand a change on campus. More often change is indirect and, for example, includes pressure on government to change laws or policy to remove support of specific actions or relations that exploit the disadvantaged. For example, in 1937 the United Auto Workers labor union pressed Frank Murphy, the governor of Michigan, to stop using the police to support the anti-labor actions of large automobile manufacturers. When General Motors realized the government would no longer enforce existing labor rules, it agreed to negotiate with the union.[46] In sociological terms, the union was able to eliminate an opportunity (police enforcement of what GM argued were the rights of private property ownership of the factory), making it much more costly for GM to maintain the structured restrictions facing the union.

Such examples of exploitation in social structures remind us of a fundamental difference between structure and culture: structure consists of objective relations among social positions, while culture consists of ideas, objects, and other things with meaningful content. People may or may not be aware of the structural relations within which they live, but culture is impossible without human awareness of, or at least an unconscious resonance with, the meanings inherent in cultural objects. Thus, exploitation in a social structure can exist without the abused being aware of it. The Dalits ("Untouchables") in India have been exploited by higher castes for centuries, but for most of that history they didn't see it that way. Women executives in a sexist business firm may not even be aware that they are being paid less than their male peers. Social structures are systems of objective relations between social positions.

This character of structure also suggests a helpful way forward for organizations that are committed to justice. Whether in a management team of a business firm, an academic department in a university, a Catholic parish council, or an NGO, a very helpful place to start is a frank discussion that identifies the restrictions, opportunities, and incentives facing the various subgroups involved. Senior faculty in a chemistry department may (or may not) deserve the greater influence (an opportunity) they have in the process of hiring new members of the department, but openly acknowledging this difference from junior faculty paves the way for healthy conversation about privilege. By themselves such discussions cannot guarantee a move to greater justice, but they are a critical first step, one facilitated by a proper understanding of *how* social structures have their causal effect.

Conclusion

Social structures are systems of relations among (preexisting) social positions. Those relations among positions—like the relation of the earth and the book—are transfactual (i.e., not sense-perceptible) and yet ontologically real. Just as the force of gravity is an emergent property of the relation between earth and book, so too restrictions, opportunities, and incentives emerge from the relation of social positions. But unlike the earth and book, the persons who take on particular social positions—whether professor in a classroom, manager of a sales team, or pedestrian in a crosswalk—are conscious agents and have the freedom to act in accord with or contrary to the restrictions, opportunities, and incentives they face. The influence of social structures is causally powerful but not deterministic.

Because persons in structures will be worse off if they violate restrictions, fail to take advantage of opportunities, or act contrary to incentives, most people most of the time "go along," and social structures are thereby reproduced. Yet persons seriously enough disadvantaged—or whose strongly held principles are violated—in social structure may be willing to "pay the price" for violating a restriction and act to transform the structure "from below."

In chapter 7 we will see how this critical realist understanding of structure can illuminate the character of markets as social structure. There is, however, one step to take before that occurs: an investigation of the nature of power, particularly as it is exercised as conditional penalties (restrictions) or rewards (opportunities), in order to understand the power that the market exercises through prices, for good and ill.

Notes

1. Hayek, "Scientism," 43.
2. Hayek, "Scientism," 43.
3. Hayek, *Law, Legislation and Liberty*, 69.
4. Bhaskar, *Naturalism*, 26.
5. Bhaskar, *Naturalism*, 28.

6. Bhaskar, *Naturalism*, 34.
7. See Witt, *Evolutionary Economics*, chap. 4. See also Nelson and Winter, *An Evolutionary Theory of Economic Change*.
8. See Henriot, "Social Sin," 129–30; Himes, "Social Sin and the Role of the Individual," 186; and Daly, "Structures of Virtue and Vice," 350–52.
9. Daly, "Structures of Virtue and Vice"; Shadle, *Interrupting Capitalism*.
10. Milbank, *Theology and Social Theory*, 71.
11. Milbank, *Theology and Social Theory*, 6.
12. Pius XI, *Quadragesimo anno*, 110.
13. Bellah et al., *Habits of the Heart*.
14. John Paul II, *Centesimus annus*, 46.
15. Porpora, "Four Concepts," 195–212.
16. Weber, *The Theory of Social and Economic Organization*, 102.
17. Homans, "What Do We Mean by Social 'Structure'?," 53–65.
18. Collins, "On the Micro-Foundations," 984–1014.
19. Giddens, *Critique of Historical Materialism*.
20. Porpora, "Four Concepts," 201. Lars Udehn argues for a distinction between strong and weak versions of methodological individualism. Udehn, "The Changing Face of Methodological Individualism," 502.
21. Comte, *Systeme de politique positive*, 181, quoted in Archer, *Realist Social Theory*, 3.
22. Durkheim, "Review of Antonio Labriola," 645, quoted in Bottomore, "A Marxist Consideration of Durkheim," 902.
23. Archer, *Realist Social Theory*, 3.
24. Blau, *Inequality and Heterogeneity*.
25. Mayhew, "Structuralism," 335–75.
26. Porpora, "Four Concepts," 195.
27. Porpora, "Four Concepts," 198.
28. Archer, *Realist Social Theory*, 33.
29. Porpora, "Four Concepts," 195.
30. Porpora, *Reconstructing Sociology*, 98–99.
31. Archer, *Internal Conversation*, 165–83.
32. Chetty et al., "Exposure to Better Neighborhoods on Children," 855–902.
33. Private email exchange with the author, February 18, 2014. Granovetter has not defined a social structure explicitly, although he talks of the embeddedness of markets within structures as a way of improving on the neoclassical explanation of such things as "sticky" prices. Granovetter and Swedberg, *The Sociology of Economic Life*, 13–14.
34. Bhaskar, *Naturalism*, 40.
35. Archer, "Structural Conditioning," 29.
36. Archer, *Realist Social Theory*, 66–79.
37. C. Smith, *What Is a Person?*, 328.
38. Archer, *Realist Social Theory*, 73.
39. Bhaskar, *Naturalism*, 34.
40. Archer, *Realist Social Theory*, 75.
41. For example, Millard Fuller, the founder and CEO of Habitat for Humanity, was fired by the Habitat board for a history of actions the board saw as sexual harassment but Fuller thought was just an affectionate manner. Alan Cooperman, "Harassment Claims Roil Habitat for Humanity: As Founder's Supporters Rally, New Allegations Emerge,"

Washington Post, March 9, 2005, http://www.washingtonpost.com/wp-dyn/articles /A18460-2005Mar8.html.

42. Marc Fisher, "Satellite Programming May Signal Trouble for Public Radio Stations," *Washington Post*, September 26, 2004, https://www.heraldextra.com/entertainment /satellite-programming-may-signal-trouble-for-public-radio-stations/article_f1e89896 -406f-5510-afd8-9f0abf705e97.html.
43. Archer, *Realist Social Theory*, 72.
44. Bhaskar, *Naturalism*, 35.
45. Goldin and Rouse, "Orchestrating Impartiality."
46. Barnard, *American Vanguard*.

CHAPTER 6

Power

In *Gulliver's Travels* the satirist Jonathan Swift describes a peculiar center of academic research called the Grand Academy of Legado. Great minds there work on such creative projects as softening marble to make pillows and developing a new breed of naked sheep. When Swift's narrator turns to the political science branch of the academy, he learns about several equally harebrained schemes. One would attempt to persuade monarchs to choose their ministers based on "their Wisdom, Capacity, and Virtue." Another would teach government ministers "to consult the Publick Good."[1] Swift's art makes the point that we ought not to trust those who wield power, for they do not have the common good in mind. Such convictions were widely held in Swift's day, and we know that power is frequently destructive today as well.

Introduction

Chapters 4 and 5 examined the philosophical foundations of critical realism, the stratified character of the social world, and consequent insights into how social structures function. Chapter 7 will apply that analysis to understand markets more adequately—as social structures. Yet before that occurs, there is one more element to add to our study to sharpen this perspective on economic life: power.

Power is arguably the most misunderstood part of daily life. It is often abused. This is true; we are all sinners. As Langdon Gilkey has put it, "When the eagle of power sits on your right shoulder, the raven of guilt sits on your left."[2] But it is a mistake to conclude from this, as many people do, that life would be considerably better if there were less power.

In this chapter we will focus on the notion of power as "power over" other people, because clarity about this most fundamental of the various meanings of power will be critically important in our understanding of markets and the sort of power that prices exert within them. We will review an insightful analysis of power provided by the philosopher Thomas Wartenberg and then compare his view with the critical realist understanding of power implicit in the causal impact of social structures. The result will be a more adequate understanding of power and the way it operates within social structures.

Power plays a central role in the harmful causal impact of markets in the lives of distant others, even though power is unacknowledged in the "perfect competition" paradigm of mainstream economics. This neglect of power pervades much of life, as reflected in another piece of art—of a sort quite different from Swift's.

The Invisibility of Power

The J. Paul Getty Museum in Los Angeles has an exhibit titled "*La machine d'argent*."[3] It includes the exquisite artistry of eighteenth-century French silver-smiths. The central piece is an elaborate silver dish that once served as a centerpiece for the dining room table. On its cover in precious metal are three-dimensional renditions of carrots and shallots, dead birds and rabbits—the fruits of the lord's estate. The serenity and artistic sensitivity of the piece are dramatic, but there is an eerie silence about the power relations in society that made its creation and daily use possible. The silver piece today does not reflect the power that separated these privileged few from the many servants whose quotidian duty was to deliver the rabbits and shallots to his lordship's table. As R. H. Tawney once said, the eighteenth century was an age characterized by "a halo of haughty benevolence and submissive gratitude."[4]

The invisibility of power—especially from the perspective of the powerful—is more pervasive than its abuse. People who live within the penumbra of influence created by the power of others are far more likely to be aware of power and more able to articulate its shades of influence, even when there is little abuse. The CEOs of very large multinational corporations are among the most powerful people on earth, but many have said that they really don't have much power. As they see it, most decisions they make are clearly indicated, with external forces often not leaving much room for discretion. As critical realist sociology would put it, CEOs make the big decisions, but they do that faced by causally powerful restrictions, opportunities, and incentives.

However, the invisibility of power occurs not only in large organizations. Parents are more frequently aware of their love of their children than of their power over them, even though for at least the pre-school years, children experience their parents as having a near monopoly on power in their lives, while love often comes from multiple sources. University faculty members are more often aware of their concern for their students than of their power over them, even though students experience the assigning of grades as exercising a power that can keep them from their preferred job or graduate program. When we exercise power, we are often unaware of doing so.

There is, of course, much more to life than power, but there are few dimensions of life that are so fundamental and yet so widely misunderstood. Life is complex, and so is power. Theorists of power have distinguished power over others (the typical form of power) from "power to" and "power for" others (defined as explicitly benevolent forms of influence).[5] For the purposes of this study, power over is central, though, as we will soon see, power over is frequently exercised benevolently.

Most theories of power focus on the power of powerful persons. Steven Lukes, one of the most perceptive of scholars in this area, argues that "when the generic sense of 'power' is used in relation to social life, it refers to the capacities of social agents" (individuals or collectivities). He adds that, as a result, "we will not attribute power to structures or relations or processes that cannot be characterized as agents,"[6] though he acknowledges that "some . . . attribute power to the structures within which agents act."[7] In this volume we are interested in exactly the power generated by social structures, which, from the sociological view, are responsible for most of the power wielded by the powerful persons Lukes focuses on. Any adequate understanding of the stratified social world we live in requires an account of power. As will be see later in this chapter, a more nuanced understanding of power will improve the critical realist analysis of social structures.

Understanding Power

In his book *The Forms of Power*, Thomas Wartenberg set out to better understand how one person has power over another, the capacity to alter the decisions that someone subject to that power would otherwise make. To do this he provides a "field theory" of power: "It treats an agent's power over another agent as a field *within* whose effect the subordinate agent acts."[8] This differs from theories that focus on power as exhibited in an event—as when the city council passes an ordinance—seeing power as existing in its exercise.[9] It also differs from theories of power as a personally possessed "dispositional property" of the one who holds it, a capacity of the powerful individual that exists before it is exercised.

Wartenberg uses the metaphor of a field, based on the notion of a magnetic field, which is the "alteration of the space surrounding the magnet in such a way that the motion of any susceptible object is affected."[10] Power similarly alters the social space for acting that is occupied by the subordinate.[11] Wartenberg follows Aristotle in saying that having power over others means that one has caused or controlled the other's actions somehow and to some degree. Although the control is never absolute, even low levels of power do "cause" others to act differently, to some extent.[12] And power operates in a field because it alters the opportunities (the options) faced by those whom power affects. Power makes some things more costly for the subordinate to do. The set of choices, what Wartenberg calls our "action-environment," is altered by power. So his definition of power is this: "A social agent A has power over another agent B if and only if A strategically constrains B's action-environment."[13] Thus, like Lukes, Wartenberg focuses on the power of one person over others.

For example, a college professor has power over her students because she will issue a grade for the course, which will appear on each student's transcript. If she assigns a low grade, the student may find that with a now lower overall GPA he cannot get into the grad school program he wants or he may be overlooked for that most desired job after college. Like life more generally, college education isn't all about grading, and grading is not all about power. At their best, grades give helpful feedback to students about how well they are grasping what's being studied, and students at their best do not worry much about grades but are motivated to study from a desire to learn. Nonetheless, creating some healthy student apprehension is part of the logic of grading. It motivates students toward more and better work. In some students there is a desire for the direct approval of the professor, but the more general incentive comes from the power.

Grading exemplifies the "field" character of power. Many students would not be much concerned whether Professor Smith gave them an A or a D if no one outside the classroom ever took notice. The power inherent in the capacity to assign a grade is dependent on those third parties whom Wartenberg calls "aligned social agents." In this case, these are the graduate admissions committees and employers that take note of the student's grades and draw some conclusions from them. College professors would have little power in assigning a grade if others didn't notice, which is why many second semester seniors who already have a job or grad school admission often care less about grades than they previously did. In this situation a faculty member's power to alter the student's alternatives is much weaker, even though the professor is doing the same thing in grading the work of her seniors and her sophomores. This same dependence of power on third parties holds true for the most powerful tyrant.

The Mechanics of Power

Power typically works because third parties employ some marker in the relation of person A to person B (in our example, grades given) as a criterion for B's access to certain things B wants (a job or grad school admission) but that the third parties control.

To take another example, the power possessed by the police officer who stops a driver for speeding is not based in what the officer might physically do to the driver (though if the driver becomes belligerent, the officer would indeed handcuff him and take him back to the police station). The most fundamental basis of the officer's power lies in what others—officers at the police station, the prosecuting attorney for the city, the judge in court—will do if the officer issues a speeding ticket.

Similarly, the power exercised by a worker's boss subsists in the fact that others will typically act in support of the boss's decisions, within the firm (supervisors up the line, human resource staff, etc.) or even outside the firm (since if the worker is fired and applies for a job elsewhere, the new HR department might call and learn of the boss's "negative assessment"). Of course, even Adolf Hitler didn't exercise his power by personally killing people. Whether we're talking about professors, police officers, job supervisors, or tyrants, power exists before it is exercised and is most frequently exercised through a field of influence, where third parties take action based on the decisions of the one wielding power.

Once again, we should be clear that power is not the only or even the dominant reality at play in most of these situations. Respect, shared values, mutual concern, and even affection often characterize relationships that simultaneously entail the exercise of power. The point is that power is present and functions through a field of influence, not typically in some direct line from A to B.

In describing power, Wartenberg distinguishes force from coercion. Force is a physical intervention by person A to *prevent* person B from doing something.[14] Force prevents action by B but cannot *make* B do anything. It closes off options and can even end in death, but, as Wartenberg explains, the person subject to force still has a choice, even if under great duress.

Contrary to what many people are instinctively inclined to think, force is not always immoral. Parents physically prevent their two-year-old children from walking into the street. Police keep citizens back from a crime scene. You yourself might physically restrain a hysterical neighbor to prevent her from reentering her burning house to search for a missing child. We need a moral analysis to evaluate the morality of power as force.

In Wartenberg's analysis, the second form of power is coercion, a threat. It occurs when person A can affect person B significantly: A threatens to do so unless B acts in a certain way, and B, because of the threat, then decides to alter what he would otherwise do.[15] Consider an example. John has been late for work several times in recent weeks and has twice been warned that he must be prompt. His boss tells him that if he's late even one more time, he will be fired. This is the threat: if you do X, Y will happen. John, needing the job, then changes his behavior and is careful to arrive on time.

Coercion is part of the "software" of every organization, part of the "operating system" that allows daily life to boot up. As such, coercion can be good or bad; we need a careful analysis to evaluate the morality of any instance of coercive power. Even the best parents coerce their children, explaining to them that they must do this or must not do that, under penalty of some consequence. Every syllabus a college professor hands out contains an implicit threat that if the student doesn't complete the course requirements, she will give the student a failing grade (and that's a threat even when the professor employs the prevailing euphemism that the student "will *earn* a failing grade"). The secretary of the chess club implicitly threatens members with eviction if they don't pay their dues. Every time I decide to drive no more than five miles per hour over the speed limit to avoid a speeding ticket, when I would otherwise prefer a higher speed, I have been coerced, for the common good. A moral judgment is required before deciding whether any particular coercion is good or bad.

Wartenberg observes that, like force, coercion cannot *make* anyone do anything. There is no determinism here. Coercion relies on the subordinate's *decision* to act in accord with what the dominant agent wants.[16] However, as Wartenberg adds, like force, coercion creates resistance: those subject to threat from coercive power often seek ways to resist the power that enables the dominant agent to alter the set of alternatives they face.

Power as Relational

Power, as Wartenberg puts it, "exists in *relationships*—it has a primary location in the ongoing, habitual ways in which human beings relate to one another."[17] Community organizers often say that the most powerful person in the city has the longest list of contacts in his cell phone. In addition, relationality is the reason power is always dynamic: it changes over time as relations change. In this sense power is like an athlete's muscle strength: it is created by consistent, recurring actions, and it slowly atrophies when the activities stop.

Power is also relational in another sense, according to Wartenberg: it is often "situated power." This notion "treats an agent's power over another agent as the result of the social field within which the two agents are themselves located."[18] He calls this kind of power "structural" because there is some structure of social mediation involved. This helps explain the power that the teacher, the boss, and the president of the student club have over the situation of those subject to that power; it is "the power that accrues to individuals when they occupy certain social roles and the power that others lose when they occupy other ones."[19] Put another way, "an agent's power over another agent is the result of a structure of a broad social network."[20] We will see how Wartenberg's notion of "structured power" can be improved by the critical realist insight into social structures.

The moral quality of power is generally no better or worse than the moral quality of the relationships within which it operates. A racist police department in the US will exercise its coercive power in racial profiling, leaving African American drivers far more frequently under threat than others. The management of a clothing factory that cares only about increased profits may coerce its seamstresses to work in unsafe conditions and with insufficient bathroom breaks.

Well-structured societies and organizations have patterns of power that are predictable and functional for both those who are charged with exercising power and those whose options are restricted by it. In fact, when institutions are operating well, the presence of coercive power within them is unobtrusive and judged to be just even by those subject to it. At its best the presence of coercion does not dominate our experience of human life, whether as students or employees or drivers. Human life is complex, and coercion is usually only present in the background. Thus, parents love their children and professors respect the autonomy of their students. Employers know that the workplace will be more productive if there is a good relationship between managers and workers. And police officers frequently work to be a nonthreatening presence when there is no criminal activity going on. It is a sign of social dysfunction when citizens fear interactions with the police, when workers cringe as the boss walks by, or when students avoid contact with their teachers.

The problem is an ancient one, of course. In Saint Benedict's sixth-century instructions for every abbot, which, like all parts of *The Rule*, were to be periodically read aloud to all the monks at mealtimes, he acknowledges the simultaneous importance of power and virtue, always striving to move each monk from being coerced by power to being enticed by virtue:

> As the occasion may call for, let him show the severity of the master and the loving affection of a father. He must sternly rebuke the undisciplined and restless; but he must exhort the obedient, meek, and patient to advance in virtue. . . . The well-disposed and those of good understanding, let him correct at the first and second admonition only with words; but let him chastise the wicked and the hard of heart, and the proud and disobedient at the very first offense with stripes and other bodily punishments.[21]

The restrictions enforced by coercive power are ever present in social structures. When is it unobtrusively in the background, and why? A critical issue here is trust. Do those subject to such threats trust "the system" and trust those charged with exercising power within it? We will investigate the importance of trust—and of the relations of reciprocity that generate trust—in chapter 9.

Although governments are different from other institutions in the severity of the penalties they can impose (e.g., incarceration), it is a mistake—frequently made by proponents of "minimal government"—to *define* the relationship between governments and their citizens in terms of the most severe penalties of coercive power available. In the vast majority of cases those powers, though present in the background, are not even noticed. Thinking of government simply as a coercive power would be like thinking of the relationship of professor and student as constituted by pass/fail grading, or of parents' relationship to their children as defined by the coercive power parents exercise. Although one can go to jail for filing a fraudulent tax return, in a well-functioning society people pay their taxes with no more anxiety about coercion than accompanies the legal requirement to pay for one's lunch at a restaurant.

Coercive power is part of the software of organizational life, of relational life. And ignoring power in any description of human life can only handicap our understanding and undercut any attempt at social transformation. Describing human life, and moral agency in particular, without attending to power is like playing ping-pong while ignoring a strong crosswind.

Implications for a Critical Realist Understanding of Structure

The understanding of power provided by Wartenberg proves to be a helpful complement to the critical realist understanding of social structures, and the two together will, in the next chapter, provide an insightful way to understand markets as social structures that exert power through the effect of prices and other economically critical structural forces. In this section we will compare these two compatible views to understand that complementarity. Put briefly, both perspectives recognize power as a social phenomenon beyond the one-to-one relationship of superior and subordinate. Wartenberg's analysis underplays the reality of structure but clarifies the influence of persons in the exercise of power. The critical realist approach to structure underplays the options of persons who exercise power but clarifies how power operates in social structures.

Differences

First, although Wartenberg explicitly rejects an individualistic interpretation of power, which sees it as the personal property of the powerful, he understands power more individualistically than critical realist sociology does. Structural power, in his view, exists within the "social relations" among persons: the one wielding power, the one subject to that power, and the third-party actors whose decisions make that power effective. Wartenberg sees power lying in the ongoing nature of interactions within "a broad social network."[22] "The power of the dominant agent is constrained by the presence of aligned social agents."[23] Even though his notion of situated power is founded on the person's taking on a social role, Wartenberg provides no analysis of the social structures within which those roles exist. Critical realist sociology, on the other hand, speaks less of the power of individuals and more of power as an emergent characteristic of social structures embodied in the restrictions, opportunities, and incentives that characterize the relations among social positions that constitute social structures, as we saw in chapter 5. Even Wartenberg's speaking about social *roles* that people take on is more individualistic and less structural than the critical realist focus on the social *positions* into which people enter. A role tends to be understood as a characteristic of a person relating to other persons. Taking on a social position emphasizes the preexistent character of relations among *positions* and not simply relations among *persons*.

Where Wartenberg would speak of the power of a college professor in assigning grades as being effective because others notice those grades in dealing with the student who receives them, critical realism would speak of the restrictions that individuals face when they take on the social role of student in a college classroom. The strength of Wartenberg's approach is to illuminate the influence of the professor. The advantage of the critical realist approach is to make clear that this influence arises from the preexisting relation (between professor and student) into which each of them enters.

Another way to articulate this difference is to consider the importance of individual persons who lead organizations. Critical realist sociologists tend to downplay the significance of personal difference. Though Margaret Archer has taken note of the causal powers of people as human beings, more typical, for example, is her argument that after the 2008 financial crisis it was a severe mistake of critics to call for greater moral virtue on the part of the CEOs of banks and investment houses to prevent future calamities in the world of finance.[24] CEOs do what they do because of the restrictions, opportunities, and incentives that they face, articulated by the boards of directors of their firms, who in turn react to the pressures of the market. If one particular CEO were to decide to ignore the restrictions before him, he would soon be replaced by another who would cooperate. Wartenberg, however, might argue that we have good reason to care who, from a list of the most likely candidates, leads the organizations we care about: whether the president of a nation, provost of a university, supervisor of our workplace, or coach of our favorite sports team. People with power can make significant changes to the organizations they lead.

The second difference between these two approaches is that Wartenberg defines power as occurring through a strategic *decision* by *a person* wielding power. He wants this to differ from "behavioristic accounts."[25] To explain, he reports that to disable a subordinate's car on purpose would be an exercise of power: as it constrains the subordinate's action-environment. Yet, he argues, "a random traffic accident" also restricts it, without any power being exercised.[26] Critical realists focus instead on the causal impact of social structures, recognizing that the restrictions generated by structures may or may not be the conscious intention of anyone. Standing back from both accounts, they are not as far apart as it might seem, since structural restrictions are not random events like traffic accidents. They may indeed be part of someone's (perhaps a leader's) strategy, but even if they emerged without a decision to create them, restrictions typically do have a purpose: the reproduction of the social structure. Violate the restriction and you will pay a price.

Third, nearly all of Wartenberg's analysis focuses on the way in which a person wielding power constrains the options of others. He makes only brief mention of the way in which a teacher herself faces constraints "within a complex social network," including the "reciprocal power" that students have through the evaluation of faculty at the end of the course.[27] Critical realist sociologists make clear that both those wielding power and those in subordinate positions face (different) restrictions, opportunities, and incentives as part of a single social structure.

Fourth, another difference arises from the sociologist's attention not just to restrictions but to opportunities as well. Translated into Wartenberg's terms, power exists not only in successful threat (a conditional penalty) but also in a successful enticement (the offer of a conditional reward): if you do X, I will do Y for you. For example, bosses don't only threaten; they also reward. If you perform well, I will raise your wages. If the subordinate earns the raise, the conditional reward was successful. Although enticement that changes the decisions of others is mentioned by Wartenberg, sociology integrates it more thoroughly. Conditional penalties and conditional rewards—both restrictions and opportunities—are forms of power, what we might call constrictive and "enticive" power.

We will investigate enticive power more in the next section. Here it will be helpful to note that "constraint" is a better description of the threat-character of power than Wartenberg's "coercion." The power of threat can have either morally good or bad effects, but the word "coercion" carries a powerfully negative connotation for most English speakers. Speaking of constraint and constrictive power better captures this double meaning.

Similarities

Yet despite such differences, the two perspectives do have much in common. First, both reject an individualistic view of power. For Wartenberg, power "exists in relationships." Critical realist sociology makes clear that those relationships are not just interpersonal; they are relations among social positions. Sociology more clearly identifies this origin of power, but both perspectives understand power as a profoundly social phenomenon.

Second, the two approaches are similar in their understanding of *how* power has its causal impact. For Wartenberg, coercion occurs because the person exercising power can change the options faced by those subject to power, and this "results in a different actions' being taken."[28] Power creates constraints in decision-making because of the action of third parties. For critical realist sociology, the restrictions people face within social structures have causal power because they tend to alter the choices those people make.[29] In both approaches, power is a constrictive causal force that alters how people decide things. Yet this causal force does not function in a deterministic manner. That is, from both perspectives, persons subject to power still make decisions; they just tend to choose differently because of the price they would have to pay if they ignored the constraints they face.

Third, both perspectives understand vividly that the exercise of power often creates resistance. Wartenberg describes power as dynamic, changing over time, often in response to opposition from those subject to that power. Sociologists speak of the structural transformation that can occur when groups disadvantaged by the restrictions, opportunities, and incentives they face choose to "pay the price," violate restrictions, and openly press for social change.

Fourth, both views endorse the morally positive role that power can and frequently does play, not simply its destructive potential. Lukes similarly observes that there are "manifold ways in which power over others can be productive, transformative, authoritative and compatible with dignity."[30] Healthy organizations constrict options to discourage dysfunctional behaviors, even when these implicit threats remain in the background and do not often enter the consciousness of those subject to the restrictions. Put in the more personalist terms of Wartenberg, a good leader in a good organization can exercise power by altering others' action-environments to encourage constructive teamwork and discourage destructive behaviors. Here we see how both Wartenberg and sociologists can encompass some of the goals and forms of "power to" or "power for" within their own frameworks.[31]

Fifth, both perspectives can provide a theoretical understanding of the invisibility of power identified at the beginning of this chapter. For Wartenberg, the frequency of the constriction of options in ordinary life entails our becoming so used to them that we often do not notice their presence. The analysis of social structures makes clear that persons continuously face the restrictions, opportunities, and incentives that those structures generate, and they most often "go along" with the system, meaning that those persons are frequently unreflective about restrictions to which they long ago acceded. The American tourist who rents a car during a vacation in England is vividly aware that the British requirement to drive on the left-hand side of the road is a restriction, but he's probably never thought of the analogous necessity at home (to drive on the right-hand side of the road) as anything but common sense.

Enticive Power

Further insight into power over others arises when we notice that Wartenberg focuses on only coercive power—a conditional threat—while sociology examines both restrictions and opportunities generated in social structures. Restrictions are a kind of conditional threat: if a student doesn't complete the requirements for the course as described in the syllabus, he will get an "F." Articulated as a form of power, the professor exercises constrictive power. But since opportunities are a form of conditional reward, isn't this also a form of power? Does not the prospect of an "A" also alter the amount of effort a student may invest in a course? Is this not a situation where one person brings about a change in another's decision?

The conditional rewards that opportunities represent are enticements to act. For the salesman Jack, the prospect of a bonus if he exceeds his sales quota encourages him to work harder. If he chooses to take up this opportunity—recall that he is not deterministically forced to do so—we can say he was enticed to act. We have all had the experience of buying something "because it was on sale." The lower price was not the only cause, of course, but it was indeed a cause of our purchase—it enticed us to act.

If we follow Wartenberg's lead and consider the person responsible for the bonus—Maria, the manager of Jack's sales group—we can recognize that Maria exercises a kind of power over Jack, or what we might call "enticive power."[32] She offers a conditional reward that functions parallel to the conditional threat embodied in, say, her decision to require a reduction in the expense accounts of her staff (reduce the amount you spend on meals with clients or you will pay a price). As Wartenberg would say, since it is the firm that pays Jack's bonus and not Maria herself, enticive power, like constrictive power, depends on aligned third-party agents and demonstrates the "field" character of both types of power.

From the perspective of those subject to power, enticive power is less objectionable than constrictive power because it doesn't threaten a penalty. But enticive power is not always morally good. There is a widespread tendency to view threats as morally wrong and enticements as morally good. But as we've seen, the power of constraint is frequently beneficent, whether in families, firms, or the Friday afternoon bridge club. Similarly, enticement can be destructive, as in a bribe offered to an elected official. Both forms of power can be employed for good or evil.

Turning to the sociological perspective, social structures generate both restrictions and opportunities, exercising both constrictive and enticive power over the decisions of persons within them. As we will see in the next chapter, a change in price exerts both kinds of power: threatening economic penalties to some actors but promising economic rewards to others if they take advantage of the situation.

Constitutive Power

One final form of power remains to be examined. It is a subtler form of influence, one that we may easily overlook in daily life. Yet its subtlety makes it all the more effective — just because those subject to that power are less likely to notice or resist it.

Joseph Nye, one of the most influential American political scientists of the past fifty years, has written extensively about power. His pathbreaking book, *Soft Power: The Means to Success in World Politics*, set out to challenge those political leaders who believe that only "hard" power is successful on the world stage.[33] Hard power, he explains, "rests on inducements ('carrots') and threats ('sticks')," which we have termed enticive and constrictive power.[34] Powerful nations do indeed have these forms of power at their disposal. But Nye proposes that soft power is too frequently overlooked. Soft power entails "getting others to want the outcomes that you want"; it "co-opts people rather than coerces them"; it "rests on the ability to shape the preferences of others." It includes influence and persuasion but extends to include "the ability to attract," resting on "an attraction of shared values."[35] Stated in practical terms, Nye argues that if the nations of the West want to end the terrorism of Islamic extremism, soft power, not hard, will be more effective.

Steven Lukes makes a similar point when he insists that there are three dimensions of power. The first dimension concerns the obvious: conflict, interests, and decision-making by the powerful. The second addresses the subtler question of whose interests get addressed; this dimension of power is the capacity to shape the agenda, to determine which issues are even discussed. The third dimension of power, the principal issue here, is the capacity to "prevent people, to whatever degree, from having grievances by shaping their perceptions, cognitions and preferences in such a way that they accept their role in the existing order of things."[36] Power can thus be active in "inducing compliance by influencing desires and beliefs."[37] Examples range from a tyrant's heavy-handed control of the media to an inspiring statesman's capacity to present a vision that people find attractive.

Both Nye and Lukes focus on the power of agents, not the power of social structures. Yet this chapter's focus on the latter allows us to recognize that structures have effects quite similar to Nye's soft power and Lukes' third dimension of power. Because this form of power alters perceptions, cognitions, and preferences, we can call it "constitutive" power. Over time, power can change who we are. Persons who initially merely conceded to structural restrictions or took advantage of structural opportunities are often changed over time by repeatedly making the same decisions week after week and come to *prefer* to act in these ways, independent of the added incentive provided by the power to which they are subject.

One simple example of the constitutive power of social structures concerns automobile seatbelts. Over the past fifty years various states have slowly stiffened requirements that drivers wear seatbelts. A few drivers were in favor from the start, but most didn't like the law. Today only a few still resent such requirements, and most now see the seatbelt as merely an ordinary part of driving a car and are so used to the practice that they would continue to use seatbelts even if the law were repealed. The constitutive power of structure has altered us and our perceptions of the world. A similar transition occurred concerning the presence of African Americans at lunch counters and as actors in movies. Racism remains a serious problem in the United States, but unlike fifty years ago, most Americans don't find these particular changes offensive. The constitutive power of markets has been recognized by some economists. As early as 1928, Joseph Schumpeter argued that "capitalism, whilst economically stable, and even gaining in stability, creates, by rationalising the human mind, a mentality and a style of life incompatible with its own fundamental conditions, motives and social institutions."[38]

Of course, this insight into constitutive power is an old one. Seven hundred years ago Thomas Aquinas recognized that because of "the discipline of laws," criminals can be "restrained from evil by force and fear" (constrictive power) and yet "by being habituated in this way, might be brought to do willingly what hitherto they did from fear, and thus become virtuous" (constitutive power).[39] And eight hundred years before Aquinas, Benedict taught that "through this love, all that he [the monk] once performed with dread, he will now begin to observe without effort, as though naturally, from habit, no longer out of fear of hell, but out of love for Christ, good habit and the delight of virtue."[40] Benedict, like Aquinas, does not mention power in this context. Yet actions "performed with dread" unmistakably occur in response to a restriction, and the formation of the habit here is the gradual effect of structural opportunities (as well as, of course, an effect of a change of the monk's ideas—participating in the culture of the monastery).

At a more local level, most of us can think of some restriction we face in the social position of employee that we occupy at our workplace that used to annoy us but that, over time, has become so taken for granted that we no longer are bothered by it. Similarly, the young lawyer who used to work sixty hours a week in order to *become* a partner in the firm becomes the sixty-year-old partner who could work less but *chooses* to skip vacations and work overtime.

Parents exercise constitutive power (we usually call it character formation) when their enticive and constrictive power, exercised in teaching their young children basic manners and morality, eventually "takes" and the kids become courteous and caring adults. Moral *agency* exercised well tends to build good moral *character*. Of course, the internal change doesn't always occur; the severe taskmaster parent can enforce specific behaviors, but the child may decide to comply only out of fear and look forward to being old enough to leave home. Constrictive and enticive power do not always result in constitutive power, another reason why power exercised in love is morally superior.

Conclusion

This chapter has outlined an understanding of power in social structures—constrictive, enticive, and constitutive. Such power is an emergent property of the relations among positions in structures, and it tends to alter the choices that persons freely make. It can operate in an impersonal way (by means of general rules or expectations "democratically" enforced by many others) or in an intensely personal way (enforced by persons who wield power due to the positions they hold). The latter approach recognizes that persons with power have some significant latitude in altering the "action-environment" of those subject to their power. In the sociological jargon, persons who wield power in a social structure frequently can alter the restrictions, opportunities, and incentives of others in the structure. Still, they rarely try to change them as much as they might like, since they themselves face the restrictive, enticive, and constitutive power of structures that discourage change.

Considered theologically, all three forms of power—constrictive, enticive, and constitutive—can be sinful. As a result, the social structures that generate these kinds of power can be sinful as well. Chapter 8 will address the moral assessment of structures and power in economic life. But first, chapter 7 will employ this analysis of power to better understand markets as social structures and show that prices and other structurally generated influences exert restrictive, enticive, and constitutive power in the lives of market participants. Markets *cause* things to happen by altering the decisions people make within them.

As we will see, the power of markets can be quite beneficial—as when the rise in price of a scarce natural resource leads us all to consume less of it. However, when the constrictive power of markets sharply limits the options of the poor and marginalized—at times denying them the necessities of life—those of us who benefit from market processes should recognize our causal role in the generation of that denial and our consequent moral responsibility for the harms caused. Power tends to be invisible to those who exercise it, particularly when they stand at a substantial psychic distance from those subject to its effects. A prime example is the causal power of consumers in sustaining markets and the harmful causal impact of markets in the lives of distant others.

Notes

I am grateful to the Catholic Theological Society of America for permission to use here much of my presidential address, "Power and Public Presence in Catholic Social Thought, the Church, and the CTSA," *CTSA Proceedings* 62 (2007): 62–77.

1. Swift, *Gulliver's Travels*, 49.
2. Jeff B. Pool, "Eagle of Power, Raven of Guilt: Historical and Religious Dimensions of the Current Global Crisis, Conversations with Langdon Gilkey," Religion and Culture Web Forum, Martin Marty Center, University of Chicago Divinity School, November–December 2005; https://divinity.uchicago.edu/sites/default/files/imce/pdfs/webforum/112005/gilkeyinterview.pdf.
3. *La machine d'argent* is a masterpiece of French eighteenth-century silver made by one of France's foremost goldsmiths, François-Thomas Germain. As the Getty describes it, "the term Machine d'Argent literally means 'machine of silver.' At the time, the French word 'machine' meant 'an invention of artistic genius or spirit' and was broadly used to describe a centerpiece on a formal dining table during the course of a meal. The Machine d'Argent includes an assemblage of two game birds, a small rabbit, and vegetables."
4. Tawney, *Equality*, 34.
5. For a treatment of "power to," see Hinze, *Comprehending Power*. For "power for," see Mercedes, *Power For*.
6. Lukes, *Power: A Radical View*, 71–72.
7. Lukes, "Power," 61.
8. Wartenberg, *The Forms of Power*, 71.
9. Wartenberg, *The Forms of Power*, 72.
10. Wartenberg, *The Forms of Power*, 74.
11. Wartenberg, *The Forms of Power*, 74.
12. A note on "cause": Even the hurricane that floods city A is not the only cause for the flooding. Why? The same hurricane would not have flooded city B for a number of reasons (such as higher elevation and stronger dikes). We focus on the "intervening" event as the cause, but it is only a new cause interacting with many preexistent causes. Mill, *A System of Logic*, 237.
13. Wartenberg, *The Forms of Power*, 85.
14. Wartenberg, *The Forms of Power*, 93–96.
15. Wartenberg, *The Forms of Power*, 96.
16. Wartenberg, *The Forms of Power*, 101.
17. Wartenberg, *The Forms of Power*, 165. Italics in the original.
18. Wartenberg, *The Forms of Power*, 142.
19. Wartenberg, *The Forms of Power*, 157.
20. Wartenberg, *The Forms of Power*, 165.
21. Benedict of Nursia, *The Rule of St. Benedict*, chap. 2.
22. Wartenberg, *The Forms of Power*, 165.
23. Wartenberg, *The Forms of Power*, 169.
24. Wartenberg, *The Forms of Power*, 30.
25. Wartenberg, *The Forms of Power*, 85.
26. Wartenberg, *The Forms of Power*.
27. Wartenberg, *The Forms of Power*, 180.
28. Wartenberg, *The Forms of Power*, 88.
29. Archer, *Realist Social Theory*.
30. Lukes, *Power: A Radical View*, 109.
31. Hinze, *Comprehending Power*; Mercedes, *Power For*.

32. The author reluctantly relies here on a neologism, enticive, for lack of a publicly authorized synonym. Attractive, assertive, and abusive are commonplace, while acceptive, adoptive, amusive, and assaultive all appear in the dictionary (though the spellchecker doesn't recognize two of these). As a result, might there not be psychic space in our vocabulary for "enticive"?
33. Nye, *Soft Power*.
34. Nye, *Soft Power*, 5.
35. Nye, *Soft Power*, 5–7.
36. Lukes, *Power: A Radical View*, 11.
37. Lukes, *Power: A Radical View*, 136.
38. Schumpeter, "The Instability of Capitalism," 385–86.
39. Aquinas, Summa Theologica I–II, q. 95, a.1.
40. Benedict of Nursia, *The Rule of St. Benedict*, chap. 7, 68–69.

CHAPTER 7

The Market as
a Social Structure

We live in a globalized world, and the products we buy, whether whole or in part, often come from several different nations around the world before they enter our homes. Throughout this volume we have focused on the example of textiles produced in one nation and worn in another, but the notion that markets, even the market for textiles, are global is not a new one.

> The woolen-coat, for example . . . is the produce of the joint labor of a great multitude of workmen. The shepherd, the sorter of the wool, the wool-comber or carder, the dyer, the scribbler, the spinner, the weaver, the fuller, the dresser, with many others, must all join their different arts in order to complete even this homely production. How many merchants and carriers, besides, must have been employed in transporting the materials from some of those workmen to others who often live in a very distant part of the country! How much commerce and navigation in particular, how many ship-builders, sailors, sail-makers, rope-makers, must have been employed in order to bring together the different drugs made use of by the dyer, which often come from the remotest corners of the world![1]

These words of Adam Smith, published in 1776, remind us that it is a daunting task to describe the long chains of relationships in the market processes that eventuate in our daily consumption. And the success of economics to date in doing so is rightly admired. As Nobel Prize-winning economist Kenneth Arrow puts it, the price system "is certainly one of the most remarkable of social institutions and the analysis of its working is, in my judgment, one of the more significant intellectual achievements of mankind."[2]

Introduction

In chapters 2 and 3 we saw the limitations and inadequacies of both mainstream economics and traditional ethical analysis for understanding how our agency as consumers is integrally related to the harms that markets help to cause for the distant producers of the goods we buy. Chapters 4 through 6 outlined a critical realist alternative that is better able to understand social structures and the place of human agency within them. In this chapter we return to consider economic markets and apply critical realist insights to understanding how the price system functions. It is helpful to start with an observation from chapter 2.

The stitches in the collar of the shirt I am wearing were sewn by a woman somewhere in Bangladesh. Her participation in the market has no doubt increased her economic well-being, since that is the fundamental reason behind her decision to work. Yet she might also be subject to unjust practices at her workplace, or she might even have died a horrific death in the fire at the Tazreen Fashions factory outside Dhaka that killed 112.[3] Moreover, unbeknownst to either her or me, there may be a woman in Mexico whose economic security was swept away when the textile firm she used to work for went bankrupt due to lower-priced clothing produced by Bangladeshi seamstresses.

Christians and others have a number of warrants for their obligation to assist others in need that are entirely independent of whether one played any role in causing the problem. Yet beyond these reasons, this volume sets out to establish an important additional warrant based on our causal participation in markets. Articulating the relation of social causality and moral responsibility provides a significant additional reason why people should be concerned about their participation in markets and why they should work to structure those markets more justly. In addition, because markets are genuinely beneficial in so many ways, without an analysis of their structural shortcomings both ignorance and economic self-interest tend to focus society's moral energy on the relief of suffering rather than its prevention.

Although these are important questions about our moral responsibility in the harms caused in the lives of those who make the products we buy, the discipline of economics does not address them. (As seen in chapter 2, economists leave moral judgments to policy makers, philosophers, theologians, and ordinary citizens.) However, underlying the question of whether I am *morally* complicit here must be the question of whether I am *causally* complicit in those harms—and causality is indeed the proper concern of science. If I buy a shirt that was sewn by women who later died in a factory fire, did I become causally involved in their deaths simply by buying that shirt? If so, how should we describe that involvement?

Such a question is rarely addressed in mainstream economics, and the view of markets articulated there does not provide much help in thinking about this issue. The market for shirts is understood in an abstract and individualistic way, with the market presenting a set of opportunities to each participant—whether consumer, department store clerk, clothing brand CEO, factory owner, or seamstress—in response to which each participant makes utility-maximizing decisions. Because any one consumer has an imperceptible effect on the market as a whole, within the neoclassical paradigm there is no sense that such a consumer has any noteworthy causal role in harms suffered by a seamstress half a world away.

This chapter will employ international trade in textiles to illustrate the stratified character of economic life, where the market exists at a "higher" level than the persons acting within it. It will employ the insights of the previous five chapters into the nature of social structures and the characteristics of power within them to understand the market as a social structure, as a long chain of ontologically real relations between preexisting economic positions, a chain of causal relations linking consumers causally to the distant producers of the products they buy.

This perspective on markets promises five contributions to economic analysis. First, it provides resources for better analysis in several subfields of economics, such as institutional evolution, international trade, and the economics of supply chains and "fair trade" consumer movements. Second, it provides a more adequate understanding of the market as a social phenomenon. It grounds traditional mainstream supply and demand explanations in real relations in the economy; it describes what goes on inside the black box of the market. Third, it connects economics today with its more practically based historical roots. Whether in the 1770s (Adam Smith's day) or the 1870s (Léon Walras's day), economists used to feel the need to make at least some effort to relate economic theory to how markets entail relations among people. Fourth, it provides a more adequate methodology for economics, grounded in a critical realist philosophy of science that explains the actions of scientists better than empiricism can and thereby better sustains an adequate economic science. By treating prices as only one of many causal forces generated within the social structure of the market, it allows room for the neoclassical view as a subset of a more comprehensive perspective (after all, some decisions *are* adequately modeled by utility maximization). In doing so it moves institutional influences from the background to the foreground of consciousness, understanding them as operating parallel to the influence of prices. Fifth, by providing a better causal account of the long chain of relations that constitute global markets today, it provides a better economic foundation for ethical deliberation (outside of economics) about those markets.

Three final introductory notes are appropriate. First, markets do not only cause harms. The same market in textiles that deprived the Mexican seamstress of her job provided jobs for women in Bangladesh. The same market in electronics that has pressed American manufacturing workers into lower-paying service jobs has raised the standard of living of millions of Chinese citizens and provides less expensive electronic goods to consumers around the world. This volume focuses on the harms that markets help to cause, but the analysis proposed to do this can articulate the beneficent effects of markets equally well.

Second, although the focus in this volume is on global markets, the analysis applies equally to local markets, as when you get a haircut from a self-employed barber or buy vegetables at a local farmers' market. The "chain" of these markets has only one link (you deal directly with the producer), and the face-to-face encounter makes structural constraints more pliable. But even those intensely local markets are social structures. The relation, for example, between the social positions of farmer and buyer at a local market generates constraints and opportunities, as all social structures do.

The third is that although this chapter and the book as a whole focus on global textiles markets, the critical realist analysis of the market as a social structure applies equally well to many other problems that are largely ignored here due to constraints of space. These include the environment, racism, sexism, homelessness, health care, and economic inequality.

How Markets Operate

Economists rightly value markets highly because markets so effectively coordinate the economic activity of billions of people. The most fundamental economic problem for any nation is resolving how to employ the many available resources—classically identified as land (including all natural resources), labor, and capital—in the production of the goods and services to be consumed each year. The questions are, "What shall we produce, and how?"

The former Soviet Union empowered a group of central planners to decide these issues—everything from how much of each kind of steel to make to what sort of trousers to produce. The intention was to ensure that national goals were accomplished. The problems associated with central planning are many, as one might end up with more than enough rolled steel for washing machines but not enough steel beams for buildings, or citizens may be left with few options but to buy and wear trousers that don't fit properly. As Friedrich Hayek famously argued, central planners cannot possibly possess the knowledge of local situations that is essential for good economic decisions.[4] Such knowledge is only available to individuals and businesses making choices in millions of unique situations all across the nation.

In contrast, markets leave these sorts of decisions to individuals and firms, each of which tries to accomplish whatever goals they have in light of the opportunities and restrictions they face. Economists point to the role of prices within markets as fundamental to the effectiveness of this process because of the information that prices relay quickly throughout the system. And this is invaluable. The owner of a lumber mill in Idaho does not need to know the details of the devastation caused when a major hurricane rocks the East Coast. All he needs to note is the rise in the price of lumber and he will increase production, a change that helps meet the now greater need for building materials.

Yet the understanding of prices in markets can be improved by employing the analysis of power developed in the previous chapter. We saw there that the most ubiquitous forms of power over others are restriction, a conditional penalty, and its parallel positive form of power, enticement, a conditional reward. Prices present the prospect of both penalties and rewards.

When the price of steel rises because it has become more difficult to find high-quality iron ore, the firms that use steel as an input to production face the constrictive power of prices, a conditional penalty: alter your behavior or you will be worse off. Some users of steel, of course, have little choice: manufacturers of washing machines will continue to buy steel to ensure that the frame of each machine is sturdy enough to do its job. They will have to raise the sale price of washing machines and hope this won't discourage too many potential buyers. Other users of steel will alter their decisions in the face of this threat. Alarm clocks used to have steel frames, but plastic works nearly as well and is cheaper.

Although a rise in the price of a product represents a threat to those who use that product, the same rise in price similarly announces a conditional reward—an enticement—to those who make and sell anything that might substitute for it. Thus, the makers of plastic, wood, and aluminum benefit from the rise in the price of steel. Prices render the economy more efficient because of their constrictive and enticive power—the conditional penalties and rewards they promise. A now higher-priced input (steel) will continue to be employed by those who value it most highly (i.e., they have no other good options), but others will switch to a lower-priced substitute. This market allocation of steel to its highest-valued use represents the essence of the efficiency of the market system.

Moreover, the same is true for a drop in prices. When the price of electronic components drops, computers and a myriad of devices guided by computer chips become cheaper than before. This provides a conditional reward—an enticement—to potential consumers, since they can now alter their behavior: they buy cheaper computers and have money left over for other expenses. And analogous to the price rise just described, a drop in price of computers has presented a conditional penalty—a threat—to those who provide goods or services that computers also provide. To take but one example, the availability of various forms of entertainment on computers, tablets, and smartphones has threatened the economic well-being of competitors who provide similar entertainment through television or cinema. They have responded to the constrictive power of prices by altering their business plans to cushion the negative impact that the drop in the price of computer devices would otherwise have caused (e.g., I can now buy pizza and a glass of wine at the local movie theater).

Technically, in economics this role of prices is referred to as a "pecuniary externality," which, as Albino Barrera's excellent study of economic compulsion puts it, is "the very dynamic that brings about allocative efficiency."[5] As we saw in chapter 2, we are most familiar with real (or "technical") externalities, such as the negative health effects of air pollution that are suffered by people downwind who are "external" to the business decisions of the owners of the plant that creates the smoke. In a similar sense the role of prices in the economy is a pecuniary externality: the initial cause of the rise in the price of steel—the increasing difficulty of mining high-quality iron ore—eventually affects persons and organizations external to the steel industry. But it is exactly the change in behavior by these external persons and organizations that increases the efficiency of the economy by allocating resources to their higher-valued uses. The constrictive and enticive power of prices brings about a myriad of changes in the use of steel and other products that help to increase our efficient use of them. This causal influence of prices illustrates the "field" character of power identified by Wartenberg in the previous chapter. Changes in the iron ore industry in northern Minnesota have the impact they do because of reactions around the globe.

None of us likes being subject to the constrictive power of price. Our personal lives would be better if this or that change in the price of a product did not make us worse off. But the benefits of market coordination over those provided by central planning are considerable. And many of the most severe problems we face require us to rely on that constrictive power—for example, putting a price on carbon to slow global climate change. Nonetheless, there are several moral problems with the operation of the price system, a theme we will return to later in this chapter when we review the constrictive, enticive, and constitutive power of markets.

The Market as a Social Structure

Mainstream economists will be quite amenable to critical realist talk about individuals making decisions in the face of opportunities, restrictions, and incentives. Economists, of course, think of prices as having precisely these effects. Business firms exist because their owners understand that at current prices they face an *opportunity* to purchase all the inputs necessary and sell their products at a profit. When consumers find their buying power *constricted* by the rise in the price of some product they currently purchase (leaving them with less money in their budget for everything else), they typically respond by consuming less of this product, often substituting another now-relatively-cheaper product that provides comparable utility. Both critical realists and neoclassical economists understand agents as making decisions to accomplish their goals (whatever those are) within the opportunities, restrictions, and incentives they face in markets.

However, most economists will have to stretch to wrestle with the underlying insight—the "realism" in critical realism—that these opportunities, restrictions, and incentives are not simply presented by a sort of "disembodied opportunity set," as neoclassical economics describes them. Nor are they presented by one individual or group to another, as methodological individualism would have it. Rather, they are generated by market *relations* that are ontologically real, in the same way that the relation between the earth and the book—and the relation between the position of professor and the position of student—are real. Since social structures exist at a "higher level" than the persons who act within and sustain them—the world is "stratified"—the causal forces at play there are different in kind from those assumed in an individualistic account of economic life.

Many economists think of prices as simply generated by the abstract interaction of supply and demand. But the history of economics as a discipline demonstrates that this abstract interaction is dependent on people negotiating prices in the market. Adam Smith talked about "the higgling and bargaining of the market."[6] Even Léon Walras, abstract though his work was, pictured an auctioneer calling out prices to potential buyers and sellers through a process of "tâtonnement" (French for "trial and error"), eventually finding the price where supply equals demand (the market-clearing price) for all commodities.[7] Critical realist sociology offers economists a scientifically founded model of social structures that roots the theory of supply and demand in the real relationships into which people enter.

Put concretely, when a freeze in Colombia damages this year's coffee crop, the eventual rise in price of a cup of Colombian dark roast at your local coffee shop begins with the very real negotiation between the person who holds the position of sales manager at a particular coffee plantation in Colombia and someone else who holds the position of purchasing agent for an international coffee company (and, of course, there are multiple plantations and several coffee companies). This is why we must be clear that the price does not rise "because of the law of supply and demand." Just like the "law" of gravity, this "law" is helpful, but it is only the economist's attempt to summarize the real but transfactual causal forces at work in the market. Like the "law" of gravity, the law of supply and demand has no causal force of itself. The price of coffee rises because of decisions that occur all along the chain of relations among positions: from plantation manager/coffee buyer to coffee shop waitress/customer. Each person holding a position in this chain of relations is subject to the constrictive, enticive, and constitutive power of price as well as other restrictions, opportunities, and incentives that affect their economic choices. Thus, although the cold weather in Colombia is the precipitating cause of the change in the price of coffee, a multitude of other causes also play a role in whether and to what extent the price of a cup of java rises at the coffee shop.

From the critical realist perspective, each market is a social structure. That is, it is a system of social relations among preexisting social positions, and individual persons move into and out of various positions in multiple markets during the ordinary activity of the day. A typical person might go to work in the morning (entering into the positions of subordinate to one's boss and of coworker with one's peers) and stop to buy a quart of milk on the way home (taking on the position of customer in relation to the clerk). She may also that evening take on the non-market position of citizen and send an email to her US senator endorsing a proposal to alter the current laws structuring the market for fossil fuels.

One significant advantage of the critical realist view of markets is that it attends to the institutional characteristics of markets that the most basic neoclassical economic model eclipses. Rather than seeing institutional features as no more than background conditions for the price system, in a stratified world both prices and other structural influences are recognized as arising from the same source. The easily monetized opportunities, restrictions, and incentives—primarily prices—on which neoclassical economists focus are generated by the same real relations among social positions that generate the nonmonetary causal impacts that, say, a business owner faces. Consider some examples.

A firm will be worse off if it ignores prices, of course, but it also won't survive if it ignores the restrictions imposed by various civil laws (concerning the character of contracts, the standards for financial reporting, the treatment of workers, etc.) or the restrictions entailed in the minimal expectations of workers in its particular market (concerning the frequency of bathroom breaks or time off at various holidays, etc.). For nearly eight decades now the calendrical five-day workweek has allowed business firms in the US to respect the traditional work restrictions of Christian and Jewish religious culture without really noticing them as restrictions. Today, the appearance of a growing number of American Muslims in the workforce and their insistence on a place and time for prayer during the workday has made economically relevant religious restrictions more noticeable. Some firms have fired Muslim workers for not "clocking out" during ten-minute prayer breaks, but many have made accommodations.[8]

In sum, although the neoclassical model privileges prices, they are but one of a multitude of opportunities, restrictions, and incentives generated by the relation of social positions that constitute a market. And because we can speak of the constrictive, enticive, and constitutive power of government regulations, industry standards, union contracts, religious expectations of workers, and many other restrictions and opportunities in the social structure of any market, we should speak more generally about the constrictive and enticive power of markets and not just of prices, a theme we will return to presently.

The Market as a Chain of Relations

The Italian sociologist Pierpaolo Donati has criticized the "black box" approach to markets. This is the prevailing tendency of economists teaching Econ 101 to millions of students each year: they present only the generalized theory of perfect competition and do not "look inside" markets to see what's happening among real persons, identifying the internal character of markets.[9] What occurs inside this black box is invisible (uninvestigated) and, as a result, some options faced by consumers and producers are largely ignored. For example, not all firms take maximizing profits as their sole aim. Workers can try to alter the restrictions they face by negotiating informally with management or through formal unionizing. Consumers are also citizens who can influence whether and how the laws structuring markets can prevent labor rights abuses or environmentally destructive side effects in the production of the products they buy. Economists, of course, can and often do respond that their theory is general enough that it can include goals of the firm other than profit. Yet when studies are done, they almost always look only at profit. As economist and theologian Mary Hirschfeld has said, even though many economists do not recognize it, "the result is that they are frequently deaf to real concerns about the ethical implications of their supposedly neutral apparatus."[10]

The critical realist analysis of markets as social structures allows for a more adequate description of the far-flung character of global markets. There is, of course, a growing body of economic literature on fair trade markets and supply-chains,[11] and a large literature in business ethics on the relation of supply chains and corporate social responsibility.[12] Yet here too the critical realist view of markets as social structures can strengthen the analysis.

Let us return to the example of a typical consumer who goes to a Macy's department store to buy a shirt that has been manufactured in Bangladesh. Here the person enters into the preexisting position of customer, which is in social relation to the position of clerk, in a long chain of social relations among preexisting positions that extends from the consumer to the seamstresses. For simplicity we will here ignore offshoots from many links in the chain to the suppliers of inputs at each stage (for example, to the firms that build the ocean-going ships that transport the clothing or the sewing machines used by the seamstresses).

The consumer interacts with the clerk in the department store, and each faces opportunities, restrictions, and incentives built into the consumer/clerk relation. These elements exist independently of the two particular persons interacting with each other. For example, the consumer at Macy's is not free to bargain over a price, even though in some places in markets such haggling is quite acceptable. At the same time, the enticive power of this social structure offers the consumer the opportunity of a "no hassle" returns policy. The clerk also faces restrictions, such as the job-imposed obligation to be unflappable even in the face of an irresponsibly irate customer, perhaps something she might never do in other parts of her life. The clerk also faces the opportunity of significant discounts on quality clothing she may want to buy for herself or her family. The relation of customer/clerk is ontologically real and has a causal impact on the choices made by the persons entering into it—just as the relation of the earth and the book causes the book to hit the floor.

In turn, the position of clerk is in relation to the position of supervisor, which is in a relation with the position of store manager, which in turn is in a relation to the corporate purchasing manager who decides which shirts Macy's will offer for sale. Simplifying the language to persons (but intending reference to the positions they hold), this person has a relation with the sales manager of a clothing brand, who in turn has a relation with corporate buyers within that firm who deal with the owner of a clothing factory, who is in a relation with the factory manager, who directs the floor supervisor, who oversees the work of the women who sew the shirt the consumer buys.

Each one of these relations between preexisting social positions is ontologically real and is one link in a long chain of causally structured relations that delivers shirts from seamstress to final customer. Prices are negotiated for various inputs (e.g., cloth and sewing machines, transport services, wages, the rent Macy's pays) and for the shirts themselves in various of these links and are signaled up and down the chain.

And, just as important, each link generates non-price, economically influential restrictions, opportunities, and incentives that influence the market for shirts (e.g., quantities, due dates, labor/management procedures, technical production requirements, legal obligations, etc.).

Often when describing the market for shirts, neoclassical economics shows little interest in how the market works "internally," as if the only thing that mattered is that there is a price for and availability of shirts. However, if we look inside the black box of the market we can clearly tell that each of the links that make up that long chain of relations includes a number of economically essential opportunities, restrictions, and incentives, and each link is causally dependent on and causally integral to what we call the market for shirts. How individual agents react to the opportunities, restrictions, and incentives in each of these relational links is critically important for whether and how the market for shirts operates; market prices are only part of the economic picture. This insight provides the rationale for attention to institutional form and cultural influence on economic life.

International Trade in Services

For simplicity, the analysis of this volume has focused on the supply and demand of goods—material objects such as textiles. But many services are traded internationally. The best known are services in insurance, business consulting, banking, and finance. Christina Traina has examined how something as personal and immediate as childcare can be part of a global chain.

> In a typical global care chain, an educated Filipina mother looking for better wages to support her children, and perhaps avoiding a difficult spouse, might emigrate to Los Angeles to work as a nanny for a professional couple. Meanwhile, she hires a nanny for her children in Manila at perhaps one-tenth the wage she herself is earning. Then her own nanny arranges for a grandmother, aunt, or older sibling to care for her children, often free of charge.[13]

The chain that constitutes this market in childcare is simpler than that for the shirts we buy, as it has fewer links, but the geographic distances involved are comparable. The shorter chain makes the causal relationships clearer. There is the position of Los Angeles employer of a nanny and the position of nanny there, into which the Philippine woman enters. There is the position of employer of a nanny in Manila (a position occupied by the nanny in LA) that is in relation to the position of nanny there. Acknowledging the nonmarket relations that always support market relations, there is then the relation of the position of young woman or grandmother within the social structure of the Philippine family. Each of these relations generates restrictions, opportunities, and incentives (notably different in LA than in Manila), and each is causally dependent on the other two.

A critical realist understanding of markets illuminates economic exchange in services as well as goods.

Competition

For simplicity, our treatment of markets as a social structure in this volume has focused on the long chain of economic relations that connect the consumer to the seamstress. The constraints of space prevent our attention to an equally important set of economic relations between competing firms that are relevant in many of the links of that long chain. Thus, Macy's competes with other stores. The shipping company that transported my shirt from Asia to North America competes with others. Most apparent in our treatment of the market for shirts, each clothing factory competes with similar factories domestically and in many other nations around the world.

Any one firm involved in this long chain holds a position in relation to the positions held by other firms producing the same goods or providing the same services. Thus, the restrictions that emerge from this competitive relation within the structure of the market alter the decisions of the owners and managers of any particular factory. It is in such relations that the constrictive and enticive power of markets is most vividly evident. We can easily imagine, then, that morally responsible managers at firms along this long chain of relations may ask themselves the same question we did in chapter 1: "Why don't we have better choices in markets?" This reality does not exonerate firms that choose to get profits by means of unjust practices, but it does make clear the constrictive power that markets exercise. Both manager and market cause the outcome.

The Power of Markets

As we have seen, the constrictive power of markets can and often does have a positive moral effect, as when the rise in the price of scarce resource leads to greater conservation or when a tax on cigarettes leads to less smoking. But constrictive market power can also lead to morally bad outcomes.

Most fundamentally, the threat of not being able to sell their products without a loss keeps producers from making things needed by those too poor to buy them. For example, there is not enough affordable housing for the poor, and pharmaceutical companies don't develop drugs to treat diseases plaguing the world's poorest people. City zoning regulations and national patent laws indeed restrict and enable these decisions, but the constrictive and enticive power of markets is also a fundamental cause of these outcomes. Second, many firms are large enough to have some control over the prices they charge. This is of lesser moral importance if Crest has a higher price than other toothpastes but a much more severe problem if pharmaceutical companies dramatically raise the price of life-saving drugs.[14]

Third, the constrictive power of markets can generate unjust results when it is faced by the poor or marginalized. When the price of fuel oil rises, the market's constrictive power may require the eighty-year-old widow living on Social Security to choose between an adequate diet and her prescription medicines. And, of course, there is the recurring example in this volume of the plight of workers in the developing world.

Many people outside of economics, particularly those committed to reducing economic injustice in the world, mistakenly blame international trade as the fundamental cause for poverty in developing nations. Economists know the benefits of international trade in ways most others do not—importantly, in the understanding of comparative advantage—and this is a critical contribution to policy debates.[15] Yet economists too often judge the arguments against trade as simply shallow and uninformed. Economist N. Gregory Mankiw has argued that resistance to the Trans-Pacific Partnership was due to isolationism, nationalism, and ethnocentrism.[16] Less ideologically, from the mainstream point of view, the lack of, say, fire escapes that contributed to fatal factory fires is usually understood as a form of government failure to enforce fire codes or managerial irresponsibility in not providing those fire escapes, not the fault of the market itself. Of course, government and management *are* causes. The point is that they are not the only ones.

A more adequate, structural analysis acknowledges the causal role that markets themselves play in such disasters, by generating the opportunities, restrictions, and incentives that press factory owners and brand name buyers to act as they do. As we saw in chapter 1, following the death of 117 garment workers in the worst industrial fire in the history of Bangladesh, the *Wall Street Journal* reported the testimony of one of the managing partners of the firm that owned the factory. He named the role of market forces in the disaster (what we have called the constrictive power of markets): they generated a substantial restriction on his choices. "It's hard to continue to improve factory compliance and safety when there is ever increasing downward pressure on the prices that global retailers are willing to pay."[17] A similar report came from another factory owner concerning child labor: "We cannot follow all the rules, not even those that cover the employment of children. If I follow the rules, I have to raise prices."[18] We don't need to approve of this man's decision to violate child labor laws, but we can recognize the causal power of markets in his life.

Such factory owners are in a preexisting social position of supplier of textiles and are thus in relation to others in the position of buyer for large clothing retailers. Among the restrictions generated in that relation is the threat that the retailer will buy from other sources if the factory owner does not lower his prices. Although mainstream economics speaks abstractly of market competition pressing firms toward greater efficiency, the constrictive causal power of prices occurs up and down the chain (between firms and between individuals and firms), within the relation of supplier and buyer. That power can cause harms to workers by threatening the economic well-being of factory owners, who (in most capitalist markets) control working conditions. Business owners and managers around the globe understand the causal power of prices and markets.

Although the constrictive power of markets exerted through the effects of prices deserves much attention, the same social structure of the market simultaneously generates nonprice constraints that affect economic decisions by individuals and businesses. These can be morally destructive, as when corporate policies penalize workers with parental duties or when a factory labor union opposes the firing of a clearly irresponsible worker. Yet the nonprice constrictive power of markets can also be morally constructive, as when corporate policies against sexual harassment threaten a sexist manager or when protests by workers press a Peruvian mining company to allow time off for church attendance during the Sunday shift.

The Enticive Power of Markets

Just as significant as the constrictive power of markets is their enticive power, the conditional offer of a reward. Markets regularly offer opportunities to individuals and firms to improve their economic well-being. This, too, is how markets cause things to occur, always, of course, by altering decisions made by persons within them.

The effects of this enticive power of markets are often highly beneficial. Examples here include the college student who seeks an education for employment in the solar energy sector, the entrepreneur who decides to start a business there, and the inventor who spends two years of unpaid effort to develop a new solar technology he hopes will be profitable. But market opportunities do not only generate good results. The chance to make a profit at the expense of workers or the environment is another illustration of the enticive power of markets. And, of course, some market opportunities represent a combination of good and bad. The development of hydraulic fracturing ("fracking") in drilling for natural gas and oil has reduced carbon emissions because the lower price for natural gas has led to the production of electricity by natural gas instead of coal. However, it has also threatened groundwater supplies in many areas near the drilling sites, and the lower price for gasoline has encouraged greater use of gas-guzzling vehicles.

Attending to the enticive power of markets is particularly important in efforts to help the poor of the world improve their economic situations. People in poverty are as creative as anyone else and often can recognize an economic opportunity to start a small business, hiring local people to meet some local need. However, many developing nations have made it extremely difficult to start a new business. In Venezuela, for example, starting a small business typically requires seventeen different permits or licenses, takes on average 144 days, and requires payments equal to 89 percent of the average Venezuelan's annual income. In Canada, by contrast, it takes on average two such procedures, thirty-six hours, and less than one-half of one percent of an average income.[19] Here is a case where freer markets—less government regulation—will surely help the poor.

In addition, government corruption makes matters considerably worse. I recall visiting a small steel fabrication business situated on the heights overlooking the fishing port of Chimbote, Peru. Because of overfishing of the ocean by boats from many nations, the fishing industry had collapsed, unemployment was over 50 percent, and the twenty manufacturing jobs this business provided were invaluable in the local economy. The factory produced steel storage sheds that the owner was hoping to export to the United States, where his products could compete favorably on both quality and price, except for one big problem: to get them from his small factory onto a docked cargo ship he pointed to down the hill, he needed to obtain an export license, which would add 20 percent to the price of a shed. The official fee for the license was small, but the required "under the table" payment to the man issuing those licenses meant his products would be too expensive abroad. The enticive power of the global market was inviting him to increase his workforce to one hundred employees, but foreign sales were not an option.

A further example where an extension of the enticive power of markets would improve the lives of the poor concerns the legal limbo within which hundreds of millions of "squatters" live—residing in shacks on the peripheries of cities around the developing world. Peruvian economist Hernando de Soto has argued persuasively that granting the poor a legal title to the land they live on would do much to help them.[20] For many people in the industrialized world, their homes are the most valuable thing they own, and many invest time, energy, and money in improving those homes, both for immediate benefit and in response to the market's promise of a higher sale price later on. In addition, most who begin a new small business rely on home mortgages to help finance it. Squatters, on the other hand, have no economic incentive to do any of this. Without ownership, any effort to improve their living quarters or even to press the city to install potable water or sanitary sewers will only make it more likely that they will be evicted from the now-more-valuable property they helped to create.

Returning to the textile example and the abject poverty facing so many families in Bangladesh, the market's enticive power has a causal impact on the decision of the young woman wanting to support her family. She chooses to take the job of seamstress even though the working conditions may be bad and the factory may have no fire escapes. The wages are above the national average and most employees never experience a fire or building collapse. Yet choices made under the constrictive and enticive power of prices can cross the line from freedom to economic compulsion and injustice. This occurs when, as Albino Barrera puts it, "market participants unavoidably incur profound opportunity costs. People give up non-trivial interests in order to satisfy, safeguard, or procure their other vital claims that are at even greater risk."[21] Knowing how to think more precisely about the progression from (always constrained) freedom to compulsion will require considerable work, employing the insights of critical realism in fundamental moral theology and Christian anthropology.

Although the presence of the constrictive power of markets harms the poor in many circumstances, the *absence* of the enticive power of markets frequently leaves them worse off than they would otherwise be. There is no better way to reduce poverty around the world than to create opportunities for poor people to work productively to improve the economic well-being of themselves, their families, and their communities. The enticive power of markets holds out just such a promise.

The Constitutive Power of Markets

As we saw in chapter 6, there is a third form of power to consider: constitutive power. When people make choices under the influence of constrictive or enticive power over the long run, the people themselves—their perceptions, cognitions, preferences, and habits—are changed. Persons become constituted differently over time. Consider an example.

From the arrival of the first Europeans until the early twentieth century, most US citizens lived in rural areas within a few miles of a town.[22] The distance between small towns was roughly twice the distance a farm family could conveniently drive their horse-drawn wagon into town to pick up supplies. All this changed after the invention of the internal combustion engine—a source of power small enough to be contained in a vehicle, whether a pickup truck or farm tractor. With a pickup the farmer could easily travel five or ten times farther for supplies if they were cheaper there. The tractor meant that a farmer could farm far more land than a pair of horses allowed. As Adam Smith predicted, easier transportation meant a broader market and labor-saving farming meant lower sale prices for farm goods.[23]

The process entails technological change, of course, but the enticive power of markets—luring inventors to develop trucks and farm machinery and leading farmers to buy and sell in larger regional centers instead of the local town—eventually altered the conceptions, cognitions, and preferences of farm people. The constitutive power of markets (along with other causal forces, of course) created farmers who were no longer "small town" people.

And as we have seen, contemporary examples include the young lawyer enticed by wealth and status to work seventy hours a week—who becomes the sixty-year-old partner who, having achieved wealth and status, still works those long hours without the incentives. Sociologist Robert Putnam argues, in *Bowling Alone*, that market relationships have contributed to a general weakening of social ties. "We sign fewer petitions, belong to fewer organizations that meet, know our neighbors less, meet with friends less frequently, and even socialize with our families less often."[24] The point here is that markets exercise constitutive power that alters who we are over time.

Conclusion

Every market is a social structure existing at a "higher" level than the persons making decisions within it. In a globalized world, the typical product market today is a very long chain of relations among preexisting social positions. Market relations—whether between the consumer and the clerk at Macy's, or the seamstress and her supervisor in Bangladesh—are structured, with a variety of opportunities, restrictions, and incentives to be faced by any person who takes on one of those positions. These persons exercise moral agency. They make decisions in light of their goals, whatever those may be, and the constraints and opportunities they face. That is, the market alters their decisions—has its causal impact—by means of its constrictive and enticive power. This is the causal role of markets in unjust market outcomes as well as in morally beneficial ones; markets alter people's decisions and, in the long run, their characters.

The outcomes of those decisions, as they interact with the decisions of others, alter the restrictions, opportunities, and incentives of the next links in the chain "above" and "below" this link. The constrictive, enticive, and constitutive power of market structures is thus transmitted up and down the chain. Some of this influence occurs through the impact of prices, but by no means all of it.

The seamstress and the customer at Macy's are causally connected by the long chain of relations we call the market for shirts. Each link in that chain is causally dependent on and causally critical to the cooperation at a distance, which the market makes possible. This means that the consumer and the seamstress are causally present in each other's lives.

Economists are not well equipped to make a judgment about the *moral* responsibility a consumer may incur by purchasing a shirt at Macy's. However, economists ought to be able to describe the chain of *causal* relations linking that consumer to the seamstresses in Bangladesh who made the shirt he buys. Critical realism, along with an enhanced understanding of the kinds of power at work in social structures, provides an explanation of those causal connections and the stratified character of reality. It holds out the possibility of a re-conceived view of the market as a social structure that allows Christians to articulate the causal foundations for moral judgments about our responsibilities in a globalized world.

The next two chapters will investigate the moral analysis of structures: chapter 8 will ask what it means to describe a social structure as sinful, and chapter 9 will look more broadly at the character of an ethics capable of a moral assessment of social structures—ethics in a stratified world.

Notes

1. A. Smith, *The Wealth of Nations*, 1.
2. Arrow, "Values and Collective Decision-Making," 221.
3. Jim Yardley, "Horrific Fire Revealed a Gap in Safety for Global Brands," *New York Times*, December 6, 2012, https://www.nytimes.com/2012/12/07/world/asia/bangladesh-fire-exposes-safety-gap-in-supply-chain.html.
4. Hayek, *Collectivist Economic Planning*.

5. Barrera, *Economic Compulsion*, 28.
6. A. Smith, *The Wealth of Nations*, 31.
7. Walras, *Elements of Pure Economics*.
8. Omar Sacirbey, "For U.S. Muslims, Work-Time Prayer a Struggle," *Huffington Post*, October 20, 2011, http://www.huffingtonpost.com/2011/10/30/for-us-muslims-work-time-_n_1064761.html; Julie Turkewitz, "Prayer Dispute Between Somalis and Plants Reshapes a Colorado Town, Again," *New York Times*, March 8, 2016, http://nyti.ms/24M5K1F; Sarah Larimer, "These Muslims in Wisconsin Were Just Fired in Prayer-Break Dispute," *Washington Post*, February 5, 2016, https://www.washingtonpost.com/news/acts-of-faith/wp/2016/02/05/these-muslims-in-wisconsin-were-just-fired-in-a-prayer-break-dispute/.
9. Donati, "The Morality of Action," 63–66.
10. Hirschfeld, *Toward a Humane Economy*, chap. 2.
11. Dragusanu et al., "The Economics of Fair Trade," 217–36; Hayes and Moore, "The Economics of Fair Trade"; Ciscel and Smith, "The Impact of Supply Chain Management," 429–37.
12. Doorey, "The Transparent Supply Chain," 587–603; Strand, "Corporate Responsibility in Scandinavian Supply Changes," 179–85; Park-Poaps and Rees, "Stakeholder Forces," 305–22.
13. Traina, "Facing Forward," 189.
14. Peter Loftus, "Drugmakers Raise Prices," *Wall Street Journal*, January 10, 2016, https://www.wsj.com/articles/drugmakers-raise-prices-despite-criticisms-1452474210.
15. Comparative advantage, an insight first explained by David Ricardo, is that international trade between two nations can benefit both even when one of them is more efficient in producing each of the goods traded.
16. N. Gregory Mankiw, "Why Voters Don't Buy It When Economists Say Global Trade Is Good," *Economic View*, July 29, 2016, http://www.nytimes.com/2016/07/31/upshot/why-voters-dont-buy-it-when-economists-say-global-trade-is-good.html.
17. Syed Zain Al-Mahmood, "Bangladesh Probe Calls Fatal Fire Sabotage," *Wall Street Journal*, December 17, 2012, https://www.wsj.com/articles/SB10001424127887323723104578185260860346712.
18. Cláudia Brandão, "The Real Cost of Cheap Shirts," *New York Times*, April 22, 2018, https://www.nytimes.com/2018/04/21/opinion/sunday/the-real-cost-of-cheap-shirts.html.
19. World Bank Group, "Starting a Business."
20. De Soto, *The Mystery of Capital*.
21. Barrera, *Economic Compulsion*, 17.
22. US Census Bureau, "Population: 1790–1990."
23. A. Smith, *The Wealth of Nations*, 1.
24. Putnam, *Bowling Alone*.

PART III
Implications

CHAPTER 8

Sinful Social Structures

Several years ago I was leaving Guatemala one Sunday morning when the newspaper ran a front-page story about a wealthy landowner who had been kidnapped a few days before. Such kidnappings for ransom occur there often enough that no one was surprised by the news, but this time things were different. The victim was forty-one years old and somehow was able to escape his captors after a few hours. He returned to his home and reported the crime to the police, who sent to investigate the incident the same three men who had kidnapped him that morning—now in their police uniforms. The man had connections, he knew the head of the nation's supreme court, and the story made it onto the front page. I asked several locals what they thought of these events, and the responses were nearly identical: a shrug of the shoulders and some version of "What can you do?"

In his monumental study *Bribes: The Intellectual History of a Moral Idea*, John T. Noonan makes clear that the problem of corrupt officeholders is an ancient one, documented in the Near East as early as four thousand years ago.[1] In addition, corruption plagues every nation, with police corruption in many major US cities an ongoing problem.[2] The point here, however, is that this kidnapping case manifests a criminal justice system so pervasively corrupt that, in the parlance of Catholic social thought, one would surely call it a sinful social structure.

In theological terms we have no problem employing the notion of sin to describe the actions of the individual kidnappers. But, given the analysis of social structures provided in chapter 5, we should understand the actions of the police officers not simply individualistically—arising only from personal decisions—but also structurally—arising from personal decisions made in a stratified social world, within the causal impact of the restrictions, opportunities, and incentives that the criminal justice system generates. Now that we have developed a more precise account of the causal forces at work in structures, we can outline a moral analysis of them, specifically asking how the notion of sinfulness can apply to them.

Introduction

Official Catholic social teaching has for decades acknowledged the destructive impact of sinful social structures, but it has never explained what a social structure is or how one operates, and thus it has not been able to articulate *how* sinful social structures have their power in the world. This chapter will briefly review this problem within theology. It will then examine several characteristics of original sin and will propose that these also characterize sinful social structures. Moreover, it will propose that any judgment that a social structure is sinful will require a specific causal framework—or causally based typology—of that particular kind of structure, whether concerning national economies, public high schools, or university student organizations. Just as original sin characterizes us all as sinners even though we often make virtuous choices, so no sinful social structure is only sinful. These social entities exist at a higher level than the person, but they share this fundamental moral ambivalence with the persons whose actions sustain them.

The idea of sinful social structures entered the vocabulary of the universal Church primarily due to its place in liberation theology and in the documents of the Latin American bishops at Medellín, Puebla, and Santo Domingo.[3] The notion raised concerns among popes and bishops because of a perceived conflict between the power of social structures and the freedom of individuals within them.

Social Structures in Catholic Social Thought

Magisterial descriptions of structural evils[4] include any violation of "the demands of human dignity,"[5] the "rights of human persons," "others' freedom," "the dignity and honor of one's neighbor," or "the common good and its exigencies in relation to the whole broad spectrum of the rights and duties of citizens."[6] More generally, such evils often "generate violence"[7] and include "situations of life which are injurious to man's dignity and freedom."[8] If these are the evils, what are the structures that cause them?

Social structures, of course, are not conscious agents and thus don't sin in any literal way. But the adjectival form "sinful" performs a helpful task, as does the word "evil" in phrases such as "an evil plan." This chapter examines what official Catholic social teaching has taken for granted. Employing the understanding of a social structure from chapter 7, it will articulate what it means for a social structure to be sinful.

A helpful way to summarize the approach of official Catholic theology to sinful social structures is provided by the view of Joseph Ratzinger, later Pope Benedict XVI, in his 1984 analysis of liberation theology.

Nor can one localize evil principally or uniquely in bad social, political, or economic "structures" as though all other evils came from them so that the creation of the "new man" would depend on the establishment of different economic and socio-political structures. To be sure, there are structures which are evil and which cause evil and which we must have the courage to change. Structures, whether they are good or bad, are the result of man's actions and so are consequences more than causes. The root of evil, then, lies in free and responsible persons who have to be converted by the grace of Jesus Christ in order to live and act as new creatures in the love of neighbor and in the effective search for justice, self-control, and the exercise of virtue.[9]

On the one hand, as Cardinal Ratzinger says, structures have causal impact: they can be evil and they can cause evil. On the other hand, he is careful to defend freedom, something necessary for religious conversion. Further, his claim that structures "are consequences more than causes" helps to focus attention on human agency and freedom.

However, this account leaves a number of important problems unaddressed. There is no description here of just *how* structures cause evil, a gap that our understanding of the critical realist view of social structures from chapter 5 can fill. Implied in the cardinal's words is the concern that freedom is threatened if one assigns too much causal impact to social structures. But what if, as we saw earlier, social structures have their impact *by means of* human freedom, by changing the options people face? In addition, he seems to assume that "structures" refers to very large institutions, whether economic, political, or social. But what if the typical Catholic parish is also a social structure? What if preaching, spiritual direction, and repentance all occur and are made possible by (beneficial) social structures? Critical realist sociology not only understands the parish as a social structure; its treatment of both restrictions and opportunities allows us to account for the positive effects of such structures. Finally, consider his claim that structures are "consequences more than causes." If your parish, the high school you attended, Stalin's government, and the Wednesday night bowling league are all social structures, is it helpful to describe them as consequences more than causes? Surely they are both. Also, the incommensurability of the ways they are both cause and consequence renders any judgment of "more" or "less" deeply questionable.

Yet twenty-five years later the same man, Pope Benedict XVI, provided a short hint on how to answer the questions his earlier statement raised. He wrote: "The Church's wisdom has always pointed to the presence of original sin in social conditions and in the structure of society."[10]

How Is Original Sin Sinful?

We have from chapter 5 a sociological description of how social structures have causal impact on human freedom, and we just saw a magisterial description of the sorts of evils sinful social structures can cause. But we are still in need of a theological construal of the relation between that impact and those results. How shall we understand such structural influences on human freedom from a theological point of view?

As we have seen, social structures are not conscious agents, so they cannot sin in the literal sense. However, since they have causal effect through the choices made by persons within them, they can be described as sinful when their constrictive or enticive power—the restrictions, opportunities, and incentives those persons encounter—encourage morally evil actions. Here Pope Benedict's comment turns out to be analytically insightful because, like the sin that can exist in social structures, original sin too is sin only analogically.[11] (We are not personally guilty for any sin committed by others in the past.)

To further this investigation, it will be helpful to review eight characteristics of original sin that also apply to the ways in which social structures can be sinful. First, both personal disposition and environment are entailed in original sin. Joseph H. McKenna notes that "much of moral evil is mediated to us by the historical situation into which we are born."[12] That is, as the quotation from Pope Benedict indicates, one dimension of original sin is evident in the influence of our environment on us. In describing the views of Karl Rahner, Kevin A. McMahon has observed that "the freedom and integrity of our decisions, already restricted by our individual sinfulness, is further compromised by the decision of others, at times in ways that make their influence, for all practical purposes, inescapable."[13]

As Rahner himself has said, "all of man's experience points in the direction that there are in fact objectifications of personal guilt in the world which, as the material for the free decisions of other persons, threaten these decisions, have a seductive effect upon them, and make free decisions painful."[14] According to McKenna, "Before the act of freedom . . . we are in a sense already affected by historical evil. Before we have experienced freedom we are deeply influenced, perhaps for life, by the world and the community into which we are born."[15]

Similarly, critical realist sociologists point to the causal impact of social structures on human choices as one of the most fundamental insights of their discipline. As we saw in chapter 5, most of us, most of the time, "go along" with the restrictions, opportunities, and incentives of the social structures we live and work within daily. Yet we are also free to take a stand that contradicts them, if we are willing to pay the price. Critical realists would also note that those structures arise not only from "objectifications of personal guilt in the world" but from a wide variety of human activities, both good and bad.

Second, original sin has long been understood as a sort of "inclination to evil." As Jesse Couenhoven has expressed it, "disordered beliefs and loves" have shaped our "most basic cognitive, affective, and volitional powers."[16] Toddlers are not morally responsible for their choices, but eventually they become responsible persons who are characterized by these disorders of original sin, which they themselves did not create. As Dorothee Sölle puts it, "I am responsible for the house which I did not build but in which I live."[17] The fundamental insight of original sin is not that it was passed down biologically from Adam and Eve but that we are morally responsible for our decisions even though they are distorted by disorders in our lives that we did not create.

Analogously, social structures are inevitably characterized by distortion, to one extent or another. At a minimum, as we saw in chapter 5, social structures generate restrictions and opportunities that tend to elicit from persons within them decisions that reproduce the structure instead of transforming it for the better. Even in structures oriented toward the common good—for example, a well-run religious charity—there will be more-advantaged subgroups whose privileges are maintained by the restrictions and opportunities the structure generates. Moreover, as Reinhold Niebuhr argued, whatever virtue might be hoped for in individuals, organizations and social groups are inevitably less capable of virtue.[18] Like humans, every social structure is to some extent a sinful one.

Third, despite all the distortion caused by original sin, Catholic theology has always endorsed the human capacity for virtue. As the *Catechism of the Catholic Church* says, "Human nature has not been totally corrupted: it is wounded in the natural powers proper to it; subject to ignorance, suffering, and the dominion of death; and inclined to sin—an inclination to evil that is called concupiscence."[19] "Man has a wounded nature inclined to evil."[20] Yet the same individual who is characterized by this inclination to evil is also capable—with the help of God's grace—of choosing the good.

This insight extends to our understanding of sin within social structures, because no social structure is only sinful, even those we rightly condemn as thoroughly sinful. The sinful structures of Nazi Germany that facilitated the utterly abhorrent extermination of millions nonetheless encouraged fortitude and valued fine music and art. There is no moral "equivalence" between evil and good here, but these latter characteristics are certainly morally commendable.

Fourth, limitations on freedom that come with original sin operate *through* our freedom, not deterministically suppressing or destroying it. As Rahner describes it, "We are a people who must inevitably exercise our own freedom subjectively in a situation which is co-determined by the objective occasions of guilt, and indeed in such a way that this codetermination belongs to our situation permanently and inescapably."[21]

To explain this statement, Rahner immediately follows up with a vivid economic example: "When someone buys a banana, he does not reflect on the fact that its price is tied to many presuppositions. To them belongs, under certain circumstances, the pitiful lot of the banana pickers, which in turn is co-determined by social injustice, exploitation, or a centuries-old commercial policy. This person himself now participates in the situation of guilt to his own advantage. Where does this person's personal responsibility in taking advantage of such a situation co-determined by guilt end, and where does it begin? These are difficult and obscure questions."[22]

A critical realist understanding of the relation of structure and agency can fill the analytical gap that Rahner points to here when he acknowledges the power of "situations" that shape the circumstances of action without articulating *how* situations

impinge on free choices. Nonetheless, the banana example vividly conveys his awareness of the moral ambiguity of free choices within the social structure of the market,
where others who produce what we consume are too frequently treated unjustly.

Fifth, under the influence of original sin, one's sinful acts occur with a sense
that only part of one's self is engaged. According to McMahon, Rahner understands
concupiscence, an effect of original sin, as an "inertia." "Rahner meant that this
inability (characteristic of any finite creature) to act with one's entire self in a given
decision precludes the whole self from being engaged whether the decision is for
good or for evil."[23]

This insight corresponds well to the critical realist understanding that any particular agent may make choices when occupying a social position within a social
structure that differ from—or may fundamentally conflict with—choices he or she
would make when in other social positions. Sometimes this difference is of little
consequence—as when we whisper after taking on the position of a patron at the
library. But every day many people face more fundamental conflicts of conscience—
as when a manager decides to "cut a corner" morally under threat of losing his job.
In a more extreme situation, the virtuous mayor of a small Latin American city may
have to decide whether to accept a $50,000 bribe from a drug cartel that simultane-
ously threatens to kidnap the mayor's child if the bribe is declined.[24]

Sixth, each sinful choice made under the condition of original sin shapes us
further. As Rahner observes, "Sin is certainly not like breaking a window which
falls into a thousand pieces, but afterwards I remained personally unaffected by it.
Sin determines the human being in a definite way: he has not only sinned, but he
himself is a sinner."[25] Part of the change in us caused by original sin is a distortion
of our understanding of ourselves and the world, as liberation theologians have long
stressed.

Critical realist sociologists understand the social world as ontologically real and
thus objective. As a result, it often appears to us who are born into it as natural, like
the flora, fauna, and terrain of the earth around us. How social structures alter the
character of persons within them is described by Dave Elder-Vass as altering internal
dispositions[26] and by Margaret Archer as entailing "reflexivity" and the internal conversation.[27] In the language developed in chapter 6, social structures have constitutive power; over the long run they shape who we are.

Seventh, because the influence of original sin is constrained by virtue, moral
character is pivotal. And moral character is shaped not only by our own prior decisions but by those of others, most important in the formation we receive as young
children. As Jesse Couenhoven puts it, not everyone has an "equal moral start" in
life. "It is clearly better for a child—morally and spiritually—to be raised in a stable
and caring home than in an abusive one."[28] The point is that the effects of original
sin can be muted by careful, virtuous upbringing by one's parents.

Things are similar with social structures. A nonprofit organization designed by its
founders for the common good is more likely to resist the inevitable distortions of
structural life than is an organized crime syndicate or a profit-above-all-else business

firm. The nonprofit cannot guarantee moral purity, but virtuous leadership in a social structure—particularly at the inception of an organization—can improve its structurally generated causal impact on decisions. And, of course, strong moral convictions are what typically motivate those willing to "pay the price" for resisting structural restrictions in order to transform the structure.

Eighth, the complexity of the situation of human freedom under original sin makes it exceedingly difficult to draw a bright line between human choice and the influence of one's environment. "Inasmuch as the social environment does affect human nature positively and negatively, it is therefore difficult to determine what is 'innate' about human evil and what is environmentally 'contracted.'"[29]

Similarly, from the critical realist point of view, agency always occurs within the causal influence of social structure; yet structure cannot exist without the choices of free agents whose actions reproduce or alter it. There is no agency without structure, and no structure without agency.[30]

In sum, there are eight characteristics of original sin that also characterize the sinfulness of social structure.

1. Original sin has its effect through both one's environment and one's personal disposition.
2. When we reach an age of moral responsibility for our actions, we are already disordered due to original sin.
3. Original sin is an inclination to evil, a reality that makes sinful choices more likely.
4. Original sin's influence on our choices occurs through our freedom and not in violation of it.
5. Under the influence of original sin, our sinful choices occur with the psychological sense that only a part of our self is engaged.
6. Each sinful choice made under the influence of original sin shapes who we are.
7. Formation in virtue by one's parents reduces the influence of original sin.
8. Given the interplay of environment and personal disposition in original sin, it is impossible to draw a bright line between our freedom in choosing and the influence of that environment.

Sinful social structures are sinful in a similar way. The opportunities, restrictions, and incentives they generate have their causal effect—their constrictive and enticive power—only through people's moral agency: they reward sinful choices and penalize virtuous ones. Although every social structure is sinful to some degree, careful design and ongoing moral attention can reduce the inevitable distortions. Persons often feel only a part of themselves is involved in these sinful choices—since they likely wouldn't have made them in other areas of their lives—and yet the choices do shape them to be more the kind of person who does make these sorts of choices. This is the effect of constitutive power. Moreover, since the sinful causal impact occurs only through the exercise of human freedom, it is usually impossible to parse precisely the respective influences of personal character and social structure.

We should note here, as earlier, that the decision to limit this volume to the sociological treatment of structure, while ignoring culture, imposes a significant cost in our discussion of original sin. This chapter argues that social structures are sinful in a way analogous to the sinfulness arising from original sin. A similar and equally significant argument could be made about the ways that culture can be sinful.

Identifying Sinful Social Structures

The final step in this chapter's investigation of how social structures can be sinful requires a causal framework—ideally a typology—that identifies causal relationships and distinguishes good from bad structures of a specific kind, whether these are kinds of economic systems, school districts, or Catholic parishes. A moral assessment of this or that characteristic of a social structure is impossible without a judgment (whether explicit or implicit) about what that characteristic will cause to happen. That is, the moral assessment relies, in part, on a set of causal assumptions.

Such descriptive typologies may be available from professional social scientists or directly from insightful participants in those structures. In each case, the sinfulness of a social structure parallels "original sinfulness." That is, the structure has causal power through the restrictions, opportunities, and incentives faced by persons within it—which incline their free choices toward evil.

Inclusive and Extractive Institutions: An Example

Let us begin with one insightful example of such a causal framework from the study of economic development. There is no claim here that everyone adopting the view of sinful social structures proposed in this volume will or should thereby adopt this particular causal analysis—because there are morally respectable differences among social analyses of economic development among sincere and well-informed Christians. The point is that the example demonstrates how causal framework functions in any adequate moral analysis of social structures.

In their book *Why Nations Fail*, Daron Acemoglu and James A. Robinson ask the same question as did Adam Smith in his famous volume, *An Inquiry into the Nature and Causes of the Wealth of Nations*: Why is it that some countries are wealthy and others poor?[31] However, these two volumes offer different approaches. For Smith, the answer is founded most basically in human nature; for Acemoglu and Robinson, it is founded in economic and political institutions.[32]

The authors open their book with a comparison of two cities divided by a fence: Nogales, Arizona, and its sister city just across the border with Mexico, Nogales, Sonora. At the time of the creation of the border dividing the one city into two in 1853, there was little difference in the people of the two areas. Festivals, religion, food, and music were the same. But the northern half of the city became part of the institutions of the United States, which encouraged innovation and the creation of business, something discouraged by the institutions of Mexico. Nogales, Arizona, is poorer than most US cities, and Nogales, Sonora, is wealthier than most Mexican cities—and both currently struggle with the violence of drug cartels. But everyone in the region knows that citizens on the north side of the border enjoy higher incomes, better health care and life expectancy, and higher-quality roads, public utilities, and police protection than do their peers to the south.

A similar example arises in a comparison between North Korea and South Korea. Before the separation into two nations in 1948, the people of the peninsula shared a common culture and tradition, shared beliefs and expectations. The critical difference after the division into two nations had to do with the political and economic institutions established. The same can be said about the division of Germany into East and West at the end of World War II.

And what is this difference in institutions? Acemoglu and Robinson propose a typology of inclusive and extractive economic institutions. The inclusive sort

> allow and encourage participation by the great mass of people in economic activities that make best use of their talents and skills and that enable individuals to make the choices they wish. To be inclusive, economic institutions must feature secure private property, an unbiased system of law, and a provision of public services that provides a level playing field in which people can exchange and contract; it also must permit the entry of new businesses and allow people to choose their careers.[33]

Although no set of institutions is perfect, Acemoglu and Robinson argue that the economic institutions of the United States, South Korea, and West Germany have generally been inclusive and ordinary people have benefited greatly. In contrast, the laws and institutional structures of Mexico, North Korea, and East Germany are "extractive" in the sense that they were "designed to extract incomes and wealth from one subset of society to benefit a different subset."[34]

This causal framework has its shortcomings. The authors attribute too much influence to structure and not enough to culture. The typology itself sounds as if the authors might think that there are no extractive institutions in the more industrially developed nations and no inclusive ones in the developing world. The historic interaction between the United States and Latin America demonstrates clearly a long history of extraction by US firms and the US government itself. Moreover, as the Great Recession of 2008 amply illustrates, most of the largest financial firms in the US were willing to fraudulently extract high profits from their clients, a fact admitted only by their payment of billions of dollars in fines to the US Securities and Exchange Commission.[35]

Nonetheless, this typology of institutions as inclusive and extractive is helpful in exploring the notion of sinful social structures because it entails an important insight and because Acemoglu and Robinson are so adamant in stressing the influence of institutions, discounting the impact of personal virtue. Consider, they would say, the difference between the economic vitality and the interest in democracy of the thirteen US colonies in 1776 and the state of the economy and polity in Latin America at that time. They do not think North Americans were more virtuous than the citizens of Latin America.

The authors point out that when the British founded the settlement at Jamestown, Virginia, in 1607, they came intending to employ the model of extractive colonization that had been so successful for the Spanish in South America. That is, the intentions of the British colonizers were no more pure than those of the Spanish. "The notion that the settlers themselves would work and grow their own food seems not to have crossed their minds."[36] Once the new arrivals understood that there was no gold to be taken, Capt. John Smith concluded that "if there were going to be a viable colony, it was the colonists who would have to work." In messages back to England he pleaded that the directors of the Virginia Company, the organization responsible for the settlement, should send more people, but especially the right kind of people. "When you send againe [*sic*] I entreat you rather to send some thirty carpenters, husbandman, gardeners, fishermen, blacksmiths, masons, and diggers up of trees, roots, well provided, than a thousand of such as we have."[37] Smith wanted neither noblemen nor goldsmiths, only more settlers who knew how to grow food or make and repair things.

The colony barely survived the first winters, but when more practical immigrants arrived, the settlement took a turn toward the self-reliance and independence of which Thomas Jefferson later spoke so highly. The point here is that it was not a more virtuous intention of British colonizers that led to a different social structure for Virginia than that of the Spanish colonies—they did, of course, turn to the extractive institutions of slavery within a few decades—but it was rather the necessities on the ground.

Acemoglu and Robinson take the next step to argue that once a formal government is set in place, whether economic institutions are inclusive or extractive depends on whether the political institutions are inclusive or extractive. For example, they argue that the difference between the US and Mexican banking systems in later decades arose not from a difference in the motivation of bankers. Earlier in history US bankers tried to establish for themselves the same monopolistic advantages as occurred in Mexico. However, it was the inclusive political system in the United States—with politicians ultimately voted out of office if they supported extractive banking monopolies—that made the difference. The structures of democracy imposed restrictions on those holding the position of member of Congress, to good effect.

Of course, Acemoglu and Robinson do not employ critical realism or Christian social thought in their analysis. But that analysis is sharpened by both. Critical realism describes the mechanisms by which the institutions have the effects they claim. Catholic social teaching provides the moral warrants—unspoken and taken for granted by Acemoglu and Robinson—necessary to judge extractive institutions as violating the rights and dignity of the persons mistreated within them.

Thus, employing the causal framework of Acemoglu and Robinson: an economic system would be judged to be sinful if, for example, large numbers of people ("squatters") cannot attain a property right to the unowned land they live on, if systems of law and public services promote the interests of the prosperous but not the poor, if monopolies (private or state-owned) exploit consumers and employers, if one has to obtain two dozen different permits to start a small business, or if people are kept from making the best use of their talents to improve the economic well-being of themselves, their families, and their community.

By these criteria the market for shirts—by which I came to own the shirt I wear— is sinful. It is not *only* sinful, of course, since at each link in the chain there are restrictions, opportunities, and incentives that encourage life-giving results. (For example, in the vast majority of cases, the economic well-being of even the seam- stresses in Bangladesh has been improved by it.) But its sinful character leaves those of us who are prosperous consumers of these shirts indicted by the injustices the seamstresses face, even by the criteria identified by Acemoglu and Robinson (less comprehensive than Catholic social thought requires).

Causality and Moral Assessment

The typology of inclusive and extractive institutions provided by Acemoglu and Robinson is insightful, but it is only one of several possible ways of identifying sinful social structures in economic and political life. A similar causal framework, distinguishing "the natural state" from "open access orders," can be found in *Violence and Social Orders* by Douglass North, John Joseph Wallis, and Barry Weingast.[38] Scholars coming from a liberationist perspective may grant Acemoglu and Robinson the importance of institutions but will undoubtedly criticize their approval of capitalist markets. Even "progressive left" critics would see capital- ism in the US today as extractive. The influence that money—particularly anony- mous "dark" money—has on the US political system is important evidence for the claim. The work of Acemoglu and Robinson is employed here only as an example of the sort of causal framework that any ethical tradition must always employ— either explicitly or implicitly—in order to assess morally the causal relationships in contemporary social events from a structural perspective. Without such a set of assumptions about "how things work," we might notice the suffering or injustice experienced by others but would be unable to diagnose their causes, rendering us helpless to prevent them.

Of course, economic and political institutions are only the largest and most frequently noticed sinful social structures. Universities, police departments, social security systems, parishes, and all other structures can themselves be sinful. In each case, specialists who know well a particular kind of social structure can develop, and often already have on hand, helpful frameworks to distinguish healthy from unhealthy forms, functional from dysfunctional, life-giving from life-diminishing, virtuous from vicious, just from unjust, grace-filled from sinful.

At times, that sinful character is evidenced in the absence of decent market options facing poor families unable to provide education, health care, or even food for their children. This is one of the greatest evils in trusting markets alone to resolve economic problems. Those with the fewest options are just "left out" and suffer the most.[39] As Pope John Paul II puts it, economic development occurs "over their heads."[40] In this sort of situation there is often no one person to point to whose decisions have left the marginalized without options.

But the sinful effects of structures more frequently arise out of the decisions of persons in social positions within a structure that directly affect the lives of others. Due to (some of) the restrictions, opportunities, and incentives facing persons in social positions, the constrictive power of a *sinful* structure penalizes rightful action and its enticive power elicits life-diminishing choices.

In nations where government corruption is taken for granted, officeholders find it easy to accept bribes or extort payments and face few restrictions in doing so. In US police departments, where an unspoken racism prevails, officers stop and harass people of color with disproportionate frequency, as there are few restrictions on these unjust choices. In firms where profit is assumed to be the only goal of the organization, decisions ranging from plant closings to work rules on the shop floor are made with no more respect for the human dignity of employees than the restrictions imposed by law require. In a church where the canonical pastor has nearly unlimited authority over parish matters, an autocratic pastor can arrive on the scene with sinfully constrictive power and can undo in a month the pastoral effectiveness of the parish that took decades to develop. In an academic department aiming to improve its national status, where decisions by senior faculty leave too many untenured colleagues vying for too few tenured positions, sinfully enticive power can tempt the untenured to destructively competitive choices. When the legal contours of an energy market have been set by decades of lobbying by carbon energy producers, structured opportunities to ignore destructive externalities lead to overproduction and a bias against alternative fuels. Many are the varieties of sinful social structures.

Moreover, of course, the moral quality of social structures will be disputed. There are good reasons to judge immoral the US campaign finance system where one wealthy individual can legally spend $100 million to influence elections, while elderly fellow citizens in poverty cannot afford the money or time it takes to obtain the photo ID now required to vote in many states. Yet others see such campaign donations as "speech" protected by the constitution and view photo IDs as a prudent device to prevent election fraud. The analysis provided here will not of itself resolve such disputes without a causal framework. But its focus on how the privileged and marginalized in any social structure face radically different restrictions and opportunities can help. It shifts conversations away from individualist interpretations of life toward a more capacious understanding of the structural forces that shape our lives, individually, as a nation, and in global markets.

Two final observations are in order. The first is a reminder that the restrictions, opportunities, and incentives people face in social positions in social structures do not only make *destructive* choices more likely. When institutions are well-structured, constrictive power can restrain sinful personal instincts, enticive power can encourage generous and life-affirming choices, and constitutive power contributes to the virtuous development of personal character. Kevin Ahern's book *Structures of Grace: Catholic Organizations Serving the Global Common Good* provides a multitude of examples of groups working to improve the restrictions and opportunities facing the poor, though it does so without employing this critical realist language.[41] Similarly titled, *Structures of Grace: The Business Practices of the Economy of Communion*, by John Gallagher and Jeanne Buckeye, describes how business affiliated with the Economy of Communion structure themselves in a self-conscious embodiment of faith values for greater service to the poor.[42] Of course, because a moral assessment of any aspect of a social structure entails a judgment (whether acknowledged or not) about what will occur *because* of that aspect, we would need a causal framework to compare the virtue of good social structures.

The second is that structures and culture exist in intimate relationship, even though culture has been largely ignored in this volume. A culture of racism will support the structural opportunity for racial profiling in a police department. A culture of democratic participation in a parish will make it more difficult for an autocratic pastor to act unilaterally, even when he has the canonical right to do so. The focus on this volume on structure should not be taken to imply a dismissal of culture.

Conclusion

Social structures are systems of human relations among (preexisting) social positions. They are ontologically real: emergent "things" that exist at a "higher level" than the individual persons from whose actions they emerge. Structures exert causal impact on persons who take on positions within them by generating restrictions (constrictive power) and opportunities (enticive power) that influence the free decisions those people make. And over time their constitutive power slowly shapes people's characters. Social structures are not conscious agents and thus cannot sin in a literal sense, but they can be sinful similar to the way original sin is sinful.

Structures can appropriately be called sinful when their causal impact—their constrictive and enticive power—encourages morally evil decisions. What "evil" means depends on the sort of social structure under discussion (i.e., political evils differ from parish evils). As a result, there is no single set of criteria precisely defining a line beyond which any structure is sinful. A more specific analysis of each particular kind of structure is required. In current ethical discourse, the phrase "sinful social structure" has been applied to only the most egregiously sinful structures, but, like persons, no structure is entirely sinful or entirely sinless.

These insights into the sinfulness of social structures also suggest a useful local practice. Any organization interested in improving its own moral character should start with a frank conversation about the restrictions, opportunities, and incentives faced by persons holding different social positions within it. Privilege and disadvantage are not necessarily unjust and when they are, naming them in an organization does not guarantee justice. But it is a necessary first step.

We saw in chapter 2 the shortcomings of traditional philosophical and theological ethics in dealing with what Christopher Kutz calls "collective wrongdoing." The arguments in this volume have laid the groundwork for a more adequate understanding of the social structures within which such wrongdoing occurs, and this groundwork now allows us to understand better what an ethics of social structures looks like.

Notes

I am indebted to *Theological Studies* for permission to use here much of my essay "What Is a Sinful Social Structure?" from *Theological Studies* 77, no. 1 (March 2016): 136–64. I am indebted to *Concilium* for permission to use several paragraphs of my essay "Confronting Ubiquitous Corruption" from *Concilium*, no. 5 (2014): 221–30.

1. Noonan, *Bribes*, 3–13.
2. One vivid example is police corruption in Baltimore, Maryland, where in 2018 a group of officers admitted to robbery, extortion, and other crimes. Timothy Williams, "In Baltimore, Brazen Officers Took Every Chance to Rob and Cheat," *New York Times*, February 6, 2018, https://www.nytimes.com/2018/02/06/us/baltimore-police-corruption.html.
3. Episcopado Latinoamericano, *Documentos Pastorales*.
4. In magisterial documents these are evils attributed to social sin, structures of sin, or sinful social structures.
5. Ratzinger, "Instruction on Christian Freedom," 74.
6. John Paul II, *Reconciliatio et paenitentia*, 16.
7. John Paul II, *Ecclesia in America*, 56.
8. Ratzinger, "Instruction on Christian Freedom," 74.
9. Ratzinger, "Instruction on Certain Aspects of the 'Theology of Liberation,'" 15.
10. Benedict XVI, *Caritas in veritate*, 34.
11. Rahner, *Foundations*, 110–11.
12. McKenna, "Original Sin," 82.
13. McMahon, "Karl Rahner and the Theology of Human Origins," 501.
14. Rahner, *Foundations*, 109.
15. McKenna, "Original Sin," 81–82. I am indebted to Christina McRorie for this reference.
16. Couenhoven, *Stricken by Sin*, 208.
17. Sölle, *Thinking About God*, 55.
18. Niebuhr, *Moral Man and Immoral Society*.
19. Libreria Editrice Vaticana, *Catechism of the Catholic Church*, 405.
20. Libreria Editrice Vaticana, *Catechism of the Catholic Church*, 407.
21. Rahner, *Foundations*, 110.

22. Rahner, *Foundations*, 110–11. I am indebted to Kristin Colberg for this reference.
23. McMahon, "Karl Rahner and the Theology of Human Origins," 501.
24. This example arises from an oral conversation with Gerardo Sanchis Muñoz of the Pontifical Catholic University of Argentina in Buenos Aires.
25. Rahner, *The Content of Faith*, 531.
26. Elder-Vass, *Causal Power*, 108–12.
27. Archer, *Internal Conversation*.
28. Couenhoven, *Stricken by Sin*, 215.
29. McKenna, "Original Sin," 86.
30. Archer, *Realist Social Theory*, 65–69.
31. Acemoglu and Robinson, *Why Nations Fail*.
32. Smith attributed the greater wealth of England as compared with nations on the Continent to increased economic productivity arising from "the division of labor" (i.e., specialization in work) and the division of labor to "a certain propensity in human nature . . . to truck, barter, and exchange one thing for another." Because people were naturally inclined to barter with each other, they soon discovered that specializing in one type of production and then trading for the other things they needed left them wealthier than trying to make everything themselves. Of course, this view led Smith to various recommendations for structures that would channel these natural inclinations toward greater national prosperity. A. Smith, *The Wealth of Nations*, 14.
33. Acemoglu and Robinson, *Why Nations Fail*, 74–75.
34. Acemoglu and Robinson, *Why Nations Fail*, 76.
35. The SEC has charged nearly every major financial firm in the US with concealing from investors risks, terms, and improper pricing or making misleading disclosures to investors about mortgage-related risks. US Securities and Exchange Commission, "SEC Enforcement Actions."
36. Acemoglu and Robinson, *Why Nations Fail*, 20.
37. Acemoglu and Robinson, *Why Nations Fail*, 23.
38. North et al., *Violence and Social Orders*.
39. For an insightful discussion of economic compulsion, see Barrera, *Economic Compulsion*.
40. John Paul II, *Centesimus annus*, 33.
41. Ahern, *Structures of Grace*.
42. Gallagher and Buckeye, *Structures of Grace*.

CHAPTER 9

Economic Ethics in a Stratified World

In 1305, in the Arena Chapel in Padua, Italy, the great Italian artist Giotto completed a series of frescoes depicting virtues and vices. He placed these in pairs—prudence and foolishness, fortitude and inconstancy, temperance and anger, justice and injustice, faith and infidelity, charity and envy, hope and desperation. Each is portrayed by a human figure. Charity is depicted by the full-length figure of a woman handing out food to the needy. The figures representing the vices are the more interesting. Desperation is a woman who has just hanged herself; envy, a woman with a snake exiting her mouth.

Most intriguing is the image for injustice. Here is a powerful (and self-important) man, perhaps the mayor of the city, sitting with his body facing forward but head turned to his right in a distant and impassive stare. Below his feet is a scene of rape and murder, while two soldiers stand by idly. Giotto's message is clear: although the criminals below are unjust, the height of injustice is the indifference of the powerful to the plight of the oppressed.

Should we today, seven centuries later, understand this man's indifferent stare as Giotto's indictment of us as consumers in global markets, looking away while those markets treat unjustly so many of the distant producers of the goods we buy?

Introduction

This chapter asks how ethics needs to be expanded, once we recognize we live in a stratified world. We saw in chapter 1 the simple example of a personal openness to greater transparency in organizational policy. Even there the complexities created by the social structure of a place of work raise critical moral and strategic issues that don't have to be faced in the differently structured environment of the living room. Appeals to personal virtue remain essential, but they will have to be joined with careful reflection on causal relations within structures. These relations are not individualistically additive; they are not merely the sum of the influence of all the persons involved. As noted in the introduction, Christian ethicist Christina Traina has compared the needed shift in ethical reflection to the move from Newtonian mechanics to Einstein's theory of relativity: "It creates challenges for accounts of moral accountability because it operates on a scale at which the effects of individuals' actions and intentions can no longer be calculated arithmetically."[1]

We saw in chapter 3 how Iris Marion Young and Onora O'Neill critiqued the individualistic bias in ethics. Christopher Kutz's example of the World War II firebombing of Dresden illustrated the inadequacy of the "individual difference principle," the common sense rule in interpersonal ethics that "I am accountable only for the difference my action alone makes to the resulting state of affairs."[2] Kutz responds that ethical analysis of collective harms cannot ultimately rest on the causal effects of individual actions. Kutz accepts that without a consideration of the social structures within which those collective harms occur, the usual understanding of causality are found wanting, and he turns elsewhere for analytical leverage.

Although ethical deliberation has gone on for thousands of years of human history, only in the last century and a half has sociology developed genuinely new insights into the causal impact of social structures, and only in the last few decades has the improved analysis of the relation of structure and agency provided by critical realism been available. Furthermore, the difference these insights make for our understanding of moral agency is still being worked out, as this volume attempts.

However, a second significant difficulty is presented by another phenomenon, noted in chapter 1. We saw there that one of the insights of *Habits of the Heart* was that people today have a much more difficult time articulating *any* intellectual foundations for the moral convictions they hold. As Michael McCarthy puts it, "In the contemporary West, we share a much broader consensus on life goods than we do on the moral sources needed to ground and sustain their responsible pursuit."[3] The sheer diversity of perspectives in contemporary pluralistic cultures is great, and there is no illusion here that this volume will overcome that diversity. Still, a more precise awareness of the character and influence of social structures can help.

As the title of this chapter indicates, just acknowledging the stratified character of the world we live in is an essential part of that greater awareness. As Christian Smith summarizes it, "objective reality is by nature not flat but stratified, existing on multiple, though connected, levels, each of which operates according to its own characteristic dynamics and processes. We live in a multilayered reality, it turns out, and our framework for understanding reality must be attuned to that fact."[4] We saw in chapter 4 that emergence is a basic fact of nature, and any reductionism (claiming that every higher-level emergent reality can be fully explained by the characteristics of the lower-level elements essential to its existence) misunderstands the natural world. The same is true in the social world, where the "causal capacities" of social structures "are not present in the mere sum total of the parts . . . because the social structure is a real emergent product of the *relationality* of the parts and not simply the features of each part added up."[5] Like the natural world, the social world is stratified.

Ethically based improvements in sinful social structures require changes to existing structural opportunities and restrictions. These are objective realities perceived psychologically as incentives and disincentives. Moreover, because these opportunities and restrictions are emergent properties of ontologically real social structures—and are not under the easy control of even those in authority—moral deliberation about them and action to address them is a more complicated process than just persuading others to change their views.

Choosing a Causal Framework

We saw in chapter 8 that we cannot assess a social structure morally (i.e., judge to what extent it encourages sinful or virtuous action) without a causal framework with which to understand such structures. Any moral assessment of a social structure requires a causal judgment of what is occurring as a result of its various features. Identifying the morally good and bad cannot be based only on moral conviction, but also on a view of the causal relationships involved. Employing our example of the global textiles industry, some people see the injustices faced by the seamstresses as arising from the greed of the owners of clothing factories and apparel brands; they judge not only the market for shirts but capitalism as a whole to be unjust. Others see the injustices arising from corrupt government officials (who accept bribes from immoral factory managers trying to dissuade them from enforcing local workplace health and safety laws), and they judge the market for shirts as fundamentally ethical but the political system as vicious. Two very different accounts of the causal forces at work are entailed here. As we have seen, either account can be made more precise by investigating the structural restrictions and opportunities that constitute (many of) the causal forces involved.

It is not the aim of this volume to persuade the reader of any particular causal framework as best for understanding the global market for shirts—or other social structures like the national government, your local parish, or the Monday evening bridge club. Still, it is essential to understand how the choice of critical realism is indeed the choice of a general causal account, which should be distinguished from the more specific causal frameworks under discussion here.

Critical Realism as a Causal Account

We saw in chapter 5 that the decision to employ critical realist sociology from among competing causal accounts in sociology is a choice. Both because it entails a more adequate philosophy of science (chapter 4) and the commitments of the Catholic intellectual tradition (chapter 5), critical realist sociology is endorsed in this volume because it is noncollectivist, nonindividualist, nondeterministic, and nonempiricist.

This, too, is a choice of a causal account of things, though at a more fundamental level than the choice of a causal framework discussed in chapter 8 and again here in chapter 9. This decision to rely on critical realism's understanding of social life is by far the more important choice for the reader and the primary recommendation of this volume.

The choice of critical realism eliminates from consideration any causal frameworks that attribute too much power to social forces (collectivist and deterministic accounts) or to individual decisions (individualistic accounts) or that restrict human knowledge to only that which is perceivable by our five senses. That is, because of the choice of critical realism, some causal frameworks for understanding markets (or universities, city governments, or other social structures) will not be acceptable.

More Specific Causal Frameworks

Yet, once we decide to employ a critical realist framework, there is still a range of defensible competing causal accounts among which an ethically responsible person must choose—in order to move to a more detailed moral evaluation of any particular social structure. In our example of injustices in the lives of the seamstresses, both people on the political left who are not deterministic and people on the political right who are not individualistic might employ the critical realist view of markets as social structures as outlined in chapter 7. Such liberationists might propose one causal account—challenging the legitimacy of capitalist markets—while such conservatives might propose another—focusing on the damaging effects of government corruption and the need to increase the virtue of corporate and government leaders.

The author's own decision about the most adequate view of causality in economic life is but one among the several defensible options. It is more critical of markets than most right-of-center defenders of capitalism and more appreciative of markets than most left-of-center critics. From this perspective there are indeed injustices faced by many of the women who make our clothing, including the denial of bathroom breaks, various forms of harassment, resistance to unionization, and the lack of fire escapes in multistory factories. Although many assert that the typical wage paid in the industry is unjust, it is nearly always above the median for the producing nation, and the warrant for the assertion is considerably weaker than for the forms of injustice just cited. It would be a sign of appropriate economic development if workers in the Global South had access to more jobs, where working conditions were safe and humane and where wages were above average for the nation. (There is hardly a city council in the United States that would not put out the welcome mat for a firm offering analogous jobs here). And, over time, wages will rise.

Of course, such judgments are based on an assessment of the causal relations of economic development in less industrialized nations, and some readers farther to the political left or right will prefer a different causal framework. However, the aim of this volume is neither to persuade the reader of the wisdom of this position nor to explore how the reader should choose among competing causal frameworks. It is to persuade the reader to understand moral agency within social structures with the assistance of critical realism.

To illustrate the assistance that critical realism can provide to moral analysis within social structures, the next two sections aim to illuminate two contemporary issues. The first is the policy differences typically found between left and right in discourse about a host of economic issues. The second is an issue in recent Catholic social thought: the importance of trust and reciprocity in economic life.

Rules and Goals in Economic Life

Public intellectual discourse is complicated, and no one framework can capture its intricacies. Still, critical realism helps to parse one of the fundamental differences among people hoping to improve the justice of the economic system: between those who recommend changing the laws and regulations that structure markets (generally those on the political left) and those who instead stress improving the virtues of market participants (generally those on the political right). The former work from a causal typology that stresses the social impact of structures, while the latter see the choices of individuals as the dominant causal force. We might say that the former stress the rules of the game, while the latter stress its goals. Within the Christian community, as we have seen, "liberationists" have stressed the need to change the unjust rules of the capitalist economic "game" to achieve justice, while neoconservatives have argued that what is needed is more persons who have internalized and act out of fundamental virtues in their daily economic lives (from corporate CEOs to low-income parents).

Those on the left, in general, aim to alter the rules of economic life because they see capitalism as a vehicle for enabling the wealthy (and, due to their influence, politicians) to impoverish many and plunder the environment. Those on the right, in general, call for a more virtuous society because they see morally weak individuals and firms undermining the otherwise beneficial outcomes of capitalism. From the perspective of the left, appeals for stronger moral commitments rarely have much effect on corporate CEOs but do provide moral cover for ongoing immoral practices. From the right, granting government more power to change the rules of the economic game subverts the economic prosperity that promises a better life for the poor and provides moral cover for those who want to gain for themselves from the political system what they cannot accomplish on their own. Such differences are characteristic of a wide range of disputes over public policy in the United States and other industrialized nations, so it is helpful to look more deeply at the underlying moral instincts of both groups.

The rules group knows the power of structures. It is convinced that if a person in a position within an organization objects on moral grounds to something he or she is expected to do, one of two things will likely happen: either the structure will bend the decisions of that person to support the goals of the organization or that person will be removed and a more "cooperative" other will be found. The goals group knows that no organization can operate well without the virtue of its members; usually taking a more individualistic perspective, it is convinced that only virtuous persons can make responsible organizations.

The rules group responds to critics in the goals group by stressing that, in a pluralistic society, discussions about developing common goals rarely succeed. Insisting on better laws and regulations is the only dependable way to improve justice. John Rawls's *A Theory of Justice* is a major representative work in this strain.[6] The goals group responds that laws do no more than specify a moral minimum, a floor below which human morality is not allowed to fall. Real human flourishing requires people to live virtuously by choice, not because some regulation would penalize them if they fail to live up to what the law requires. A pessimistic view of government's power imbues St. Augustine's classic, *The City of God*.[7] Even if the discussion about the rules and goals of economic life occurs only within religious groups, finding agreement there would be a significant accomplishment.

Virtue and Vice under Structural Constraints

Christian ethics needs to attend to both the rules and the goals of economic life, and the critical realist understanding of human decision within social structure makes this obvious. Throughout the day, persons act within numerous social structures, from organizations like the firm they work for, the local grocery store, or their child's soccer league to broader institutions like their city's scheme for traffic control, their bank's system for credit-card processing, or any of a myriad of markets for consumer products. Within each of these, people seek their goals (whatever those may be) under the influence of the restrictions and opportunities that such structures generate.

Good moral outcomes begin with the moral virtue of persons making decisions, since structures do not "do" anything. Only people are conscious agents. It is a grave mistake to think that all we need for a just world is appropriately structured organizations. But it is equally wrong to believe that all we need are virtuous people. Ours is a stratified world, and in any organization, structural restrictions penalize some activities and structural opportunities reward others. And this constrictive and enticive power of structures regularly alters how persons make decisions. Even a virtuous person may act badly in the face of penalties for good behavior or in response to rewards for bad. Even a vicious person may act well to avoid a penalty for immoral action or to achieve a benefit that accompanies a virtuous choice. Moreover, because social structures typically emerge from the action of individuals with unintended characteristics, sinful social structures can arise even from the choices of virtuous people.

In addition, because most of us make the same decisions again and again under the same structural influences, structures have habituating, constitutive power. As Daniel Daly has argued, "People become, in part, who they are socially structured to become."[8] Structures shape us over the long run, forming our characters and rendering us as either more or less virtuous people.

The recognition that we live in a stratified world leads us to conclude that our attempts to improve the moral quality of economic life must encompass both an improvement of virtue in persons and a transformation of social structures. Neither is easy. But, because Christian ethics, education, spiritual direction, and pastoral care have long wrestled with how to accomplish the former, we need to expend similar energy and effort on the latter. Critical realism helps us understand that the transformation of structures is not about getting different leaders or reorganizing agencies and offices. These may or may not help. The essential transformation needs to be a change in the prevailing pattern of restrictions and opportunities that shape decisions.

Three Periods of Market Activity

Another way to identify this dual importance of virtue and structure in a stratified economic world is provided by Pierpaolo Donati in his analysis of three hypothetical "temporal periods" of market transactions.[9] This envisions the lapse of time from before an agent takes action in the market, to what occurs within the market, to what is then present "after" the market has its effects in the face of the agent's action.

First, there is the "premarket" situation, including the uneven distribution of income, wealth, knowledge, and skills among various individuals and groups at any one time. Second is the "intramarket" period, when an agent's market activity occurs and has its effects within the structure of the market. Third is the "postmarket" situation, again including the uneven distribution of income, wealth, skills, and knowledge.

"Before" and "After" the Market

Employing our distinction of rules and goals, those who stress the primacy of goals emphasize the premarket period. When market participants, particularly the poor, begin with better values and skills fundamental to a successful work life—including habits such as punctuality, industry, honesty, perseverance, and the deferral of gratification—the overall result will improve. Those who stress rules agree on the importance of good education for market participants but worry that those with different economic backgrounds are differently prepared for the market.

Both groups care about what happens in the postmarket phase, but their emphases differ. The goals group stresses alterations that will improve values, or "culture" more broadly, so that people can enter into market transactions with better goals and motivation in the next "period" of the market. This is the essence of the "culture of poverty" argument: the poor are poor because they have not learned from their parents those habits of life that contribute so strongly to economic success.[10] The rules group tends to focus on how a redistribution of "postmarket" resources (greater access to jobs, income, education, health care, nutritious foods, etc.) can enable the poor and marginalized to enter the next period of the market better equipped for economic success. For example, Democrats far more than Republicans support government funding for education and trade adjustment assistance (i.e., providing retraining and relocation funds to US citizens whose jobs have been lost to international trade).

"Within" the Market

Those stressing rules tend to focus on the intramarket phase, aiming to alter the operation of markets by changing its rules, altering the constraints and opportunities that are generated within market relations and that shape the decisions of individuals within them. Examples include changes in laws to prevent discrimination against minorities or changes in a firm's internal policies that reward managers for mentoring younger colleagues. The goals group stresses the importance of virtue for both business and labor in market activity but largely relies on the unimpeded interaction of virtuous persons in markets to generate good results. And both conservatives and liberationists might agree that one way to improve the circumstances of workers in the developing world is for consumers to join together and purchase products appropriately certified by effective "fair trade" nongovernmental organizations. We will see more on this theme in chapter 10.

One of the most fundamental challenges to the usual efficiency-inducing forces within the market has come from Elinor Ostrom, as articulated in her formal address when she accepted the Nobel Prize in economics:

> The most important lesson for public policy analysis derived from the intellectual journey I have outlined here is that humans have a more complex motivational structure and more capability to solve social dilemmas than posited in earlier rational-choice theory. Designing institutions to force (or nudge) entirely self-interested individuals to achieve better outcomes has been the major goal posited by policy analysts for governments to accomplish for much of the past half century. Extensive empirical research leads me to argue that instead, a core goal of public policy should be to facilitate the development of institutions that bring out the best in humans.[11]

Put in the terminology employed here, Ostrom is claiming that, when properly configured, the restrictions and opportunities generated within social structures can do more than alter the decisions of individuals toward better choices (the usual aim of neoclassical economic policy); they can, over the long run, shape individuals to be the sort of persons who want to make those better choices, even without external incentives. The constrictive and enticive power of structures shape individual decisions, and the constitutive power of structures shapes the decision-makers themselves. Put more theologically, the moral agency of individuals is constrained toward more virtuous choices and, in the longer run, moral character changes; those individuals become more virtuous.

Trust and Reciprocity

A second example illustrating the usefulness of critical realism in economic ethics concerns the role of trust in economic life, a positive feature of economic relations that has been emphasized in recent research in sociology, economics, and management theory.[12] Trust is difficult to create. As a result, a particularly significant change within market processes would entail increasing the role of trust and resisting the long-term trend toward greater dependence on legal contracts, formal agreements, and penalties for noncompliance in economic relations within and between firms.

Trust and reciprocity were central concerns in Pope Benedict XVI's *Caritas in veritate*, where he called for attention to the "logic of gift" in economic life, saying that "the church's social doctrine holds that authentically human social relationships of friendship, solidarity, and reciprocity can also be conducted within economic activity, and not only outside or 'after' it."[13] Some have criticized this proposal as unrealistic and even romantic in modern markets. Attending to this argument here will not only identify a significant way to "humanize" markets but will also illustrate how the critical realist insight into how social structures shape our choices can sharpen ethical analysis and suggest concrete steps for structural transformation.

The notion of reciprocity is not well developed in *Caritas in veritate*, but a person influential in the drafting of that encyclical, Italian economist Stefano Zamagni, has written extensively about it. In their book *Civil Economy*, Zamagni and Luigino Bruni argue that standard economics has misunderstood economic life due to its focus on only two of the three primary activities that occur in markets.[14] Mainstream economics understands well the notion of a contract, written or oral, in which there is an agreed-on obligation to fulfill one's duties as specified in the contract. The discipline also understands the notion of a gift: the transfer of some worthwhile good or service from one person to another where there is no counterpayment in the other direction. Zamagni and Bruni argue that this view ignores actions of reciprocity, which are pervasive and morally essential for a vibrant economy.

Reciprocity is a *mix* of contract and gift and begins when a person does another person "a favor." Unlike a contract, there is no strict obligation for the other to reciprocate. Yet reciprocity is not a pure gift, because in reciprocity there is an expectation of some action by the recipient in response, whether the return of a favor to the initial person or to a third party. Anthropology has long studied this notion in cultures where reciprocal gift-giving is a sustaining part of a social system.[15]

The classic example of reciprocity is the simple act of holding the door for someone else whose arms are full. Most of us regularly provide this courtesy to others, including complete strangers. We understand that there is no contract here; the other person is not under a strict obligation to hold the door for us when our situations are reversed. And yet our action is not a pure gift either, in that we expect that the other person *will* act similarly if they have the opportunity to assist us or, more likely, someone else having difficulty opening a door. The "or someone else" here indicates that reciprocity is not merely a one-to-one relationship. At its best it is a characteristic of a group of people, a community. In fact, reciprocity is a big part of what turns a group of people *into* a community.

The uncertainty of the response is essential to reciprocity. That is, the gift character of the initial action resides in the fact that the first person is willing to provide this service without any certainty that the other will reciprocate. Sometimes they don't, and reciprocity does not emerge. This structure—of a gift freely given, followed by uncertainty, followed by a reciprocal action—is what builds trust between two persons and, even more important, in a community. Contracts are not immoral, as there are many situations where a legally enforceable "trust" is essential. However, such trust is as much trust in the court system that will enforce the contract as in the other person who signed it. The critical insight of reciprocity is that the moral fragility of the relationship is what builds the trust.

Reciprocity occurs frequently in economic life. Consider the owner of a small factory who receives a request from a customer for a job under time pressure, with the client needing the products faster than the factory would typically produce them. The owner may well turn to his shop foreman and ask him if he would be willing to work the next three Saturdays and persuade his crew to do the same thing. Such overtime is not part of the contract and would be a gratuitous decision on the part of the foreman, and he may well agree to do so. However, the foreman simultaneously knows that at some future date he might ask for a similar favor from his boss (for example, getting the afternoon off to watch his son play football). The foreman, of course, then goes through the same process with his crew: asking them to work for the next three Saturdays, recognizing that they too will expect some unspecified reciprocal consideration in the future. A version of reciprocity can occur even within large firms, for example, between the purchasing agent for one and the supplier in another. Many such exchanges occur in a long sequence over time, where a temporary advantage for one is balanced by a later advantage for the other. Stronger trust is built if each party does more than the contract requires. And with an increase in trust comes greater transparency and more just workplace relationships—whether in a garment factory in Bangladesh or an architect's office in New York.

We should note that the actions entailed in reciprocity *can* be interpreted within the economist's self-interest paradigm of "utility theory," but doing so misreads the actual character of the human relationships involved. Economic models interpret the behavior of holding a door open for a complete stranger as an effort to accomplish one's interests. The argument is that these interchanges happen multiple times in unpredictable ways and thus it is rational for a self-interested person to contribute to his own good reputation (understood as an intangible asset) so that he will be seen as worthy of such benefits from others in the future.[16] But this distorts what's actually going on in reciprocity, where self-interest plays a smaller role and concern for the other and community plays a larger one.[17]

Much more could be said about the role of reciprocity in economic life.[18] But reciprocity occurs frequently in the other dimensions of human social life as well: between community volunteers, faculty and students, pastors and parishioners, and among friends. Even within business firms, when reciprocity is lively, the resulting relationship is one of trust: persons in such relationships possess evidence that their trust of others is well-founded. Firms, voluntary organizations, and society itself depend on a necessary threshold level of social trust. Social scientists have studied the level of general trust—often termed "social capital"—in all these settings.[19] Like water flowing into a bathtub to increase the stock of water, reciprocity creates the "flow" of trust that increases the "stock" of social capital.

The Contribution of Critical Realism

This stress of Catholic social thought on the importance of reciprocity and the logic of gift also provides an opportunity to demonstrate the analytical benefits of the critical realist grasp of the stratification of the world. An individualistic ethical analysis might point to the greed of top business management and stockholders as undermining trust among employees and between firms. Critical realism's insight—that social structures exist at a higher level than the persons within them and that they exert causal force on them—enables us to name more precisely what's going on and to suggest more specific paths to the transformation of contemporary economic life.

The pressures of the market, the structure of the firm, and US case law (requiring corporate boards of directors to put the interests of stockholders first[20]) generate restrictions and opportunities facing managers at all levels of the firm to put profits ahead of other goals. Yet many contemporary theories of management argue that corporate goals can be better achieved by "flatter" hierarchies and the creation of trust within and between departments in the firm. If we recognize that the path to trust is reciprocity, we are led to identify and change the restrictions and opportunities that tend to squeeze out of the system the "frailty" necessary for reciprocity.

Consider the incentives (i.e., the opportunities and restrictions) established by a business firm for accomplishing goals—whether those goals are measured in dollars, in the number of tasks completed in a week, or in some other way. The constrictive and enticive power of such incentives push the employees facing them to choose the quickest and more certain path to the goal. In many situations this will lead them to avoid the insecurity entailed in reciprocity—for example, not offering help to another department lest it reduce the profitability of one's own, or shunning even the expense of time needed to do favors for others. This can occur even though the personal morality of those workers might otherwise lead them to offer help willingly. Further, the constitutive power of such incentives slowly transforms even virtuous persons into employees who value the quicker and more certain path over the slower and uncertain road of reciprocity.

A firm or even an individual manager that wants to take advantage of the long-term benefits of greater trust among employees will need to alter the prevailing restrictions and opportunities. For instance, they will need to be more tolerant of failures or delays that result from bona fide but unsuccessful attempts at reciprocity than they are of setbacks that result from inattention or lack of effort. And, of course, managers who want greater trust and try to *mandate* reciprocity may be able to increase cooperation but will not improve trust. Trust arises when a reciprocal action is not required but does occur. If a manager is not sure of what to do to increase trust, meeting with subordinates to identify the restrictions and opportunities that undermine reciprocity will generate a variety of suggestions.

From Market Causality to Moral Responsibility

We saw in chapter 7 how the global market for shirts is a long chain of relationships between social positions, from the relation between consumer and clerk at a department store to the relation of the factory floor manager and the seamstresses who make the garment.[21] Every market has this same character, even though some chains are not nearly so long nor so geographically extensive. Each link in the chain is causally dependent on and causally critical to the other links just "above" or "below" it. Without every link, the seamstresses' shirt is not available for the consumer to buy. The market for shirts is a social structure: a system of relations among social positions in which the consumer is in an ontologically real causal relation with the scamstress.

This conclusion differs from the one provided by the individual difference principle, which asserts that "I am accountable only for the difference my action alone makes to the resulting state of affairs." As we saw in chapter 3, the individual difference principle is founded on an accurate insight into the relation of causality and moral responsibility but depends on an inadequate view of causality itself. It accurately assumes that if I am a part of the cause of injustice, I have a consequent moral responsibility to rectify it. But this principle depends on an individualistic, unstratified view of causality. Because an individual consumer has no perceptible impact on the global market for shirts (you could stop buying shirts for the rest of your life, and the global market for shirts would not change), there is no sense of a causal relation with the seamstress attributable to any one consumer. Without any causal connection it is much less persuasive to assert that the purchase of the shirt creates a moral responsibility for harms that occur in the lives of the seamstress half a world away.

From a critical realist perspective, however, I *am* causally related to the seamstress who sewed the stitches in the collar of the shirt I wear, and that causal relation generates a moral responsibility, which traditional ethical reflection has always taken for granted. If she is being treated unjustly at her workplace, I have participated causally in that injustice, even at a distance. I have some moral responsibility to rectify the problem.

How much responsibility? Similar questions concern whether to ascribe blame or guilt to consumers. (Iris Marion Young, for example, makes clear that in her assigning of moral responsibility to consumers, she does not assign blame.[22]) These questions will not be addressed here. Much work in fundamental moral theology and in Christian anthropology is yet to be done in light of the insights of critical realist sociology into the causal impact of social structures on moral agency. Yet several observations are in order.

First, the fact that all consumers bear some moral responsibility when buying a shirt does not mean that all consumers are equally obligated. The poor in the industrialized world, for example, face far more restrictions and fewer opportunities than do those of us who are prosperous. And while a man making minimum wage in Chicago and I may both be wearing shirts made in the same factory in Dhaka—thus we are both causally related to any injustices occurring there—my relative advantages create a stronger obligation for me.

Second, although each of us is complicit in the harmful causal impact of markets in the lives of those who make the products we buy, we are not the *most* morally responsible persons. People from the owner and manager of the clothing factory to the cost-conscious corporate buyers in department store chains are more deeply involved and more responsible.

Third, behind our deliberations about the moral responsibility of actors within markets lies a necessary moral assessment of the market system as a whole, assumed but avoided here (and dealt with elsewhere).[23]

Fourth, each of us is a consumer in a dizzyingly large number of economic markets. We have in this volume focused on clothing because some of the most serious injustices to which markets contribute occur in the textiles market. Yet the same analysis applies to markets for energy (where global climate change presents a crisis), to the market for transportation (where the move to cleaner vehicles and more public transit is all too slow), and to a host of other problems, from racism to sexual harassment to rising economic inequality.

The point here is that an awareness that our daily decisions within structures tend to sustain those structures leaves us complicit in a multitude of evils. The conclusion must be that we lead indicted lives. Yet this sense of indictment must be enlivening and not deadening. It must lead us to action and not to an overwhelming sense of disheartened powerlessness.

None of us can address all the problems in which we each are complicit. With families to care for and jobs to do, no one has a moral obligation to give it all up, move to Bangladesh, and try to improve the lives of seamstresses there. How each of us addresses our obligations will depend on a multitude of factors and cannot be prescribed wholesale. Yet it seems prudent to suggest that each should be more deeply involved in addressing one or two issues, while reading, speaking up, and voting about a broad range of issues, because of our awareness that our lives are not as innocent as psychic distance and an individualistic conception of moral responsibility might lead us to believe.

Conclusion

This chapter has summarized the results of this volume in its analysis of our complicity as consumers in the injustices suffered by the people around the world who make the products we buy. It reviewed the inadequacy of individualistic approaches to ethics and the need for a robust understanding of how social structures influence decisions made within them.

It stressed the choice of a causal framework. Everyone has (at least) one, but most people do not realize they are operating with one among many alternatives. This volume has recommended critical realism as the most fundamental causal framework, excluding both individualist and collectivist accounts of social causality. Yet, at a less fundamental level, this choice of critical realism leaves options that are both left and right of the political center.

To illustrate the helpfulness of the critical realist perspective, the chapter investigated two examples. The first examined two major political "sides" in many disputes about economic life and policy: those who stress the rules of the game and those who stress the goals (moral values) of the participants. These two groups tend to propose different places for transformative action in the three hypothetical periods—before, during, and after market activity. In the second example, we explored the trust-creating character of reciprocity and how the critical realist insight into structure sharpens the advice available for any leader wanting to create more trust in an organization. The structural language of critical realism will at first feel more foreign to those who are right of the political center than to those farther left, but its capacity to sharpen our ideas of what is necessary to encourage virtuous decisions and strengthen character will make it equally valuable to both groups.

The analysis of this chapter culminates in the fundamental insight of the volume as a whole: we as consumers *are* causally related to the distant producers who make the products we buy. Moreover, this causal relationship is a fundamental reason why we then have a moral responsibility (with many others) for any injustices that markets cause in their lives, because we understand that markets cause injustices (and beneficial outcomes) only by altering decisions made within them. We lead indicted lives.

Christians have a number of other reasons why we should feel a moral responsibility for injustices suffered by others in distant lands. But such arguments are not persuasive to nonbelievers. And even for Christians, a critical realist analysis of market complicity makes clear that our causal participation in distant harms is an additional warrant for the moral responsibility of consumers.

What then to do about those injustices is another question, and to that we now turn.

Notes

1. Traina, "Facing Forward," 174.
2. Kutz, *Complicity*, 16.
3. McCarthy, "Living beyond Our Means," 87.
4. C. Smith, *What Is a Person?*, 95.

5. C. Smith, *What Is a Person?*, 30. Italics in the original.
6. Rawls, *A Theory of Justice*.
7. Augustine of Hippo, *The City of God*.
8. Daly, "Structures of Virtue and Vice," 22.
9. Donati, "The Morality of Action," 63–66.
10. Lewis, "Culture of Poverty," 187–220.
11. Ostrom, "Beyond Markets and States."
12. Fukuyama, *Trust*.
13. Benedict XVI, *Caritas in veritate*, 36.
14. Bruni and Zamagni, *Civil Economy*.
15. See, for example, Mauss, *The Gift*.
16. Mauss, *The Gift*, 170.
17. At stake here, too, are larger questions in the philosophy of social science. Some philosophers argue that social science should use the same methods as the natural sciences. See, for example, Mill, *A System of Logic*, 619–30. Others argue that because social scientists study people and not things, imposing a system of meanings (like the maximization model) without asking what meanings are held by the persons being studied is a serious methodological mistake. See, for example, Winch, *The Idea of the Social Science*, 66–94.
18. See, for example, Kolm and Mercier Ythier, *Handbook of Economics*.
19. Portes, "Social Capital," 1–24.
20. Among the earliest cases is *Dodge v. Ford* in 1919. Due to a suit by a minority stockholder, the court told Henry Ford that he was not free to use corporate money to expand production and make cars cheaper. If Ford wanted to be generous, "he should do it with his own money, not the corporation's." Cited in Nelson, *Economics for Humans*, 97.
21. For simplicity we ignore here the further complexity required to trace the cloth and sewing machines to their ultimate sources. These also entail a chain of relations among social positions that constitute every market.
22. Young, *Responsibility for Justice*, 117.
23. Finn, *The Moral Ecology of Markets*.

CHAPTER 10

What Can Be Done about Market Injustice?

In northeast Kenya, an area beset by Muslim extremists from Somalia, a bus filled with passengers was sprayed with bullets by the jihadist group al-Shabaab. During the previous twelve months al-Shabaab had killed 28 people, mostly Christian teachers, in Mandera County, and 148 others, mostly Christian students, at Garissa University College.[1] The attackers entered the bus and insisted that the 62 Muslim passengers identify the handful of Christians on board. The Muslims refused and told the jihadists that they would have to either kill everyone or leave. The militants left.[2]

The moral integrity and personal courage demonstrated by the Muslim passengers on that bus is extraordinary. Although few of us will ever be faced with so dramatic and dangerous a test of our convictions, integrity and courage are essential for our life together. Without these we are all too likely to sit where we are, like Giotto's impassive personification of injustice, content to participate in what Pope Francis has called "the globalization of indifference."[3]

Still, it is the argument of this volume that a disproportionate emphasis in Christian ethics has been placed on personal virtue and action and too little attention has been paid to the character of the social forces that powerfully shape both moral agency and, over time, moral character. Those social forces are culture and social structure, and if we consider the attention paid in Christian ethics to these two realities, by far the greater has been paid to culture. As a result, the focus of this volume has been on the characteristics and effects of the causal power generated by social structures.

Chapter 2 examined the various reasons why mainstream economics today operates with a strong individualistic bias. This occurs in both the underlying philosophy of science and policy recommendations. On the one hand, economic events are understood as being caused by the decisions of individual economic actors, whether persons or firms. On the other hand, policy recommendations (whether conservative or liberal) are made on the presumption that people are mostly self-interested so policy should be designed to nudge self-interested behavior in the desired direction.[4] This is how mainstream economics attends to social structures. It is how most economists would interpret the analysis of critical realist sociology into the restrictions, opportunities, and incentives that structures generate.

However, this individualistic commitment eclipses morally important goals for the shaping of social structures. As we saw in chapter 9, Elinor Ostrom addressed this issue in her acceptance of the Nobel Prize in economics. Argentine economist Gerardo Sanchis Muñoz has made a similar argument in his insistence that the well-intentioned anticorruption policies of the World Bank and other international institutions mistakenly rely on incentives aiming to alter self-interested behavior away from corrupt practices. As Sanchis asserts: "The need today is not to persuade these civil servants to become self-interested rational maximizers. The urgent need is to reinforce the ethos of public service, the merit system, and the professional career."[5]

Put in the terminology employed here, both Ostrom and Sanchis are arguing for the importance of personal moral virtue within social structures. Both claim that, when correctly configured, the restrictions and opportunities generated within social structures can not only alter the decisions of individuals toward more virtuous choices but can, over the long run, shape persons to be more virtuous. The constrictive and enticive power of structures shapes individual decisions and the constitutive power of structures shapes the decision-makers themselves. Understanding of moral agency within social structures must take structural forces into consideration.

Taking Action to Counter Market Harms

Many people have asserted that our participation in the global economic system renders us morally accountable for the injustices within it. But this claim is typically made without demonstrating that our market activity has had any *causal* relation to the injustices experienced by distant others. This volume has argued that a proper understanding of causality in a stratified world reveals that when I purchase a shirt made in a distant country by unnamed seamstresses, I enter into a causal relationship with them. When injustices occur in their work lives, whether the denial of bathroom breaks or their tragic deaths in a factory fire, I am part of the causal chain of relationships that we call the market for shirts that has, in part, brought about those injustices. As a result, I have a moral responsibility for those injustices. There are other reasons, of course, that we have moral responsibilities toward those treated unjustly around us, near and far. But the argument that we are part of the *cause* of distant injustice is, for most people, a more powerful reason to recognize a moral obligation to act.

Having decided to act, the first problem we face is that most of us have no direct access to the shop floors, the neighborhoods, or often even the nations where these distant injustices occur. And, of course, our moral obligation is not so strong that we would need to "drop everything" and move to Honduras, Indonesia, or Bangladesh to improve things there. Still, there are a number of things we can do.

Consumption Patterns

As we have noted, when I buy a shirt I participate causally in the restrictions and opportunities that markets generate in the lives of those many other persons in the long chain of economic relations that stretches from me to the seamstresses in a distant land. Our first instinct when discovering that we are complicit in injustice is to stop doing what we are doing or at least change our actions in a way that improves the situation.

In some situations this can be done satisfactorily. Consider taxis in large US cities. It is an unfortunate fact of life that the bell captains helping customers get a cab to the airport from many large downtown hotels extort five or ten dollars from each cab driver for the privilege of getting the large fare. We can avoid participation in this abuse simply by telling this hotel employee that we need a cab to go across town and then telling only the driver that we are headed for the airport. The analogous action when buying an item of clothing is to look for a store, or more likely a clothing brand, that buys only from supply chains known for their just treatment of workers.

Fair Trade and Ethical Trade

The best-known options here are fair trade organizations. The Fair Trade Federation is a trade association of businesses and organizations in North America committed to fair trade. Members are evaluated for their full commitment to FTF's nine principles:

1. Create opportunities for economically and socially marginalized producers
2. Develop transparent and accountable relationships
3. Build capacity
4. Promote fair trade
5. Pay promptly and fairly
6. Support safe and empowering working conditions
7. Ensure the rights of children
8. Cultivate environmental stewardship
9. Respect cultural identity[6]

Similar organizations include Fair Trade International, Fair Trade Proof, and Fair Trade America.

Another option is known as "ethical trade." Some US-based international religious service organizations, including Catholic Relief Services (CRS), Lutheran World Relief, and the Unitarian Universalist Service Committee, have found that relying only on formally certified fair trade organizations is overly restrictive.

Instead, they have taken on themselves the task of vetting small businesses and non-profit organizations in the developing world. In this process they appeal to their constituent base to rely on their own "stamp of approval" as sufficient evidence of the worthiness of the producers.

The primary motivation behind this shift from "fair trade" to "ethical trade" is an interest in including not only issues of the just treatment of workers but a broader range of moral concern. The two primary goals added to this vetting process are the treatment of the environment (in particular, reducing carbon footprint) and the impact on the local economy through productive investment. It also allows religious organizations to include the full range of ethical issues important to their denomination. Thus CRS incorporates all of the social and moral criteria stipulated by the US Catholic bishops for responsible investment, concerning issues such as family planning, land mines, and abortion. This level of effort is only possible for global organizations with large staffs. Catholic Relief Services, for example, has more than five thousand employees worldwide.

Each of these organizations takes a slightly different approach to the issue of ethically responsible consumption. For example, Lutheran World Relief produces its own brand of coffee, and it markets Divine Chocolate products of the Ghanaian cooperative Kuapa Kokoo, which is co-owned by its eighty-five thousand farmer members. The Unitarian Universalist Service Committee has established relationships with cooperatives in the Global South, such as Fundación entre Mujeres in Estelí, Nicaragua, and markets products in its "good buy" program.

These well-organized efforts to promote more responsible consumer behavior aim not just at influencing small global producers in a positive way. In addition, each is designed to assist and influence its constituent members. Put in the language employed in this volume, the social structures that we call the religious denominations that sponsor these organizations generate enticive power, new structural opportunities for ethically sound purchases that will alter the choices of their members. They also bring about change in those members themselves, as the constitutive power of social structures beneficially, though slowly, shapes the moral characters of persons making decisions under its influence.

Buying from Responsible Companies

Fair trade and ethical trade products provide only a few of the thousands of different products consumers purchase each year. So another critical response to our moral responsibility as consumers is to buy from companies who do more than their competitors to structure morally responsible supply chains.

One noteworthy organization in this effort is the Fair Labor Association (FLA). Its members include socially responsible companies, colleges and universities, and civil society organizations in some twenty nations around the globe. Among the US corporations are Burton Snowboards, Fruit of the Loom, New Balance, Nike, Patagonia, and Under Armour. FLA aims to end abusive labor practices through structural change "by offering tools and resources to companies, delivering training to factory workers and management, conducting due diligence through independent assessments, and advocating for greater accountability and transparency from companies, manufacturers, factories and others involved in global supply chains."[7]

We will look more carefully at Nike later in this chapter, but consider the ongoing efforts of Patagonia. Like other firms in the clothing industry, it does not own the factories that produce its clothes, and most factories that produce for Patagonia also produce for many other brand names as well. In addition to corporate efforts to increase fire safety standards in factories, Patagonia is working toward a "living wage" for all factory workers. Refusing to end its concerns at the factories that sew the clothing, Patagonia is pushing to improve labor conditions in the textile mills and dye houses that sell inputs to those factories.[8] For simplicity this volume has focused on the long chain of relations in the market for shirts, from the consumer/clerk relation to the factory manager/seamstress relation, but at each link in that chain there are other links going out "sideways" to the various firms and workers that produce the things needed within that link. Thus, not only textile mills are in the picture but also the cotton farmers that precede them.

It is beyond the purview of this volume to provide a list of "responsible" brand name companies. Many are the organizations and websites that strive to take on this enormously difficult and ever-changing effort, always requiring a judgment as to how much responsibility, and on which issues, is required to qualify as responsible.

No Relief from Indictment

Such options for buying products made responsibly are important, but it is likely that there will never be fair trade tires, toothpaste, toasters, or televisions. And we are a long way off from even having companies that claim to be "responsible" in producing those and the many other things we buy. That is, the sense of indictment under which we live in global markets cannot be relieved by a commitment to buy only products whose production processes we can be confident were just. Try as we might, the indictment cannot be lifted.

Theologically, this situation of permanent indictment is more uncomfortable for Catholics than it is in the Protestant traditions most deeply shaped by Augustinian theology. While both traditions depend on the grace of God, many Protestants are more accustomed to seeing human nature as fundamentally corrupt; Catholics see human nature as fallen but more capable of virtuous action. It puts it too simply, but from two bad options Catholics tend to see the better of the two as "the right thing" to do; Protestants tend to see it as a wrong thing "that I must do." The permanent indictment of consumers means that we can never be assured that we have fulfilled the responsibilities arising from our purchases. Here, this Protestant characteristic is more adequate.

Yet, interestingly, this "optimistic" perspective of the Catholic tradition led to high moral expectations for the primary social structure addressed throughout premodern

Christian history: government. This is also why, in the last two centuries, Catholic social teaching has a well-developed vocabulary and analysis of economic life.

So what do we—whether Catholic or Protestant or atheist—do under this permanent indictment? If I stop buying shirts, I do not improve the lives of the seamstresses. If we all stop buying shirts, they are out of a job, surely leaving them worse off than before. Our response needs to focus on the ways that we—along with many others, of course—can transform the market system to make it more just.

The remaining responses identified below—efforts to transform social structures—are thus essential in a stratified world, even though they may be less personally reassuring because we as individuals play only a small part within larger structural processes.

Altering Corporate Structures and Practice

The structural analysis provided in this volume makes it clear that improving the structure of corporations would improve the decisions made within them. The US case law that requires corporate boards of directors to put their stockholders' interests first is a structural restriction contrary to the common good. The law should not prevent stockholders from electing directors who value both profit and broader social goals. A more fundamental change would be the corporate structure embodied in "co-determination," the requirement for worker representation on corporate boards in large corporations in many European countries.[9]

But altering the practices of large multinational corporations is a daunting challenge. As a consumer at the store, we have no direct way to inform the clothing company of our convictions. Yet consumers have been heard through nongovernmental organizations that engage corporations collectively, whether through direct talks with leadership or public protests. The combination of the two is the most effective.

The Change at Nike

One noteworthy example of corporate change occurred at Nike, the largest sports clothing retailer (and second-largest apparel maker) in the world. The story involves both outside pressure and inside principle, and leadership from a Nike board member. Jill Ker Conway, former president of Smith College, both a runner and a feminist, was invited to join the Nike board of directors in 1987. At the time Nike was looking to improve its sales among women athletes, but it soon came to appreciate Conway's presence on the board for other reasons.

Well-organized groups on college campuses across the country had been protesting against the "sweatshops" that Nike was relying on to produce its athletic shoes and apparel. After a contentious stockholders' meeting, where college students interrupted the proceedings, Conway proposed to Nike CEO Phil Knight that on her way back from a trip home to Australia she might stop in at some of the factories that make Nike products in Southeast Asia.[10] This began a long process at Nike's board that led to the creation of one of the first board-level corporate responsibility committees in the United States and brought about profound structural changes in Nike's global supply chain.

Needing more, and more accurate, information, Nike contracted with an international NGO to interview some sixty-five thousand individual workers, mostly women, in Asia, at the dormitories where they lived rather than on the shop floor, to create a nonthreatening atmosphere. Long hours and denial of bathroom breaks were among the complaints, but some were deeply cultural. In many settings the fathers of the young women would gather at the factory gate on payday and confiscate their daughters' pay envelopes. Nike pressed for the installation of ATMs inside the factory, which allowed the women to deposit their earnings before leaving, giving them greater control over their lives. One of the findings that was not expected was that the women workers reported very little sexual harassment across hundreds of factories and the tens of thousands of workers interviewed.[11]

One of the most careful studies of efforts to improve the working conditions of factories in the developing world has been conducted by Richard M. Locke, a political scientist at MIT. Studying a number of global firms but focusing on Nike, Locke articulates both the complexity of the problem and the difficulty of achieving good results. Nike, for example, deals with more than nine hundred factories stretched across fifty nations.[12] Some of those factories, such as in the production of footwear, work exclusively for Nike. But in the realm of clothing, Nike depends on hundreds of factories that produce for a number of other international brands at the same time. In nations where government and social structures, as well as culture more generally, have not historically attended to issues of justice for factory workers, it is difficult to bring labor standards up to those expected in the industrialized world—even when a factory produces for only a single firm that insists on it. It is far more difficult when the international firm pressing for changes accounts for only 20 percent of the factory's production.

Locke's study concluded that "arm's length" insistence on better labor standards has a significant yet insufficient impact. Far more productive are the efforts of firms that not only insist on change but also assist in capacity building, i.e., providing staff to help develop the skill set of local managers. Nike, for example, employs over a 150 people to oversee compliance and provide managerial support.[13]

Yet beyond standards and support, Locke found that a third element turns out to be crucial in the actual transformation of work environments: the existence and enforcement of local laws that require higher labor standards. In the language of critical realism, the issue for us is how to alter the social structure existing in a typical clothing factory. Nike's requirements are a form of structural restriction; its offer of staff to improve the skills of managers is a structural opportunity; local laws are structural restrictions. Yet as we have seen throughout the book, such structural forces do not create determinism. Local factory owners and managers still make the decisions (based on whatever goals they hold). They can ignore restrictions (and pay a price) and ignore opportunities (and forgo a benefit).

Locke's conclusion is that efforts by producers have led to fundamental improvements in some areas, such as health and safety, but that other areas have proven much more difficult to change (for example, forced overtime and resistance to union organization). As one might expect, the resistance to change, as in any social structure, indicates the presence of other more basic structural forces.

Consider forced overtime, a pervasive problem. A study of thirteen factories in China producing products for Hewlett-Packard found that more than half the workers exceeded the agreed-on standard of a sixty-hour maximum per week.[14] A fundamental structural market force at work here is the "just-in-time" managerial practices of large multinational firms, which create pressure on factories to produce quickly. This is even more problematic in the clothing industry, where brand name clothing companies want to respond to the latest fashion trends and want products available quickly, before trends change. The factory owners involved respond by pressing their workers to work longer hours. It is quicker and cheaper than training new employees, and there is then no need to lay off employees when demand slackens.

Broader Changes

There have indeed been many good results from the consumer-led efforts to press large multinational companies to insist on stronger labor standards in the distant factories that make their products. Much more remains to be done, but there are some signs that firms may be getting the message that consumers expect more than low prices. One of the more dramatic, and unexpected, indications came from Blackrock Inc., the single biggest investor in the world, with over $6 trillion of investments. Larry Fink, Blackrock's chairman and CEO, sent a letter to the firms it invests in, saying that "society is demanding that companies, both public and private, serve a social purpose. To prosper over time, every company must not only deliver financial performance but also show how it makes a positive contribution to society. Companies must benefit all their stakeholders, including shareholders, employees, customers, and the communities in which they operate."[15] Fink went on to explain that "without a sense of purpose" a company "will ultimately lose the license to operate from key stakeholders."

It is reasonable to conclude that the efforts of various consumer-led organizations to press large companies like Nike to be more responsible (by creating structural restrictions they had to face) has created at least some change in how hard-headed investors like Blackrock think about the future of successful firms in capitalism. While there are also profound cultural issues involved here, the focus in this volume on social structures leads to an awareness of a growing set of structural restrictions placed on firms by groups of consumers large enough to make a difference for long-term profitability. There is no guarantee of success, because countervailing structural forces exist that press firms to ignore social issues to provide investors with a better return. Still, actions like those of Blackrock indicate some shift even in the structural forces coming from investors.

Financial Support for International Organizations

Another possible response to the indictment under which we as consumers live is to contribute our financial resources to those "capacity-building" organizations that are working to improve the lives of ordinary people around the world.

This might include a financial contribution to socially responsible institutions in the Global South. St. Xavier's College in Kolkata, India, began a systematic outreach to one of the very poorest nearby regions, first creating a school system and then, years later, a branch of the college there. Constansia Mumma-Martinon outlines a number of organizations requiring support in efforts to achieve sustainability in urban planning in Kenya.[16] Similarly, financial support for church-based international service organizations can fund efforts to improve the lives of the poor around the world by providing new structural opportunities. Catholic Relief Services, for example, conducts tens of thousands of women's circles in India and elsewhere. These are locally led and designed to improve the economic well-being of local families. Often combined with opportunities for micro-credit, women not only improve their economic well-being but the process fosters "empowerment, education, and participation in public life, while liberating many from domestic violence."[17] The Catholic Church has played an important role in empowering local communities in Ghana and many other nations in the Global South.[18]

It should be clear that most of the persons assisted by such efforts are not the same as those who made the products that you or I have purchased. However, this too is a response to our moral responsibilities with which our purchases encumber us in a stratified world. Contributing to the integral economic development of the Global South is a morally appropriate response.[19]

Political Support

Finally, we must recognize the role that our national political leaders play in the issues we have been examining. As indicated just above, the success of company-led efforts to improve labor standards anywhere in the world is heavily dependent on the presence of adequate laws and their effective enforcement. Not even the United States has the power to force such changes in law, but it can emphasize the importance of structural change through just labor standards in ambassadorial contacts, congressional visits, international trade agreements, and active support for international organizations such as the United Nations and its subsidiary, the International Labor Organization.

One of the most critical issues to address is government corruption. It exists in every nation to some degree, but often is worse in poorer nations, due to weaker structural supports for transparency and budgetary accountability as well as the willingness of firms, both multinational and local, to offer bribes to local officials. In critical realist terms, a corrupt system generates opportunities for businesses to get ahead by bribing government officials and generates few restrictions that penalize such behavior. Just as important, even though businesses as a group would be better off if no bribery payments were ever made to officials, competitive market pressures make it difficult for one or a few to stop. There are two structural approaches to reducing government corruption. The first is through laws in (or treaties among) other nations. For example, the US Foreign Corrupt Practices Act, passed in 1977, makes it illegal for any US company to pay a bribe to an official of any foreign government. Since 1977 over five hundred enforcement actions have been undertaken.[20] International treaties, like the UN Convention against Corruption, have the same aim, though enforcement is left to the individual signatory nations.[21]

The second approach is a local solution. All nations have laws against government corruption, but weak oversight, a long-standing culture of corruption, and the secrecy inherent in corrupt practices lead to laws that are often ineffective. Similarly, every nation has small groups of people committed to reducing corruption, but it's difficult to incite many ordinary citizens to be active in anticorruption efforts. Because the high price of corruption is paid by all citizens, no one citizen loses very much—and thus the average person has little financial incentive to spend time and energy trying to reduce corruption.

The most successful efforts focus on altering the structures of governmental activities so that local citizen groups play a role in the oversight and decision-making processes of government expenditures. The best-known example here is the city of Porto Alegre, Brazil. Since 1989 the city has employed "participatory budgeting," where citizens are directly involved in decision-making and oversight of a portion of the budget for city services as a means of reducing corruption and directing tax dollars where they are most needed. The opportunities for corruption previously generated by the relation of officeholder and citizen were altered by the structural reform that put certain expenditures under the control of intensely interested citizen committees.[22] This has been a real boon to the poor: the World Bank reports that the proportion of households in the city with water and sewer connections rose from 75 to 98 percent during just the first decade of the program.[23]

Independent of party loyalty, all citizens should prioritize the positions of candidates for national office on these crucial questions.

Conclusion

As this discussion briefly outlines, there is a wide variety of things that we can do in response to the moral responsibilities that arise because of the injustices suffered by the distant people who make the products we buy. These are appropriate responses to the sense of indictment that we cannot escape because of the numerous things each of us buys every year. Few if any of these actions will directly affect the specific people who have made the shirts I wear or built the machine that washes them for me. But this too is a feature of living in a world that is both stratified and globalized.

Notes

1. Nzwili, "Kenyan Muslims."
2. Nzwili, "Kenyan Muslims," 4.
3. Francis, *Laudato Si*, 52.
4. Thaler and Sunstein, *Nudge*.
5. Muñoz, "Public Service, Public Goods, and the Common Good," 148.
6. Fair Trade Federation, "Fair Trade Federation Principles."
7. Fair Labor Association, "Improving Workers' Lives Worldwide."
8. Patagonia, "Corporate Responsibility"
9. See, for example, Summers, "Codetermination in the United States," 155.
10. Paine, "A Conversation with Jill Ker Conway."
11. Oral interview with Jill Ker Conway, July 12, 2014.
12. Locke, *The Promise and Limits of Private Power*, 46.
13. "NIKE, Inc. FY14/15 Sustainable Business Report."
14. The sixty-hour standard has been set by the Electronics Industry Citizenship Coalition. Locke, *The Promise and Limits of Private Power*, 139.
15. Fink, "Annual Letter to CEOs."
16. Mumma-Martinon, *Toward Sustainability*.
17. Korgen and Gallagher, *The True Cost of Low Prices*, 169. See also Chalupnicek, "Empowered to Hope."
18. Dassah, *Transnational Land Deals*.
19. The notion of "integral" economic development has been explored in Catholic social teaching. See, for example, Paul VI, *Populorum Progressio*.
20. Hale, "Foreign Corrupt Practices Act Alert."
21. See, for example, "United Nations Convention against Corruption."
22. For related anticorruption efforts, see Landell-Mills, *Citizens Against Corruption*.
23. World Bank Group, "Participatory Budgeting in Brazil."

Conclusion

It is a grave mistake to think that all we need for a just world is properly structured institutions. As we saw in chapter 8, Pope Benedict affirmed that original sin characterizes structures as well as persons. However, it is equally wrong to believe that all we need are virtuous people. We live out each day passing through one social structure after another, largely unreflective about the casual impact structures have on our decisions and even less aware of how they shape who we are over the long run.

The Steps in the Argument

The fundamental premise of this volume is that we can fully understand our *moral* responsibility as consumers in the market only if we understand our *causal* participation as consumers in the harms that markets cause in the lives of those distant others who produce the things we buy. Comprehending that causal link requires several steps in the argument.

First is the recognition that the dominant individualistic views of life—whether of an average person or the mainstream economist—are generally incapable of recognizing a causal link because no single consumer has any discernible impact on what occurs in factories thousands of miles away and none of us intends those harms in the first place.

Second is the set of issues in the philosophy of science that, at first thought, may seem all too distant from concerns about justice. Despite all its advantages, empiricism has had a dramatically negative impact on our thinking and actions. Critical realism provides a more adequate understanding of the two kinds of scientific knowledge: transitive objects of knowledge (like Newton's "law" of gravity), that are human creations aiming to describe how things work (like Newton's "law" of gravity) and intransitive objects of knowledge that are the forces and mechanisms that cause things to happen and that exist whether or not humans know about them (like the force of gravity). Critical realism recognizes ontologically real things that are not sense-perceptible (like the relation between the book and the earth, that causes the book to fall to the floor) and the reality of emergence and the stratification of the natural and social worlds.

Third, critical realist sociology then applied these insights to the social world. Social structures are systems of relations among (preexisting) social positions. They are ontologically real but not sense-perceptible. They originally emerge from the actions of persons (typically long dead) and are sustained by persons (alive today). They exist at a "higher" level than persons and have causal impact on persons within them because of the restrictions (conditional penalties) and opportunities (conditional rewards) they generate. These are experienced psychologically as incentives and disincentives. They do not *determine* decisions, as people are free to ignore them, but they often *alter* decisions, because people most often "go along" instead of "paying the price" that defiance of restrictions would entail.

Fourth, employing insights into power, we saw that by means of those restrictions and opportunities, structures exert constrictive power through restrictions (if you do X, something bad will happen to you) and enticive power through opportunities (if you do Y, something good will happen for you). The constrictive power of peer complaints tends to keep people waiting patiently on queue, and the enticive power of a sale price tends to lead people to make purchases when they had not yet decided to buy. We can say that structural restrictions *cause* this or that to occur, while recognizing that the causal power of structures can have effect only *through* the choices of persons. At first this might seem odd, but this too is a part of the character of causality in a stratified world. A similarly incomplete claim balances it: we say that manager Bill Smith's decision caused this or that to occur, but we mean (or should mean) that Bill's decision, under the influence of the structural restrictions and opportunities he and his subordinates faced, caused the outcome. To think that structural power causes things to occur without the free choice of persons is the error of collectivism. To think that Bill causes things to occur without the causal impact of ontologically real structures is the error of individualism.

Because we often make the same structurally influenced decisions week after week, in the long run structures have constitutive power, shaping who we are. Thus, to understand moral agency within social structures, we need to recognize how structures affect decisions and how, over the long run, they shape moral character. Understanding moral agency requires an understanding of social structure.

The causal power of social structures is a fundamental part of the software of society that allows life to boot up each morning. In well-functioning social structures this causal power is mainly in the background, present but unnoticed. Thus, we pay for lunch at the restaurant because we know we should, not because we could be arrested if we tried to leave without paying. But some people might be tempted, and the power helps keep order. The university professor works hard to entice students to enjoy learning, but the potential of an "F" (or even a "B" for some students) is present in the background as an incentive for student effort when other uses of their time might have greater appeal.

Fifth, critical realism describes how structures can be changed. Because most of us most of the time go along with the restrictions we face, we help to sustain the structure. Yet the least privileged in a structure—those who face the most restrictions and the fewest opportunities—sometimes choose to ignore restrictions, pay the price for that action, and if enough others do the same, can transform the structure. Martin Luther King Jr. and a multitude of others brought about dramatic changes in the United States, and African Americans today continue that struggle against racist structures.

Sixth, applying these insights to economics, we can understand each market (such as the market for shirts, examined in this volume) as a social structure, a system of relations among social positions into which persons enter. When I buy a shirt at Macy's I enter into the position of customer, which is already in relation to the position of clerk, into which the woman who helps me has entered. By taking on those positions we each face restrictions and opportunities that have causal impact on our decisions.

A long chain of relations between positions extends from us "up the line" to the relation of positions of factory manager and seamstress in a distant land. Each link in the chain is an ontologically real but not sense-perceptible relation between positions, and each link is causally dependent on and has causal impact on the links just above and below it.

This grasp of causality in social structures is different in kind from the individualistic understanding of causality that works reasonably well in more-direct relationships, where the test of causality is whether there is a perceptible impact. We can affirm the traditional ethical insight, that being part of the cause of an injury creates a moral responsibility for rectifying it. We consumers are indeed responsible (to some degree and with many others) for the injustices that markets cause in the lives of distant others, recognizing that this causality only occurs through the market's influence on the decisions of persons within it.

Seventh, moving from causality within social structures to the morality of them, structures can be sinful in many of the same ways that original sin is sinful. For example, both original sin and a sinful structure make destructive decisions more likely, not by canceling our freedom but through our free choices. In both cases we know we can make a better decision, but we don't. Moreover, just as every one of us is a sinner, it is safe to say that every social structure is in some ways sinful and in need of transformation.

Markets do many things well and in many ways cause improvements in the economic well-being of those who participate in them. If this were not so, the seamstresses would not have taken their jobs. But markets also cause injustice, and our causal participation in this injustice renders us morally responsible for it, along with many others. How each one of us tries to fulfill that responsibility will vary greatly, depending on personal virtue, capacities, positions, and circumstance.

Eighth, these insights into how social structures can be sinful lead to a concrete suggestion for how an organization led by well-meaning leaders can more adequately address issues of injustice within it. A meeting for everyone (or representatives of various subgroups in large organizations) could be organized where the agenda focuses on identifying the various restrictions and opportunities facing the different groups in attendance. The relevant groups may be based on age, sex, race, seniority, or any of a dozen other criteria. Even in deeply democratic organizations some subgroups face more restrictions and fewer opportunities than others. The advantages of some, and the relative disadvantages of others, may be justifiable. Or not. The exercise itself cannot guarantee an increase in justice, but it is a constructive first step.

Finally, beyond its application to global markets, the critical realist understanding of how social structures affect and are affected by moral agency is also helpful in understanding the full range of issues attended to in Christian social ethics, from the crisis of climate change to racism, from sexual harassment to economic inequality, from the ethics of hospitalization and treatment to corporate social responsibility, from immigration to war, from homelessness to religious freedom. Critical realists have much to say about culture, the other great reality of social life, something largely ignored in this volume due to the constraints of space.

The Brief Summary

Even these nine points can be further simplified. If a reader wishes to ignore the sources in philosophy and sociology and the details of power and the specific application to markets, the most basic implication for Christian theology can be summarized:

> A social structure is a system of relations among preexisting social positions into which persons enter. Structures affect moral agency because the incentives and disincentives they generate tend to alter the decisions of persons within them. Personal moral responsibility requires not only virtuous decisions within structures (resisting restrictions and opportunities that encourage morally evil decisions) but also effective efforts to alter social structures so that restrictions and opportunities make morally good decisions more likely and, in the long run, shape us to be morally better persons.

Ethics, both theological and philosophical, has for millennia attended to the character of human moral agency. Its analysis can be deepened with attention to the social scientific insights into structure and culture over the past century and with the more precise analysis provided by critical realist sociologists over the past three decades. Christian ethics has much to gain in a more precise articulation of the interplay of moral agency and the many social structures within which daily life unfolds. By providing a causal warrant for moral responsibility within global markets, this analysis provides a concrete way to counter "the globalization of indifference" and to live out the Gospel call more faithfully.

Bibliography

Acemoglu, Daron, and James A. Robinson. *Why Nations Fail.* New York: Crown, 2012.

Ahern, Kevin. *Structures of Grace: Catholic Organizations Serving the Global Common Good.* Maryknoll, NY: Orbis, 2015.

Ahmed, Leila. *A Border Passage: From Cairo to America—A Woman's Journey.* New York: Penguin, 1999.

Aquinas, Thomas. *Summa Theologica.* New York: Benziger Brothers, 1947. https://dhspriory.org/thomas/summa/.

Archer, Margaret. *Realist Social Theory: The Morphogenetic Approach.* Cambridge: Cambridge University Press, 1995.

———. "Structural Conditioning and Personal Reflexivity: Sources of Market Complicity, Critique, and Change." In *Distant Markets, Distant Harms: Economic Complicity and Christian Ethics,* edited by Daniel Finn, 25–53. New York: Oxford University Press, 2014.

———. *Structure, Agency and the Internal Conversation.* Cambridge: Cambridge University Press, 2003.

Arrow, Kenneth J. "Values and Collective Decision-Making." In *Rationality in Action: Contemporary Approaches,* edited by Paul K. Moser, 337–53. New York: Cambridge University Press, 1990.

Augustine of Hippo. *The City of God.* New York: Modern Library, 1950.

Barnard, John. *American Vanguard: The United Auto Workers During the Reuther Years, 1935–1970.* Detroit: Wayne State University Press, 2004.

Barrera, Albino. *Economic Compulsion and Christian Ethics.* New York: Cambridge University Press, 2005.

———. *Market Complicity and Christian Ethics.* New York: Cambridge University Press, 2011.

Becker, Gary S. "Crime and Punishment: An Economic Approach." *Journal of Political Economy* 76, no. 2 (March–April 1968): 169–217.

Bellah, Robert N., Richard Madsen, William M. Sullivan, Ann Swidler, and Steven M. Tipton. *Habits of the Heart: Individualism and Commitment in American Life.* Berkeley: University of California Press, 1985.

Benedict of Nursia. *The Rule of St. Benedict.* Translated by Leaonard J. Doyle. Collegeville, MN: Order of Saint Benedict, 2001. http://archive.osb.org/rb/text/toc.html#toc.

Benedict XVI. *Caritas in veritate*. Vatican website, June 29, 2009. http://w2.vatican.va /content/benedict-xvi/en/encyclicals/documents/hf_ben-xvi_enc_20090629_caritas-in -veritate.html.

Bentham, Jeremy. *Introduction to Principles of Morals and Legislation*. London: T. Payne, 1789.

Berger, Peter, and Thomas Luckmann. *The Social Construction of Reality: A Treatise in the Sociology of Knowledge*. Garden City, NY: Doubleday, 1966.

Bhaskar, Roy. *The Possibility of Naturalism: A Philosophical Critique of the Contemporary Human Sciences*. London: Routledge, Taylor, and Francis Group, 1979.

———. *A Realist Theory of Science*. 4th ed. London: Verso, 2008.

Blau, Peter. *Inequality and Heterogeneity: A Primitive of Social Structure*. New York: Free Press, 1970.

———, ed. *Approaches to the Study of Social Structure*. New York: Free Press, 1975.

Bottomore, Tom. "A Marxist Consideration of Durkheim." *Social Forces* 59, no. 4 (June 1981): 902–17.

Bruni, Luigino, and Stefano Zamagni. *Civil Economy: Efficiency, Equity, Public Happiness*. Oxford: Peter Lang, 2007.

Chalupnicek, Pavel. "Empowered to Hope: The Impact of Social Entrepreneurship on Social Exclusion." In *Driven by Hope: Economics and Theology in Dialogue*, edited by Steven C. van den Heuvel and Patrick Nullens, 169–84. Leuven, Belgium: Peeters, 2018.

Chetty, Raj, Nathaniel Hendren, and Lawrence F. Katz. "The Effects of Exposure to Better Neighborhoods on Children: New Evidence from the Moving to Opportunity Experiment." *American Economic Review* 106, no. 4 (April 2016): 855–902.

Ciscel, D. H., and B. E. Smith. "The Impact of Supply Chain Management on Labor Standards: The Transition to Incessant Work." *Journal of Economic Issues* 39, no. 2 (June 2005): 429–37.

Clean Clothes Campaign (website). "At Least 28 More Garment Workers Die in Bangladeshi Factory Fire." December 14, 2012. https://cleanclothes.org/news/2010/12/14/at-least-28 -more-garment-workers-die-in-bangladeshi-factory-fire.

Collins, Randall. "On the Micro-Foundations of Macro Sociology." *American Journal of Sociology* 86 (1981): 984–1014.

Comte, Auguste. *Systeme de politique positive: Extraits des tomes II et III publiés entre 1851 et 1854*. Paris: Georges Crès & Cie, 1912. AnthropoMada. http://anthropomada.com/biblio theque/COMTE-auguste-Systeme-de-politique-positive.pdf.

Couenhoven, Jesse. *Stricken by Sin, Cured by Christ: Agency, Necessity, and Culpability in Augustinian Theology*. New York: Oxford University Press, 2013.

Daly, Daniel J. "Structures of Virtue and Vice." *New Blackfriars* 92, no. 1039 (May 2011): 341–57.

Dassah, Emmanuel Zumabakuro. *The Church, Transnational Land Deals and Empowering Local Communities in Northern Ghana: A Christian Socio-ethical Perspective*. Paderborn, Germany: Verlag Ferdinand Schoeningh, 2018.

De Soto, Hernando. *The Mystery of Capital: Why Capitalism Triumphs in the West and Fails Everywhere Else*. New York: Basic, 2000.

Devastating Disasters (website). "Qinghe Special Steel Corporation Disaster, 2007." http:// devastatingdisasters.com/qinghe-special-steel-corporation-disaster-2007/.

Donati, Pierpaolo. "The Morality of Action, Reflexivity, and the Relational Subject." In *Distant Markets, Distant Harms: Economic Complicity and Christian Ethics*, edited by Daniel Finn, 54–89. New York: Oxford University Press, 2014.

Doorey, D. J. "The Transparent Supply Chain: From Resistance to Implementation at Nike and Levi-Strauss." *Journal of Business Ethics* 103, no. 4 (2011): 587–603.

Dragusanu, Raluca, Daniele Giovannucci, and Nathan Nunn. "The Economics of Fair Trade." *Journal of Economic Perspectives* 28, no. 3 (Summer 2014): 217–36.

Durkheim, Emile. "Review of Antonio Labriola, *Essais sur la conception materialiste de l'histoire.*" In *Revue Philosophique* 44. Paris: Girard et Brière, 1897.

Elder-Vass, Dave. *The Causal Power of Social Structures: Emergence, Structure and Agency.* Cambridge: Cambridge University Press, 2010.

———. *The Reality of Social Constriction.* New York: Cambridge University Press, 2012.

Episcopado Latinoamericano Conferencias Generales. *Río de Janeiro, Medellín, Puebla, Santo Domingo: Documentos Pastorales.* Santiago, Chile: San Pablo, 1993.

Fair Labor Association (website). "Improving Workers' Lives Worldwide." http://www.fairlabor.org/. Accessed February 11, 2018.

Fair Trade Federation (website). "Fair Trade Federation Principles." http://www.fairtradefederation.org/fair-trade-federation-principles//. Accessed May 5, 2018.

Fink, Larry. "Annual Letter to CEOs: A Sense of Purpose." BlackRock, Inc., January 2018. https://www.blackrock.com/corporate/en-no/investor-relations/larry-fink-ceo-letter.

Finn, Daniel K., ed. *Distant Markets, Distant Harms: Economic Complicity and Christian Ethics.* New York: Oxford University Press, 2014.

———. *The Moral Ecology of Markets.* New York: Cambridge University Press, 2006.

———. "What We Should and Should Not Learn from Economics." In *Christian Economic Ethics: History and Implications*, 217–34. Minneapolis: Fortress, 2013.

Francis. *Laudato si.* Vatican website, May 24, 2015. http://w2.vatican.va/content/francesco/en/encyclicals/documents/papa-francesco_20150524_enciclica-laudato-si.html.

Friedman, Milton. "The Methodology of Positive Economics." In *Essays in Positive Economics*, 3–45. Chicago: University of Chicago Press, 1953.

Fukuyama, Francis. *Trust: The Social Virtues and the Creation of Prosperity.* New York: Free Press, 1995.

Gallagher, John, and Jeanne Buckeye. *Structures of Grace: The Business Practices of the Economy of Communion.* Hyde Park, NY: New City Press of the Focolare, 2014.

Getty Museum. "Casting Nature: François-Thomas Germain's *Machine d'Argent.*" http://www.getty.edu/art/exhibitions/casting_nature/. Accessed July 9, 2018.

Giddens, Anthony A. *Contemporary Critique of Historical Materialism.* Berkeley: University of California Press, 1981.

Goldin, Claudia, and Cecilia Rouse. "Orchestrating Impartiality: The Impact of 'Blind' Auditions on Female Musicians." National Bureau of Economic Research Working Paper no. 5903, January 1997. http://www.nber.org/papers/w5903.

Granovetter, Mark, and Richard Swedberg, eds. *The Sociology of Economic Life.* 2nd ed. Boulder, CO: Westview, 2001.

Hale, Wilmer. "Foreign Corrupt Practices Act Alert: Global Anti-Bribery Year-in-Review: 2017 Developments and Predictions for 2018," January 12, 2018. https://www.wilmerhale.com/uploadedFiles/Shared_Content/Editorial/Publications/WH_Publications/Client_Alert_PDfs/2018-01-12-FCPA-Alert.pdf.

Hayek, Friedrich. *Collectivist Economic Planning: Critical Studies on the Possibilities of Socialism.* London: George Routledge & Sons, 1935.

———. *Law, Legislation, and Liberty.* Vol. 2 of *The Mirage of Social Justice.* Chicago: University of Chicago Press, 1976.

——. "Scientism and the Study of Society: Part 2." *Economica* 10, no. 37 (February 1943): 34–63.

Hayes, Mark, and Geoff Moore. "The Economics of Fair Trade: A Guide in Plain English." Durham University Community, June 2005. http://community.dur.ac.uk/m.g.hayes/weft /The%20Economics%20of%20Fair%20Trade%20plain%20guide.pdf.

Heckman, James, Rodrigo Pinto, and Peter Savelyev. "Understanding the Mechanisms through which an Influential Early Childhood Program Boosted Adult Outcomes." *American Economic Review* 103, no. 6 (October 2013): 2052–86.

Henriot, Peter. "Social Sin: The Recovery of a Christian Tradition." In *Method in Ministry: Theological Reflection and Christian Ministry*, edited by James D. Whitehead and Evelyn Eaton Whitehead, 127–44. New York: Seabury, 1980.

Himes, Kenneth R. "Social Sin and the Role of the Individual." *The Annual of the Society of Christian Ethics* (1986): 183–218.

Hinze, Christine Firer. *Comprehending Power in Christian Social Ethics*. Atlanta, GA: Scholars, 1995.

Hirschfeld, Mary. *Toward a Humane Economy: Aquinas and the Modern Economy*. Cambridge: Harvard University Press, 2018.

Holbraad, Martin, and Morten Axel Pederson. *The Ontological Turn: An Anthropological Exposition*. Cambridge: Cambridge University Press, 2017.

Homans, George C. "What Do We Mean by Social 'Structure'?" In *Approaches to the Study of Social Structure*, edited by Peter Blau, 53–65. New York: Free Press, 1975.

Hume, David. *Enquiry Concerning Human Understanding*. Edited by L. A. Selby-Bigge. 2nd ed. Oxford: Clarendon, 1902. http://oll.libertyfund.org/titles/hume-enquiries-concerning -the-human-understanding-and-concerning-the-principles-of-morals.

——. *A Treatise of Human Nature*. Kitchner, ON: Batoche, 1999.

Hutt, William Harold. "The Concept of Consumers' Sovereignty." *Economic Journal* 50, no. 197 (March 1940): 66–77.

Jevons, William Stanley. *The Theory of Political Economy*. Edited by D. Collison Black. Middlesex, England: Penguin, 1970.

John Paul II. *Centesimus annus*. Vatican website, May 1, 1991. http://w2.vatican.va/content /john-paul-ii/en/encyclicals/documents/hf_jp-ii_enc_01051991_centesimus-annus.html.

——. *Ecclesia in America*. Vatican website, January 22, 1999. http://w2.vatican.va/con tent/john-paul-ii/en/apost_exhortations/documents/hf_jp-ii_exh_22011999_ecclesia-in -america.html.

——. *Reconciliatio et paenitentia*. Vatican website, December 2, 1984. http://w2.vatican .va/content/john-paul-ii/en/apost_exhortations/documents/hf_jp-ii_exh_02121984_recon ciliatio-et-paenitentia.html.

Kolm, Serge Christophe, and Jean Mercier Ythier. *Handbook of Economics of Giving, Altruism and Reciprocity*. 1st ed. Oxford: Elsevier, 2006.

Korgen, Jeffrey Odell, and Vincent A. Gallagher. *The True Cost of Low Prices: The Violence of Globalization*. 2nd ed. Maryknoll, NY: Orbis, 2013.

Kutz, Christopher. *Complicity: Ethics and Law for a Collective Age*. New York: Oxford University Press, 2001.

Landell-Mills, Pierre. *Citizens Against Corruption: Report from the Front Line*. Leicestershire: Partnership for Transparency Funding, Matador, 2013.

Lewis, Oscar. "Culture of Poverty." In *On Understanding Poverty: Perspectives from the Social Sciences*, edited by Daniel P. Moynihan, 187–220. New York: Basic, 1969.

Libreria Editrice Vaticana. *Catechism of the Catholic Church*. Collegeville, MN: Liturgical Press, 1994.

Locke, John. *An Essay Concerning Human Understanding*. London: Awnsham and Churchill, 1706.

Locke, Richard M. *The Promise and Limits of Private Power: Promoting Labor Standards in a Global Economy*. New York: Cambridge University Press, 2013.

Lonergan, Bernard, SJ. *Insight, A Study of Human Understanding*. 3rd ed. New York: Philosophical Library, 1970.

Lukes, Steven. *Power: A Radical View*. 2nd ed. New York: Palgrave Macmillan, 2005.

———. "Power." *Contexts* 6, no. 3 (August 2007): 59–61.

MacIntyre, Alasdair. *After Virtue: A Study in Moral Theory*. 3rd ed. Notre Dame: University of Notre Dame Press, 2007.

Mauss, Marcel. *The Gift: Forms and Functions of Exchange in Archaic Societies*. London: Routledge, 1990.

Mayhew, Bruce. "Structuralism versus Individualism, Part 1: Shadowboxing in the Dark." *Social Forces* 59 (1980): 335–75.

McCarthy, Michael. "Living beyond Our Means: The Troubling Gap between Ontology and Advocacy." *Method: Journal of Lonergan Studies* 5, no. 1 (Spring 2014): 73–94.

McKenna, Joseph H. "Original Sin and the Tractability of Evil." *New Theology Review* 10 (1997): 78–88.

McMahon, Kevin A. "Karl Rahner and the Theology of Human Origins." *Thomist* 66, no. 4 (2002): 499–517.

Menger, Carl. *Principles of Economics*. Translated by James Dingwall and Bert F. Hoselitz. New York: New York University Press, 1976.

Mercedes, Anna. *Power For: Feminism and Christ's Self-Giving*. New York: T&T Clark, 2011.

Milbank, John. *Theology and Social Theory: Beyond Secular Reason*. Oxford: Basil Blackwell, 1990.

Mill, John Stuart. *Auguste Comte and Positivism*. 5th ed. London: N. Trübner, 1907.

———. "On the Definition of Political Economy: And on the Method of Investigation Proper to It." In *Essays on Some Unsettled Questions*. 2nd ed. Clifton, NJ: A. M. Kelley, 1974.

———. *A System of Logic: Ratiocinative and Inductive; Being a Connected View of the Principles of Evidence and the Methods of Scientific Investigation*. New York: Harper & Brothers, 1874.

Mirowski, Philip. *More Heat than Light: Economics as Social Physics, Physics as Nature's Economics*. Cambridge: Cambridge University Press, 1989.

———. "Three Ways to Think about Testing in Econometrics." *Journal of Econometrics* 67 (1995): 25–46.

Mumma-Martinon, Constansia. "Toward Sustainability in Urban Planning: The Case of Kenya." In *Just Sustainability: Technology, Ecology, and Resource Extraction*, edited by Christina Z. Peppard and Andrea Vincini, 81–93. New York: Orbis, 2015.

Muñoz, Gerardo Sanchis. "Public Service, Public Goods, and the Common Good: Argentina as a Case Study." In *Empirical Foundations of the Common Good: What Theology Can Learn from Social Science*, edited by Daniel K. Finn, 142–69. New York: Oxford University Press, 2017.

Neeley, Tsedal. "Global Business Speaks English." *Harvard Business Review*, May 2012. https://hbr.org/2012/05/global-business-speaks-english.

Nelson, Julie A. *Economics for Humans*. Chicago: University of Chicago Press, 2006.

Nelson, Richard R., and Sidney G. Winter. *An Evolutionary Theory of Economic Change*. Cambridge: Belknap, 1982.

Niebuhr, Reinhold. *Moral Man and Immoral Society*. Louisville, KY: Westminster John Knox, 1932.

"NIKE, Inc., FY14/15 Sustainable Business Report." *Sustainable Brands* (website), May 11, 2016. 52. https://www.sustainablebrands.com/digital_learning/csr_report/next_economy /nike_inc_fy1415_sustainable_business_report.

Noonan, John T., Jr. *Bribes: The Intellectual History of a Moral Idea*. Berkeley: University of California Press, 1984.

North, Douglass C., John Joseph Wallis, and Barry R. Weingast. *Violence and Social Orders: A Conceptual Framework for Interpreting Recorded Human History*. Cambridge: Cambridge University Press, 2009.

Nye, Joseph S., Jr. *Soft Power: The Means to Success in World Politics*. New York: Public Affairs, 2004.

Nzwili, Fredrick. "Kenyan Muslims Protect Christian Fellow Passengers when Militants Attack Bus." *Christian Century* 133, no. 2 (January 2016). https://www.christiancentury .org/article/2015-12/kenyan-muslims-protect-christian-fellow-passengers-when-militants -attack-bus.

O'Neill, Onora. *Towards Justice and Virtue: A Constructive Account of Practical Reasoning*. Cambridge: Cambridge University Press, 1996.

Ostrom, Elinor. "Beyond Markets and States: Polycentric Governance of Complex Economic Systems." *American Economic Review* 100, no. 3 (June 2010): 641–72.

Paine, Lynn S. "A Conversation with Jill Ker Conway." *Harvard Business Review*, July–August 2014. https://hbr.org/2014/07/a-conversation-with-jill-ker-conway.

Park-Poaps, H., and K. Rees. "Stakeholder Forces of Socially Responsible Supply Chain Management Orientation." *Journal of Business Ethics* 92, no. 2 (2010): 305–22.

Patagonia (website). "Corporate Responsibility." http://www.patagonia.com/corporate -responsibility-history.html. Accessed February 11, 2018.

Paul VI. *Populorum Progressio: On the Development of Peoples*. Vatican website. March 26, 1967. http://w2.vatican.va/content/paul-vi/en/encyclicals/documents/hf_p-vi_enc _26031967_populorum.htm.

Peppard, Christina Z., and Andrea Vicini, eds. *Just Sustainability: Technology, Ecology, and Resource Extraction*. New York: Orbis, 2015.

Pius XI. *Quadragesimo anno*. Vatican website. May 15, 1931. http://w2.vatican.va/content /pius-xi/en/encyclicals/documents/hf_p-xi_enc_19310515_quadragesimo-anno .html.

Popper, Karl. "Three Worlds." University of Michigan Tanner Lecture on Human Values, April 7, 1978. https://tannerlectures.utah.edu/_documents/a-to-z/p/popper80.pdf.

Porpora, Douglas V. "Four Concepts of Social Structure," *Journal for the Theory of Social Behavior* 19, no. 2 (1989): 195–212.

——. *Reconstructing Sociology: The Critical Realist Approach*. Cambridge: Cambridge University Press, 2015.

Portes, Alejandro. "Social Capital: Its Origins and Applications in Modern Sociology." *Annual Review of Sociology* 24 (August 1998): 1–24.

Putnam, Robert. *Bowling Alone* (website). http://bowlingalone.com/. Accessed March 26, 2018.

Rahner, Karl. *The Content of Faith: The Best of Karl Rahner's Theological Writings.* Edited by Karl Lehmann and Albert Raffelt. Translated by Harvey D. Egan. New York: Crossroads, 1993.

———. *Foundations of Christian Faith: An Introduction to the Idea of Christianity.* New York: Seabury, 1978.

Ratzinger, Joseph. "Instruction on Certain Aspects of the 'Theology of Liberation.'" Vatican website. August 6, 1984. http://www.vatican.va/roman_curia/congregations/cfaith/documents/rc_con_cfaith_doc_19840806_theology-liberation_en.html.

———. "Instruction on Christian Freedom and Liberation." Vatican website, March 22, 1986. http://www.vatican.va/roman_curia/congregations/cfaith/documents/rc_con_cfaith_doc_19860322_freedom-liberation_en.html.

Rawls, John. *A Theory of Justice.* Cambridge: Harvard University Press, 1971.

Rist, J. M. *Stoic Philosophy.* London: Cambridge University Press, 1969.

Robbins, Lionel. *An Essay on the Nature and Significance of Economic Science.* London: Macmillan, 1937.

Roscher, Wilhelm. *Principles of Political Economy.* Translated by J. J. Lalor. Chicago: Gallaghan, 1854.

Samuelson, Paul. "A Note on the Pure Theory of Consumers' Behaviour." *Economica* 5, no. 17 (1938): 61–71.

Schumpeter, Joseph. "The Instability of Capitalism." *Economic Journal* 38, no. 151 (September 1928): 361–86.

Shadle, Matthew A. *Interrupting Capitalism: Catholic Social Thought and the Economy.* New York: Oxford University Press, 2018.

Smith, Adam. *The Theory of Moral Sentiments.* Indianapolis: Liberty Classics, 1978.

———. *The Wealth of Nations.* New York: Modern Library, 1937.

Smith, Christian. *What Is a Person? Rethinking Humanity, Social Life, and the Moral Good from the Person Up.* Chicago: University of Chicago Press, 2010.

Sölle, Dorothee. *Thinking about God: An Introduction to Theology.* Philadelphia: Trinity Press International, 1990.

Spencer, Andrew J. Review of *Distant Markets, Distant Harms: Economic Complicity and Christian Ethics,* edited by D. K. Finn. *Journal of Markets and Morality* 17, no. 2 (2014): 549–52.

Strand, Robert. "Corporate Responsibility in Scandinavian Supply Chains." *Journal of Business Ethics* 85, no. 1 (2009): 179–85.

Summers, Clyde W. "Codetermination in the United States: A Projection of Problems and Potentials." *Journal of Comparative Corporate Law and Securities Regulation* 4 (1982): 155–91.

Swift, Jonathan. *Gulliver's Travels.* London: Jones, 1826.

Tawney, R. H. *Equality.* 4th ed. New York: Putnam, 1956.

Taylor, Charles. *Human Agency and Language.* New York: Cambridge University Press, 1985.

———. *A Secular Age.* Cambridge: Harvard University Press, 2017.

Thaler, Richard H., and Cass R. Sunstein. *Nudge: Improving Decisions About Health, Wealth, and Happiness.* New Haven, CT: Yale University Press, 2008.

Traina, Christina L. H. "Facing Forward: Feminist Analysis of Care and Agency on a Global Scale." In Finn, *Distant Markets, Distant Harms,* 173–201.

Udehn, Lars. "The Changing Face of Methodological Individualism." *Annual Review of Sociology* 28 (2002): 479–507.

"United Nations Convention against Corruption." *United Nations Office on Drugs and Crime.* https://www.unodc.org/unodc/en/corruption/uncac.html. Accessed February 19, 2018.

Urbinati, Nadia. "A Brief History of Individualism." In *The Tyranny of the Moderns.* Translated by Martin Thom, 49–69. New Haven, CT: Yale University, 2015.

US Census Bureau. "Population: 1790–1990." https://www.census.gov/population/census data/table-4.pdf. Accessed July 16, 2017.

US Patent and Trademark Office. "Trademark Basics." https://www.uspto.gov/trademarks -getting-started/trademark-basics. Accessed August 6, 2018.

US Securities and Exchange Commission. "SEC Enforcement Actions: Addressing Misconduct That Led To or Arose From the Financial Crisis." https://www.sec.gov/spotlight/enf -actions-fc.shtml. Accessed April 18, 2016.

Van den Huevel, Steven C., and Patrick Nullens, eds. *Driven by Hope: Economics and Theology in Dialogue.* Walpole, MA: Peeters, 2018.

Veblen, Thorstein. "Why Is Economics Not an Evolutionary Science?" *Quarterly Journal of Economics* 12, no. 4 (July 1898): 373–97.

Von Mises, Ludwig. *Human Action: A Treatise on Economics.* New Haven, CT: Yale University Press, 1949.

Walras, Léon. *Elements of Pure Economics, or, The Theory of Social Wealth.* Translated by William Jaffé. Homewood, IL: Richard D. Irwin, 1954.

Wartenberg, Thomas E. *The Forms of Power: From Domination to Transformation.* Philadelphia: Temple University Press, 1990.

Weber, Max. *The Theory of Social and Economic Organization.* New York: Free Press, 1964.

Whitehead, Alfred North. *The Concept of Nature.* Cambridge: Cambridge University Press, 1920.

———. *An Enquiry Concerning the Principles of Natural Knowledge.* Cambridge: Cambridge University Press, 1919.

Wilson, Edward O. *Sociobiology: The New Synthesis.* Cambridge: Harvard University Press, 1975.

Winch, Peter. *The Idea of the Social Science and Its Relation to Philosophy.* London: Routledge, 1958.

Witt, Ulrich. *Evolutionary Economics.* Hants, England: Edward Elgar, 1993.

World Bank Group (website). "Participatory Budgeting in Brazil." http://siteresources .worldbank.org/INTEMPOWERMENT/Resources/14657_Partic-Budg-Brazil-web.pdf. Accessed July 9, 2014.

———. "Starting a Business." June 2017. http://www.doingbusiness.org/data/exploretopics /starting-a-business.

Young, Iris Marion. *Responsibility for Justice.* New York: Oxford University Press, 2011.

Yuengert, Andrew M. *Approximating Prudence: An Aristotelian Practical Wisdom and Economic Models of Choice.* New York: Palgrave MacMillan, 2012.

Ziliak, Stephen T., and Deirdre M. McCloskey. *The Cult of Statistical Significance: How the Standard Error Costs Us Jobs, Justice, and Lives.* Ann Arbor: University of Michigan Press, 2008.

Index

About the Author

Daniel K. Finn is Clemens Professor of Economics and Professor of Theology at St. John's University and the College of St. Benedict and is the director of the True Wealth of Nations research project at the Institute for Advanced Catholic Studies. He is a former president of the Catholic Theological Society of America, the Society of Christian Ethics, and the Association for Social Economics. His books include *Christian Economic Ethics: History and Implications* (Fortress), *The Moral Ecology of Markets: A Framework for Assessing Justice in Economic Life* (Cambridge), and *Empirical Foundations of the Common Good: What Theology Can Learn from Social Science* (Oxford).